# Prentice Hall
# MATHEMATICS
## Course 1

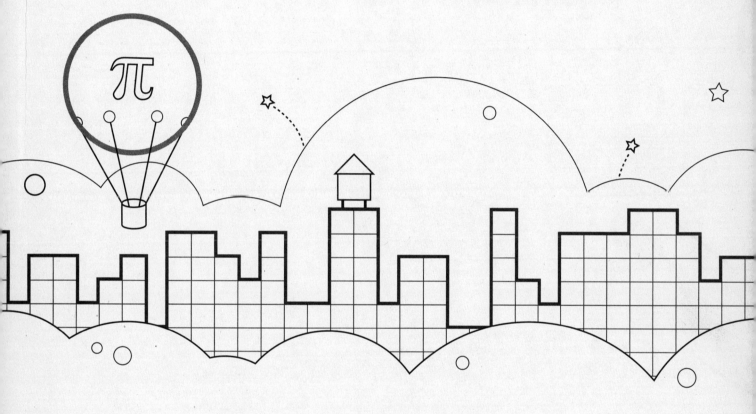

# ALL-IN-ONE
## Student Workbook
### VERSION B

Boston, Massachusetts • Chandler, Arizona • Glenview, Illinois • Upper Saddle River, New Jersey

ISBN-13: 978-0-13-372143-0
ISBN-10:   0-13-372143-4

3  4  5  6  7  8  9  10  V012  13  12  11  10

# Daily Notetaking Guide

# Daily Notetaking Guide (continued)

# Practice, Guided Problem Solving, Vocabulary

## Chapter 1: Whole Numbers and Decimals

## Chapter 2: Data and Graphs

## Chapter 3: Patterns and Variables

## Chapter 4: Number Theory and Fractions

# Chapter 5: Adding and Subtracting Fractions

# Chapter 6: Multiplying and Dividing Fractions

# Chapter 7: Ratios, Proportions, and Percents

# Chapter 8: Tools of Geometry

## Chapter 9: Geometry and Measurement

## Chapter 10: Exploring Probability

# Chapter 11: Integers

# Chapter 12: Equations and Inequalities

## A Note to the Student:

This section of your workbook contains notetaking pages for each lesson in your student edition. They are structured to help you take effective notes in class. They will also serve as a study guide as you prepare for tests and quizzes.

# Lesson 1-1                                    **Understanding Whole Numbers**

| **Lesson Objective** | **NAEP 2005 Strand:** Number Properties and Operations |
|---|---|
| To write and compare whole numbers | **Topic:** Number Sense |
| | **Local Standards:** _____ |

## Vocabulary

The standard form of a number uses _____

_____

## Example

❶ **Writing Whole Numbers** Write $42,046,708,002 in words.

| Billions | | | Millions | | | Thousands | | | Ones | | |
|---|---|---|---|---|---|---|---|---|---|---|---|
| 0 | 4 | 2 | 0 | 4 | 6 | 7 | 0 | 8 | 0 | 0 | 2 |

**Words:** Forty-two billion, forty-six million, seven hundred eight thousand, two dollars

## Quick Check

**1.** Write the value of $26,236,848,080 in words.

|  |
|  |
|  |

Daily Notetaking Guide  L1

## Examples

❷ **Comparing Whole Numbers** Use < or > to complete: 60,201 � 60,102.

**Method 1** Use a number line.

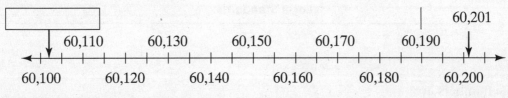

60,201 is to the right of [     ].

So 60,201 [  ] 60,102.

**Method 2** Use place value.

The first two
digits are the
same.

60,2̱01
60,1̱02

2 is [              ] than 1.

Since 2 is greater than 1 in the hundreds place, 60,201 [  ] 60,102.

❸ **Ordering Whole Numbers**

Write in order from least to greatest: 12,374; 13,341; 12,472.

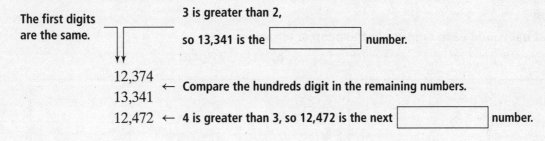

The first digits
are the same.

3 is greater than 2,

so 13,341 is the [              ] number.

12,374
13,341    ← Compare the hundreds digit in the remaining numbers.
12,472    ← 4 is greater than 3, so 12,472 is the next [              ] number.

The order from least to greatest is 12,374; [              ]; [                ].

## Quick Check

**2.** Use < or > to complete: 129,631 [  ] 142,832.

**3.** Write in order from least to greatest: 9,897; 9,987; 978.

[          ]; [          ]; 9,987

# Lesson 1-2

**Estimating With Whole Numbers**

| Lesson Objective | NAEP 2005 Strand: Number Properties and Operations |
|---|---|
| To estimate by rounding and by using compatible numbers | Topic: Number Sense |
| | Local Standards: _____ |

## Vocabulary

Compatible numbers are _____

The symbol ≈ means _____

## Example

**❶ Estimating by Rounding** Estimate 29 + 74 + 58. First round each number to the nearest ten.

29  → 9 ≥ 5, so round up.  →  30

74  → 4 < 5, so round [    ].  →  [    ]

+ 58  → 8 [ ] 5, so round [    ].  →  + 60

[    ]

## Quick Check

1. Estimate. First round each number to the nearest ten.

   **a.** 97 + 22 + 48              **b.** 94 − 32 − 41

## Examples

**❷ Estimating with Compatible Numbers** Use compatible numbers to estimate 483 ÷ 5.

483 ÷ 5    ← **483 is close to 500, which is easy to divide by 5.**

500 ÷ 5    ← **Round 483 to 500.**

500 ÷ 5 = [　　　]    ← **Divide.**

483 ÷ 5 ≈ [　　　]

**❸ Fundraising** Ms. Sanchez's classes raised money for charity. Each class raised about $405. If she teaches 9 different classes, about how much money did her class raise in all?

**A.** $40          **B.** $415          **C.** $2,000          **D.** $4,000

405    →  [　　　]  is easier to work with than 405.  →  [　　　]

× 9    →  [　　　]  is easier to work with than 9.  →  × [　　　]

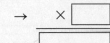

So 405 × 9 ≈ [　　　]. The correct answer is choice [　　].

## Quick Check

2. Estimate using compatible numbers.

   **a.** 8 × 39

   **b.** 672 ÷ 52

3. You have 324 cards for a strategy game. To play the game, a person needs 12 cards. About how many different people can play using your set of cards?

# Lesson 1-3                                                    **Properties of Numbers**

| Lesson Objective | NAEP 2005 Strand: Number Properties and Operations |
|---|---|
| To understand and use the properties of numbers | Topic: Number Sense |
|  | Local Standards: _____ |

## Key Concepts

**Properties of Addition**

**Commutative Property of Addition**

Changing the [    ] of the addends does not change the sum.

$9 + 5 = 5 + $ [  ]

**Associative Property of Addition**

Changing the [    ] of the addends does not change the sum.

$9 + (5 + 4) = ($ [  ] $ + $ [  ] $) + 4$

**Identity Property of Addition**

The sum of [  ] and any number is that number.

$0 + 9 = $ [  ]

**Properties of Multiplication**

**Commutative Property of Multiplication**

Changing the [    ] of factors does not change the product.

$4 \times 6 = $ [  ] $ \times $ [  ]

**Associative Property of Multiplication**

Changing the [    ] of factors does not change the product.

$4 \times (6 \times 2) = ($ [  ] $ \times $ [  ] $) \times 2$

**Identity Property of Multiplication**

The product of [  ] and any number is that number.

$4 \times 1 = $ [  ]

## Examples

**❶ Using the Properties of Addition** Use mental math to find $64 + 26$.

Look at the addends and notice that they end in 6 and 4, which combine to make [ ].

**What you think**

First I will think of 64 as $(60 + 4)$. Next, I will add $4 + 26$ to get 30.

$60 + 30$ is [ ]. So $64 + 26 = $ [ ].

**Why it works**

$64 + 26 = (60 + 4) + 26$    ← **Rewrite 64 as (60 + 4).**

$= 60 + ([\ ] + [\ ])$    ← **Use the Associative Property of Addition.**

$= 60 + ([\ ])$    ← **Add inside the parentheses first.**

$= [\ ]$    ← **Simplify.**

**❷ Using the Properties of Multiplication** Find $25 \times 7 \times 4$.

**What you think**

First I will multiply 25 and 4.

$25 \times 4 = [\quad\quad]$, and $[\quad\quad] \times 7 = [\quad\quad]$.

**Why it works**

$25 \times 7 \times 4 = 25 \times 4 \times 7$    ← **Commutative Property of Multiplication**

$= (25 \times 4) \times 7$    ← [\quad\quad\quad\quad] **Property of Multiplication**

$= [\quad\quad] \times 7$    ← **Multiply inside the parentheses.**

$= [\quad\quad]$    ← **Simplify.**

## Quick Check

**1.** Find the total cost of three pencils with prices of 36¢, 25¢, and 34¢.

[ ]

**2. Mental Math** Find $20 \times (6 \times 5)$.

[ ]

# Lesson 1-4

**Order of Operations**

| Lesson Objective | NAEP 2005 Strand: Number Properties and Operations |
|---|---|
| To use the order of operations to simplify expressions and solve problems | **Topic:** Properties of Number and Operations |
| | **Local Standards:** _____ |

## Vocabulary and Key Concepts

**Order of Operations**

1. Do all operations within [       ] first.
2. [       ] and [       ] in order from left to right.
3. [       ] and [       ] in order from left to right.

An expression is _____

_____

## Example

**❶ Finding the Value of Expressions** Find the value of each expression.

a. $(5 + 7) \div 6 \times 3 = $ [       ] $\div 6 \times 3$ ← **Add 5 and 7 within the parentheses.**

$= 2 \times 3$ ← **Divide 12 by 6.**

$= $ [       ] ← **Multiply.**

b. $20 - 5 \times 8 \div 2 = 20 - $ [       ] $\div 2$ ← **Multiply 5 by 8.**

$= 20 - 20$ ← **Divide 40 by 2.**

$= $ [       ] ← **Subtract.**

## Quick Check

1. Find the value of each expression.

a. $17 - 4 \times 2$

b. $34 + 5 \times 2 - 17$

c. $(6 + 18) \div 3 \times 2$

## Example

❷ **Using Expressions to Solve Problems** The table shows items Sandy bought at the hardware store. What is the total cost of Sandy's purchase (do not include tax)?

| Items Purchased | |
| --- | --- |
| 1 Bottle Glue | @ $3.00 each |
| 8 Decals | @ $1.00 each |
| 2 Coupons | @ $4.00 each |

**A.** $3 **B.** $7 **C.** $8 **D.** $11

Write an expression to help you find the total cost.

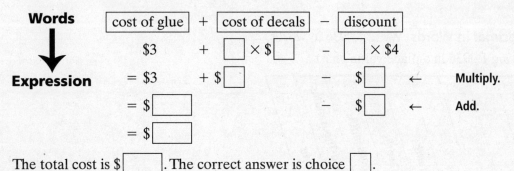

The total cost is $\boxed{\phantom{00}}$. The correct answer is choice $\boxed{\phantom{0}}$.

## Quick Check

2. You are paid $7 per hour to rake leaves. Your brother is paid $5 per hour. You worked 4 hours and your brother worked 3 hours. How much did the two of you earn together?

# Lesson 1-5

**Understanding Decimals**

| **Lesson Objective** | **NAEP 2005 Strand:** Number Properties and Operations |
|---|---|
| To read, write, and round decimals | **Topic:** Number Sense |
| | **Local Standards:** _____ |

## Examples

**❶ Writing a Decimal in Words** Write 1.0936 in words.

Begin by writing 1.0936 in a place value chart

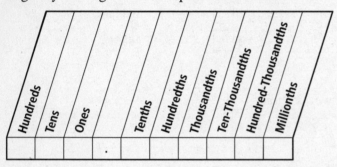

1.0936 ← **Four decimal places indicate ten-thousandths.**

[ ] **and** nine hundred thirty-six ten-thousandths

**❷ Standard Form and Expanded Form** There are four thousand five hundred thirty-six ten-thousandths kilograms in one pound. Write this number in standard form and in expanded form.

[ ] .        ← **Write the whole number part. Place the decimal point.**

0. ▓ ▓ ▓ ▓    ← **Ten-thousandths is [ ] places to the right of the decimal point.**

0. [      ]    ← **Place 4536.**

**Standard form:** [          ]

**Expanded form:** [      ] + [        ] + [        ] + [        ]

Name _____ Class _____ Date _____

**❸ Rounding Decimals** Round 20.32 to the nearest tenth.

20.32 ← **Look at the digit to the right of the tenths place.**

 ↑

 **2 < 5, so round** [            ].

So 20.32 rounded to the nearest tenth is 20.3.

## Quick Check

**1.** Write each decimal in words.

 **a.** 67.3

 [                                                    ]

 **b.** 6.734

 [                                                    ]

 **c.** 0.67

 [                                                    ]

**2.** The winning car in a race won by fifteen hundredths of a second. Write the decimal in standard and expanded forms.

 [                                                    ]

**3.** Round each decimal to the underlined place.

 **a.** 2.3<u>4</u>28

 **b.** 0.173<u>4</u>7

 **c.** 9.<u>0</u>53

Name ________________ Class ________________ Date ________________

# Lesson 1-6

## Comparing and Ordering Decimals

| **Lesson Objective** | **NAEP 2005 Strand:** Number Properties and Operations |
|---|---|
| To compare and order decimals using models and place value | **Topic:** Number Sense<br>**Local Standards:** ____________________ |

### Examples

**1 Using Models to Compare Decimals** Use Models to compare 0.5 and 0.54. Which number is greater?

**Method 1** Use grid models.

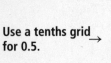

**Use a tenths grid for 0.5.** →

0.5
0.54


← **Use a hundredths grid for 0.54.**

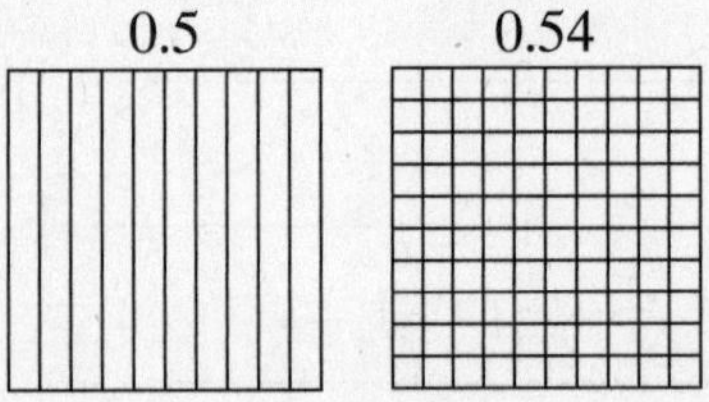

Since a larger area is shaded for 0.54 than 0.5, 0.54 is ________ than 0.5.

**Method 2** Use a number line.

Make a number line showing hundredths. Graph the points.

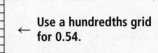

0.49
0.50
0.51
0.52
0.53
0.54
0.55


Since 0.5 is to the ________ of 0.54, 0.5 is ________ than 0.54.

**2 Comparing Decimals** Use <, =, or > to complete the statement 0.28 ■ 0.82. Compare digits starting with the highest place values.

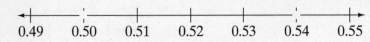

**The ones digits are the same.**

**The tenths digits are different. 2 is less than ________.**

0.28
0.82

Since the 2 tenths in 0.28 is ________ than the 8 tenths in 0.82, 0.28 ____ 0.82.

Name _____ Class _____ Date _____

**❸ Ordering Decimals** Order 0.8, 0.084, 0.48, and 0.84 from least to greatest.

Write zeros at the end of 0.8, 0.48, and 0.84. Then compare the digits starting with the highest place values.

0.800

0 is the ☐ tenths digit,  →  0.084

so 0.084 is the least decimal.  0.480 ← **4 is the next least tenths digit, so**

0.840     **0.480 is the second-☐ decimal.**

↑

**8 is the ☐ tenths digit, 0 hundredths**

**is less than 4 hundredths, so 0.800 is the third-**

**least decimal and 0.840 is the ☐ .**

The decimals from least to greatest are ☐ , 0.48, ☐ , and 0.84.

**Quick Check**

1. Use models to compare 0.59 and 0.6. Which number is greater?

   ☐ .

   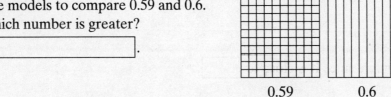

   0.59     0.6

2. Use <, =, or > to complete the statement 0.56 ▨ 0.543.

   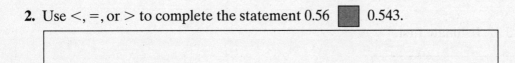

3. Order 3.059, 3.64, and 3.46 from least to greatest.

# Lesson 1-7

**Adding and Subtracting Decimals**

| **Lesson Objective** | **NAEP 2005 Strand:** Number Properties and Operations |
|---|---|
| To add and subtract decimals and to solve problems involving decimals | **Topic:** Number Operations |
| | **Local Standards:** _____ |

## Example

❶ **Finding Decimal Sums** Find $6.8 + 4.65 + 2.125$.

**Step 1** Estimate $6.8 + 4.65 + 2.125 \approx$ ☐ $+ 5 +$ ☐ , or 14

**Step 2** Add.

```
    6 . 8  0  0    ← Line up the decimal points.
    4 . 6  5  0    ← Write zeros so that all decimals have
  + 2 . 1  2  5       the same number of digits to the right
  ┌─┐ 3 .┌─┐ 7  5      of the decimal point.
  └─┘    └─┘
```

**Check for Reasonableness**

The sum ☐ is reasonable since it is close to ☐ .

## Quick Check

**1.** Find $0.84 + 2.0 + 3.32$. Estimate first.

## Examples

**2** **Using Front-End Estimation** A lemonade costs $1.79, sodas cost $1.29, and water costs $1.49. Use front-end estimation to estimate the total cost of buying one of each drink.

**Step 1** Add the front-end digits. These are the the dollar amounts.

$1.79
1.29
+ 1.49
‾‾‾‾‾
$3

**Step 2** Estimate the total cents. Then adjust dollar amounts.

$1.79 ⎤ ← about $ ☐
  1.29 ⎦
+ 1.49    ← about $ ☐
‾‾‾‾‾
  $3      ← about $ ☐

The total cost is about $3 + $ ☐ , or $4.50.

**3** **Finding a Difference** First estimate and then find 16 − 8.79.

**Estimate** 16 − 8.79 ≈ 16 − ☐ , or 7.

| Write 16 with a decimal point and two zeros. | Rename 16 as 15 and ☐ tenths. | Rename 10 tenths as 9 tenths and 10 hundredths. |
|---|---|---|
| 16.00 <br> − 8.79 | 15 10 <br> 16.00 <br> − 8.79 | 9 <br> 15 10 10 <br> 16.00 <br> − 8.79 ← Subtract. <br> ☐ |

**Check for Reasonableness** The difference 7.21 is reasonable since it is close to ☐ .

## Quick Check

**2.** Use front-end estimation to estimate the total cost of one small popcorn and two large popcorns.

Popcorn
Small $3.98
Medium $6.49
Large $9.08
Junior $3.47

☐

**3.** Use the graph at the right. How much greater is the women's record discus throw than the men's throw?

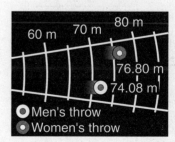

80 m
70 m
60 m
76.80 m
74.08 m
○ Men's throw
◉ Women's throw

☐

Name _____ Class _____ Date _____

# Lesson 1-8                                    **Multiplying Decimals**

| Lesson Objective | NAEP 2005 Strand: Number Properties and Operations |
|---|---|
| To multiply decimals and to solve problems by multiplying decimals | Topic: Number Operations |
| | Local Standards: _____ |

## Examples

❶ **Multiplying by a Decimal**  Find the product 2.73 × 4.

$$2.73 \leftarrow \textbf{2 decimal places}$$
$$\underline{\times \quad 4} \leftarrow + \boxed{\phantom{0}} \textbf{ decimal places}$$
$$\boxed{\phantom{0}}0.9\boxed{\phantom{0}} \leftarrow \boxed{\phantom{0}} \textbf{ decimal places}$$

❷ **Multiplying Decimals**  Find the product 0.6 × 0.42.

$$0.42 \leftarrow \boxed{\phantom{0}} \textbf{ decimal places}$$
$$\underline{\times \ 0.6} \leftarrow + \ \textbf{1 decimal place}$$
$$\boxed{\phantom{0}}.\boxed{\phantom{0}}52 \leftarrow \boxed{\phantom{0}} \textbf{ decimal places}$$

## Quick Check

1. **a.** Find 6 × 0.13.

   **b.** Find 4.37 × 5.

   **c.** Find 7 × 0.8.

   **d.** Find 0.22 × 3.

2. Find each product.

   **a.** 0.3(0.2)

   **b.** 1.9 · 5.32

   **c.** 0.9 × 0.14

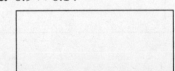

## Example

❸ Cameron can read 196 words in a minute. Robert reads 1.6 times as fast.
How many words can Robert read in a minute?

**Estimate** 196 × [         ] ≈ 200 × 1.5, or [         ] .

```
      1   9   6   ← 0 decimal places
   ×  1.  6   ← [  ] decimal place
  1   1   7   6
+ 1   9   6
[  ] [  ]  3.  6   ← [  ] decimal place
```

Robert can read about [         ] words in a minute.

**Check for Reasonableness** [         ] is reasonable since it is close to 300.

## Quick Check

3. One pound of tomatoes costs $1.29. To the nearest cent, how much do
2.75 pounds of tomatoes cost?

[                                                                        ]

# Lesson 1-9

**Dividing Decimals**

| Lesson Objective | NAEP 2005 Strand: Number Properties and Operations |
|---|---|
| To divide decimals and to solve problems by dividing decimals | Topic: Number Operations |
| | Local Standards: _____ |

## Example

❶ **Dividing by a Whole Number** A class of 27 students held a picnic. They purchased food and drinks for the picnic for a total cost of $93.15. What was the price for each student's meal?

Since you are looking for prices of equal meals, you need to divide.

**Estimate** $93.15 \div 27 \approx 90 \div$ ⬜, or 3.

```
      3 . ⬜ ⬜
 27)9 3 . 1  5     ← Divide as with whole numbers. Place
  −8 1  ↓              the decimal point in the quotient above
   1 2  1              the decimal point in the dividend.
  −1 0  8  ↓
     1  3  5
    −1  3  5
            0
```

Each student's meal cost $⬜.

**Check for Reasonableness** ⬜ is reasonable since it is close to ⬜.

## Quick Check

1. **a.** Find $8)\overline{385.6}$

**b.** Find $9.12 \div 6$.

**Example**

❷ **Dividing a Decimal by a Decimal** Find the quotient $9.674 \div 0.7$.

$0.7\overline{)9.674}$ $\longrightarrow$

$$
\begin{array}{r}
1\ 3\ .\ \boxed{\phantom{0}}\ \boxed{\phantom{0}} \\
7\overline{)\ 9\quad 6\ .\ 7\quad 4} \\
\underline{-7}\phantom{\ 6.74} \\
2\quad 6 \\
\underline{-2\quad 1} \\
5\quad 7 \\
\underline{-5\quad 6} \\
1\quad 4 \\
\underline{-1\quad 4} \\
0
\end{array}
$$

← Divide as with whole numbers. Place the decimal point in the quotient above the decimal point in the dividend.

Since the divisor has one decimal place, multiply the dividend and the divisor by ☐ so that the divisor is a whole number.

**Quick Check**

2. You have $2.75. You want to buy trading cards that cost $0.25 each. How many can you buy?

<br>

Name _____ Class _____ Date _____

# Lesson 2-1

**Finding the Mean**

| Lesson Objective | NAEP 2005 Strand: Data Analysis and Probability |
|---|---|
| To find and analyze the mean of a data set using models and calculations | Topic: Characteristics of Data Sets |
| | Local Standards: _____ |

## Vocabulary

The [        ] is the sum of a set of data divided by the number of data items.

An outlier is _____

## Example

**1** **Using a Model to Find the Mean** In five days Rebecca spent $3, $4, $2, $1, and $5. Find the mean amount of money spent.

Shade in the cubes to model the situation.

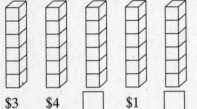

$3    $4    □    $1    □

← Shade the cubes to model the amount of money spent each day.

There are 15 shaded cubes altogether.

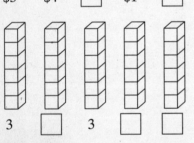

3    □    3    □    □

← Next, shade in the correct number of cubes so that the height of each stack is the same.

## Quick Check

1. Use a model to find the mean of 3, 6, 3, 4, 2, and 6.

← Shade the cubes to model the amount of money spent each day.

There are □ shaded cubes altogether.

← Next, shade in the correct number of cubes so that the height of each stack is the same.

## Examples

**❷ Calculating the Mean** Find the mean test score of 78, 85, 94, 88, and 91.

78 + 85 + 94 + 88 + 91 = [　　　　]    ← **Add the test scores.**

$$\frac{[\quad]}{[\quad]} = [\quad]$$    ← **Divide by the number of tests.**

The mean test score is [　　　　].

**Check for Reasonableness** The mean is between the lowest value, [　　　　], and the greatest value, [　　　　]. So, the answer [　　　　] is reasonable.

**❸ Analyzing the Mean** Identify the outlier in the data set 64, 66, 61, 91, 68 and 59. Find the mean with and without the outlier. What effect does the outlier have on the mean?

The outlier is [　　].

Calculate the mean with the outlier.

$$\frac{64 + 66 + 61 + [\quad] + [\quad] + [\quad]}{6} \approx [\quad]$$

Calculate the mean *without* the outlier.

$$\frac{64 + 66 + 61 + [\quad] + [\quad]}{5} = [\quad]$$

The outlier increased the mean by about [　　].

## Quick Check

**2.** You play a word game. Your scores are 12, 23, 19, 32, and 26. Find your mean score.

[　　　　　　　　　　　　　　　　　　　　　　　　]

**3.** You keep track of the number of hours you baby-sit for six days: 1.25, 1.50, 1.50, 1.75, 2.0, 5.5. What effect does the outlier have on the mean?

[　　　　　　　　　　　　　　　　　　　　　　　　]

# Lesson 2-2

**Median and Mode**

| Lesson Objective | NAEP 2005 Strand: Data Analysis and Probability |
|---|---|
| To find and analyze the median and mode of a data set | **Topic:** Characteristics of Data Sets |
| | **Local Standards:** _____ |

## Vocabulary

The [          ] is the middle number in a set of ordered data.

The mode is _____

0  1  1  2  2  3  3  3  12

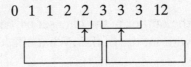

## Example

❶ **Finding the Median** A bird-watcher keeps a count of the number of birds she sees each week. The results are 23, 35, 27, 55, 41, 23, 45, and 69. Find the median number of birds.

$$23, 23, 27, 35, 41, 45, 55, 69 \leftarrow \text{Order the data.}$$

$$23, 23, 27, 35, 41, 45, 55, 69 \leftarrow \text{Since there are 8 items (an even number), use the 2 middle values.}$$

$$\frac{35 + \boxed{\phantom{0}}}{2} = \frac{\boxed{\phantom{0}}}{2} = \boxed{\phantom{0}} \leftarrow \text{Find the mean of 35 and } \boxed{\phantom{0}}.$$

The median number of birds is $\boxed{\phantom{0}}$.

## Quick Check

1. Weekly sales of comics at a store are 39, 19, 28, 9, 32, 35, and 17 comics. What is the median number of comics sold?

[                                                    ]

## Examples

❷ **Finding the Mode** The list shows the favorite colors of 12 children. Find the mode.

blue, red, blue, yellow, yellow, blue, red, blue, yellow, blue, red, yellow
Group the data.

blue, blue, blue, blue, blue
red, red, red
yellow, yellow, yellow, yellow

[_____] occurs the most. It is the mode.

❸ **Analyzing Data** The ages of everyone at a family reunion are listed. Find the mean, median, and mode. Which one best describes the typical age of the family members at the reunion?

22, 100, 26, 4, 30, 33, 21, 44, 47, 83, 47

mean $\dfrac{22 + 100 + 26 + 4 + 30 + 33 + 21 + 44 + 47 + 83 + 47}{11} = \dfrac{457}{\boxed{\phantom{00}}} \approx \boxed{\phantom{00000}}$

median  4, 21, 22, 26, 30, 33, 44, 47, 47, 83, 100: $\boxed{\phantom{00}}$

mode  47

The $\boxed{\phantom{000}}$ and the mode are only close to some of the data points.

The $\boxed{\phantom{000}}$ best describes the typical age of the family members at the reunion.

## Quick Check

2. In Example 2, how many children would have to switch from yellow to red as their favorite color for red to be the only mode?

[_____]

3. The top five women's 1-meter diving scores are 288.75, 261.83, 254.85, 254.1, and 246.8. Does the mean, median, or mode best describe these data? Explain.

[_____]

# Lesson 2-3

**Frequency Tables and Line Plots**

| Lesson Objective | NAEP 2005 Strand: Data Analysis and Probability |
|---|---|
| To analyze a set of data by finding the range and by making frequency tables and line plots | Topic: Data Representation |
| | Local Standards: _____ |

## Vocabulary

A [ ] is a table that lists each item in a data set with the number of times the item occurs.

A [ ] is a graph that shows the shape of a data set by stacking ✗'s above each data value on a number line.

The [ ] is the difference between the least and greatest values.

## Example

① **Frequency Table** The favorite lunch choice of ten students are: pizza, pizza, chicken, hamburger, chicken, pizza, chicken, pizza, pizza, pizza. Organize the data in a frequency table. Find the mode.

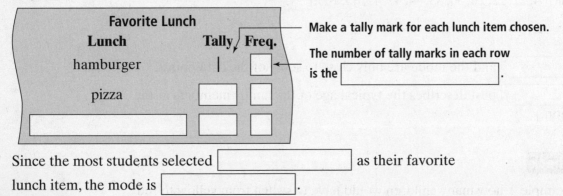

Make a tally mark for each lunch item chosen.

The number of tally marks in each row is the [ ].

Since the most students selected [ ] as their favorite lunch item, the mode is [ ].

## Quick Check

1. The first initials of the names of 15 students are listed below.

A J B K L C K D L S T D V P L

Organize the data in a frequency table. Find the mode.

| Initial | A | B | C | D | J | K | L | P | S | T | V |
|---|---|---|---|---|---|---|---|---|---|---|---|
| Tally | | | | | | | | | | | |
| Frequency | | | | | | | | | | | |

The mode is [ ].

## Examples

❷ **Using a Line Plot** Make a line plot to display the dinner hour for seven families:

5:00  7:00  6:00  6:00  8:00  7:00  6:00

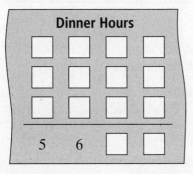

**Dinner Hours**

5    6

← Each ✗ represents one family.

← The scale of a graph includes all of the data values. The scale is ☐ to ☐ in this line plot.

❸ **Finding the Range** Find the range of the data in Example 2.

☐ − 5 = ☐  ← Subtract the least from the greatest value.

The range of dinner times is ☐ hours.

## Quick Check

2. Use a line plot to interpret the number of sales calls made each hour: 2, 3, 0, 7, 1, 1, 9, 8, 2, 8, 1, 2, 8, 7, 1, 8, 6, 1.

**Number of Phone Calls**

0    1    2    3    4    5    6    7    8    9
Phone Calls

3. The numbers of pottery items made by students are 36, 21, 9, 34, 36, 10, 4, 35, 30, 7, 5, and 10. Find the range of the data.

# Lesson 2-4

**Bar Graphs and Line Graphs**

| Lesson Objectives | NAEP 2005 Strand: Data Analysis and Probability |
|---|---|
| To make and analyze bar graphs and line graphs | Topic: Data Representation |
| | Local Standards: _____ |

## Vocabulary

A [ _____ ] uses vertical or horizontal bars to show comparisons.

A [ _____ ] uses a series of line segments to show changes in data.

## Example

❶ **Bar Graph** Make a bar graph to display the data in the table. Compare the number of 16-year-olds to the number of 14-year-olds with employer jobs.

**Students With Employer Jobs**

| Age | Number of Students |
|---|---|
| 14 | 33 |
| 15 | 60 |
| 16 | 74 |

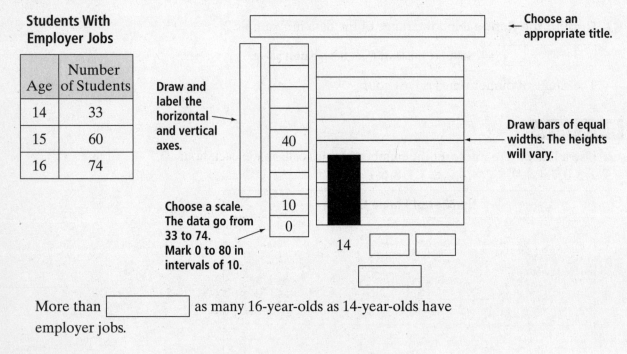

Draw and label the horizontal and vertical axes.

Choose a scale. The data go from 33 to 74. Mark 0 to 80 in intervals of 10.

Choose an appropriate title.

Draw bars of equal widths. The heights will vary.

More than [ _____ ] as many 16-year-olds as 14-year-olds have employer jobs.

## Quick Check

1. Find the difference between the number of 14-year-olds and the number of 15-year-olds with employer jobs.

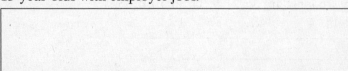

## Examples

❷ **Using a Line Graph** Use the data in the table to make a line graph. Describe the change in sales between March and May.

**The data range from 45 to 121. Mark 0 to 140 in units of 20.**

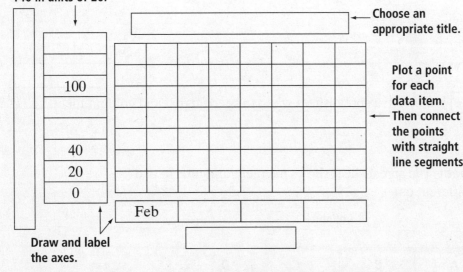

Choose an appropriate title.

Plot a point for each data item. Then connect the points with straight line segments.

Draw and label the axes.

**Running Shoes Sold**

| Month | Pairs Sold |
|---|---|
| February | 54 |
| March | 86 |
| April | 121 |
| May | 115 |

Sales increased from March to April. Then they began to decrease.

❸ **Selecting a Type of Graph** Which type of data display is the most appropriate to show a comparison of the data in the table at the right? Explain.

Use a [               ], since you want to show comparison.

**Favorite Sandwiches**

| Type of Sandwich | Number of Students |
|---|---|
| Egg salad | 8 |
| Peanut butter | 15 |
| Tuna | 12 |
| Turkey | 17 |

## Quick Check

2. Based on the graph in Example 2, are the sales of running shoes in June likely to be greater or less than 70 pairs? Explain.

3. Which type of data display is the most appropriate to display the data at the right? Explain.

**Ticket Sales**

| Week | 1 | 2 | 3 | 4 |
|---|---|---|---|---|
| Tickets Sold | 22 | 35 | 33 | 46 |

# Lesson 2-5

| Lesson Objectives | NAEP 2005 Strand: Data Analysis and Probability |
|---|---|
| To use spreadsheets to display data and solve problems | Topic: Data Representation |
| | Local Standards: _____ |

## Vocabulary

A spreadsheet is _____

_____

A [            ] is a box in a spreadsheet where a specific row and column meet.

## Example

**1** **Reading a Spreadsheet** The spreadsheet shows payment amounts in two categories for three different dates.

Column [   ]

|   | A | B | C | D |
|---|---|---|---|---|
| **1** | Date | Phone | Utilities | Total |
| **2** | 10/15 | $68 | $118 | |
| **3** | 11/15 | $55 | $143 | |
| **4** | 12/15 | $72 | $159 | |

Row [   ]

Cell [   ]

**a.** What is the value in cell C3?

$[            ]

**b.** What does this number represent?

[                                                                              ]

## Quick Check

**1.** What is the value in cell B4? What does this number represent?

[                                                                              ]

## Example

❷ **Formulas in a Spreadsheet** Use the same spreadsheet as in Example 1. Write a formula for cell D3 that will calculate the total for 11/15.

|   | A | B | C | D |
|---|---|---|---|---|
| 1 | Date | Phone | Utilities | Total |
| 2 | 10/15 | $68 | $118 | |
| 3 | 11/15 | $55 | $143 | |
| 4 | 12/15 | $72 | $159 | |
| 5 | Total | | | |

← **Add the entries in cells** ☐ **and C3.**

The formula that should go in cell D3 is ☐ .

## Quick Check

**2.** For cell B5, write a formula that will calculate the total amount for the phone bills from 10/15, 11/15, and 12/15.

# Lesson 2-6

**Stem-and-Leaf Plots**

| Lesson Objective | NAEP 2005 Strand: Data Analysis and Probability |
|---|---|
| To make and analyze stem-and-leaf plots | Topic: Data Representation |
| | Local Standards: _____ |

## Vocabulary

A stem-and-leaf plot is a graph that uses _____

to show _____

## Example

**❶ Interpreting a Stem-and-Leaf Plot** The times customers waited for haircuts are shown below.

**Wait Times for Haircuts**

```
0 | 1 1 3 4 5 6 9
1 | 0 0 1 3 4 4 9
2 | 1 2 4 6
3 | 0 2
```
**Key:** 0 | 5 means 5 min.

11 customers waited more than 10 minutes.
Their times were 11, ☐, 14, 14, ☐, 21,
22, ☐, 26, 30, and 32.

The longest wait was ☐ minutes.

**a.** How many customers waited more than 10 minutes?

☐ customers waited more than 10 minutes.

**b.** How long was the longest wait?

The longest wait was ☐ minutes.

## Quick Check

**1.** What is the range of the data?

☐

## Example

❷ **Making a Stem-and-Leaf Plot** Make a stem-and-leaf plot of the following bowling scores.

| 130 | 90 | 141 | 128 | 133 | 142 |
|-----|----|-----|-----|-----|-----|
| 123 | 148 | 105 | 93 | 108 | 130 |
| 133 | 100 | 124 | 146 | 97 | 108 |

**Step 1** Write the stems in order. Use the numbers in the tens and hundreds places. Draw a vertical line to the right of the stems.

**Step 2** Write the leaves in order. Use the values in the ones place.

**Step 3** Choose a title and include a key. The key explains what your stems and leaves represent.

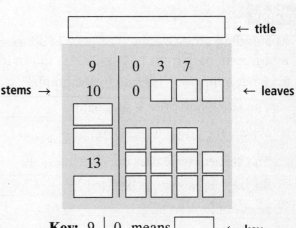

← title

stems →

← leaves

**Key:** 9 │ 0 means ☐ . ← key

## Quick Check

2. The data below show the number of students who voted for class president each year. Make a stem-and-leaf plot.

137, 125, 145, 123, 181, 132, 155, 141, 140, 133, 138, 127, 150, 126, 124, 130, 125, 138, 144, 121, 136

(*Hint:* Use the ones digits for the leaves.)

**Key:** ☐ │ ☐ means ☐ .

# Lesson 2-7

**Misleading Graphs and Statistics**

| Lesson Objective | NAEP 2005 Strand: Data Analysis and Probability |
|---|---|
| To identify misleading graphs and statistics | **Topic:** Data Representation |
| | **Local Standards:** _____ |

## Example

**①** **Misleading Line Graphs** The price of admission to an amusement park from 1985 to 2000 is shown in the graph.

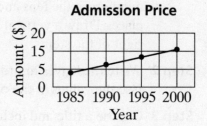

**Admission Price**

**a.** What impression is given by the graph?

The admission price is gradually ⬚.

**b.** Why is the graph misleading?

The vertical scale uses unequal intervals.

So, the increase from 1990 to ⬚

does not look so large.

## Quick Check

**1.** Redraw the graph in Example 1 so that it is not misleading.

**Examples**

❷ **Misleading Bar Graphs**

    **a.** What impression does the graph give?

    The number of females enrolled is more than

    ☐ the number of males enrolled.

    **b.** Why is the graph misleading?

    The vertical scale does not start at 0. So you are looking

    at just the ☐ of the graph.

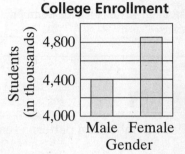

**College Enrollment**

❸ **Identifying Misleading Statistics** Five hourly wages are $5, $8, $7.50, $35, and $7. Explain why the mean may not be the best measure for describing the wages.

Only one person makes more than the mean of $☐ . The $35

hourly wage is an ☐ and greatly increases the mean.

**Quick Check**

    **2. a.** In Example 2, how many times as tall is the bar for Females
        as the bar for Males?

        ☐

    **b.** How many more females were enrolled?

        ☐

    **3.** In Example 3, which would better describe the hourly wages, the median or
    the mode? Explain.

    ☐

# Lesson 3-1

**Describing a Pattern**

| Lesson Objective | NAEP 2005 Strand: Algebra |
|---|---|
| To find and write rules for number patterns | Topic: Patterns, Relations, and Functions |
| | Local Standards: _____ |

## Vocabulary

Each number in a pattern is called a [        ].

A conjecture is _____

A [        ] is a set of numbers that follows a pattern.

## Example

① **Finding Number Patterns** Write the next two terms in this number
pattern: 5, 12, 19, 26, …

Each term is [  ] more
than the previous term. → + 7 + [  ] + [  ] + [  ] + [  ]

← Add 7 to 26 to get the fifth term.

5, 12, 19, 26, [      ], [      ], …

Add 7 to 33 to get the sixth term.

The fifth and sixth terms are [      ] and [      ].

## Quick Check

1. Write the next two terms in each number pattern.
   a. 1, 11, 21, 31, [      ], [      ], …
   b. 56, 48, 40, 32, [      ], [      ], …
   c. 29, 36, 43, 50, [      ], [      ], …

## Examples

**❷ Using a Rule to Write a Pattern** Write the first six terms in the number pattern described by this rule: *Start with 47 and subtract 3 repeatedly.*

**The first term is 47.**

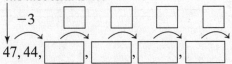

−3 ☐ ☐ ☐ ☐  ← Subtract 3 from each term to find the next term.

47, 44, ☐ , ☐ , ☐ , ☐

**❸ Writing a Rule** Write a rule to describe this number pattern: 2.3, 4.4, 6.5, 8.6, … Then write the next three terms.

+2.1 +2.1 +2.1 +2.1 +2.1 +2.1

2.3, 4.4, 6.5, 8.6, ☐ , ☐ , ☐  ← To get from one term to the next, add ☐ .

The rule is: *Start with* ☐ *and add* ☐ *repeatedly.*

## Quick Check

**2.** Write the first six terms in each number pattern.

  **a.** Start with 90 and subtract 15 repeatedly.

  **b.** Start with 1 and multiply by 3 repeatedly.

**3.** Write a rule for each pattern. Then write the next three terms.

  **a.** 1.5, 4.5, 13.5, 40.5, …

  **b.** 256, 128, 64, …

# Lesson 3-2

**Variables and Expressions**

| **Lesson Objective**<br>To evaluate algebraic expressions | **NAEP 2005 Strand:** Algebra<br>**Topic:** Variables, Expressions, and Operations<br>**Local Standards:** _____ |
| --- | --- |

## Vocabulary

A numerical expression is _____

_____

A variable is _____

_____

An algebraic expression is a _____

_____

To evaluate an algebraic expression is to _____

_____

## Example

**❶ Modeling with Algebra Tiles** Model the expression $2x + 3$ with algebra tiles.

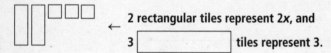

← 2 rectangular tiles represent **2x**, and

3 [ ] tiles represent **3**.

## Quick Check

**1.** Draw algebra tiles to model the expression $x + 2$.

**Examples**

❷ **Evaluating an Algebraic Expression** Evaluate $8x + 2$ for $x = 3$.

$8x + 2 = 8\left(\boxed{\phantom{xx}}\right) + 2 \quad \leftarrow$ **Replace x with 3.**

$\phantom{8x + 2} = \boxed{\phantom{xxx}} + 2 \quad \leftarrow$ **Multiply 8 and 3.**

$\phantom{8x + 2} = \boxed{\phantom{xxx}} \quad\quad\; \leftarrow$ **Add 24 and 2.**

❸ **Canoe Rental** The cost to rent a canoe at the lake is a $6 basic fee plus $4 for each hour $h$ the canoe is rented. The expression for the total cost of a canoe rental is $6 + 4h$. Complete the table for the given number of hours.

| Hours | Total Cost |
|:-----:|:----------:|
| $h$   | $6 + 4h$   |
| 1     |            |
| 2     |            |
| 3     |            |

Substitute each number of hours for $h$.

$\leftarrow 6 + 4 \times 1$

$\leftarrow 6 + 4 \times \boxed{\phantom{x}}$

$\leftarrow 6 + 4 \times \boxed{\phantom{x}}$

**Quick Check**

2. Evaluate each expression for $x = 7$.

   **a.** $3x + 15$

   **b.** $5x \div 7$

   **c.** $56 - 4x$

3. In Example 3, how much will it cost to rent a canoe for 6 hours?

# Lesson 3-3

**Writing Algebraic Expressions**

| Lesson Objective | NAEP 2005 Strand: Algebra |
|---|---|
| To use algebraic expressions to solve problems | Topic: Variables, Expressions, and Operations |
| | Local Standards: _____ |

## Examples

❶ **From Words to Expressions** Write an expression for "the quotient when $y$ is divided by 12."

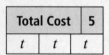

❷ **Retail** A newspaper advertisement reads, "Buy 3 T-shirts of the same kind, take $5 off the total price." Let $t$ represent the cost of one T-shirt. Write an algebraic expression that describes the situation.

| Total Cost | 5 |
|---|---|
| $t$ \| $t$ \| $t$ | |

**Write the cost of 3 T-shirts as 3$t$.**

An expression is [    ] − [    ] .

## Quick Check

**1.** Write an expression for "2 more than $x$."

**2.** Brandon is 28 years younger than his father. Write an expression using Brandon's age to describe his father's age.

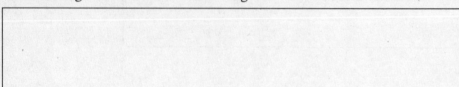

## Example

❸ **From a Pattern to an Expression** Write an expression to describe the relationship of the data in the table.

| n | ■ |
|---|---|
| 1 | 3 |
| 4 | 12 |
| 5 | 15 |

$1 \times 3 = 3$

$4 \times \boxed{\phantom{0}} = 12$  ←

$5 \times \boxed{\phantom{0}} = 15$

**Multiplying each number in the first column by** $\boxed{\phantom{0}}$ **gives you the number in the second column.**

The expression $\boxed{\phantom{0000}}$, or $\boxed{\phantom{0000}}$, describes the pattern.

## Quick Check

**3.** Write an algebraic expression to describe the relationship in the table.

a.

| n | ■ |
|---|---|
| 2 | 1 |
| 6 | 3 |
| 9 | 4.5 |

$\boxed{\phantom{00000000000000}}$

b.

| n | ■ |
|---|---|
| 2 | 6 |
| 5 | 9 |
| 7 | 11 |

$\boxed{\phantom{00000000000000}}$

# Lesson 3-4

| Lesson Objective | NAEP 2005 Strand: Algebra |
|---|---|
| To use mental math to estimate and solve equations | Topic: Equations and Inequalities |
| | Local Standards: _____ |

## Vocabulary and Key Concepts

### Number Properties

**Identity Properties**

The sum of 0 and any number is that number.

**Arithmetic** $0 + 9 = \boxed{\phantom{0}}$    **Algebra** $0 + a = \boxed{\phantom{0}}$

The product of 1 and any number is that number.

**Arithmetic** $1 \cdot 9 = \boxed{\phantom{0}}$    **Algebra** $1 \cdot a = \boxed{\phantom{0}}$

**Commutative Properties**

Changing the $\boxed{\phantom{00000}}$ of the addends or factors does not change the sum or the product.

**Arithmetic** $9 + 6 = \boxed{\phantom{0}} + \boxed{\phantom{0}}$    $9 \cdot 6 = \boxed{\phantom{0}} \cdot \boxed{\phantom{0}}$

**Algebra** $a + b = b + a$    $a \cdot b = \boxed{\phantom{0}} \cdot \boxed{\phantom{0}}$

**Associative Properties**

Changing the $\boxed{\phantom{0000000000}}$ of numbers does not change the sum or the product.

**Arithmetic** $9 + (6 + 4) = \boxed{\phantom{000}} + \boxed{\phantom{0}}$    $9 \cdot (6 \cdot 4) = \boxed{\phantom{000}} \cdot \boxed{\phantom{0}}$

**Algebra** $a + (b + c) = (a + b) + c$    $a(bc) = \boxed{\phantom{00}} \cdot \boxed{\phantom{0}}$

An equation is _____

An open sentence is _____

A solution of an equation is _____

## Example

**❶ True Equations and False Equations** Is the equation $24 - 16 = 8$ true or false?

$24 - 16 \overset{?}{=} 8$ ← **Write the equation.**

$\boxed{\phantom{00}}$ ← **Subtract 16 from 24.**

$\boxed{\phantom{00}} \overset{?}{=} 8$ ← **Compare.**    The equation is $\boxed{\phantom{0000}}$.

**❷ Using Mental Math** Use mental math to solve each equation.

**a.** $y - 7 = 15$

**b.** $d \div 9 = 6$

**What you think**

$\boxed{\phantom{xx}} - 7 = 15$, so the solution is $\boxed{\phantom{xx}}$.

**What you think**

$\boxed{\phantom{xx}} \div 9 = 6$, so the solution is $\boxed{\phantom{xx}}$.

**❸ Guess, Check, and Revise** Use the strategy *Guess, Check, and Revise* to solve $n + 14 = 42$.

**Estimate** Round numbers to get a good starting point.

$$n + 14 = 42$$
$$\downarrow \quad \downarrow \quad \downarrow$$
$$n + 10 = 40$$

**What you think**

Using mental math you know $\boxed{\phantom{xx}} + 10 = 40$, so $n$ is close to $\boxed{\phantom{xx}}$.

I can try substituting $n = \boxed{\phantom{xx}}$ in the equation: $\boxed{\phantom{xx}} + 14 = \boxed{\phantom{xx}}$.

The number 30 is too high. I will try $n = 25$:  $25 + 14 = \boxed{\phantom{xx}}$.

The number 25 is $\boxed{\phantom{xx}}$. I will try $n = 28$:  $28 + 14 = \boxed{\phantom{xx}}$.

Since $28 + 14 = 42$ is $\boxed{\phantom{xx}}$, the solution of $n + 14 = 42$ is $\boxed{\phantom{xx}}$.

## Quick Check

**1.** Tell whether each equation is true or false.

**a.** $7 \times 9 = 63$

**b.** $4 + 5 = 45$

**c.** $70 - 39 = 41$

**2. Mental Math** Use mental math to solve each equation.

**a.** $17 - x = 8$

**b.** $w \div 4 = 20$

**c.** $4.7 + c = 5.9$

**3. Use the Strategy** *Guess, Check,* and *Revise* to solve $k + 39 = 82$.

# Lesson 3-5

**Solving Addition Equations**

| **Lesson Objective**<br>To use subtraction to solve equations | **NAEP 2005 Strand:** Algebra<br>**Topic:** Equations and Inequalities<br>**Local Standards:** _____ |
| --- | --- |

## Vocabulary and Key Concepts

**Subtraction Property of Equality**

If you [ ] the same value from each side of an equation, the two sides remain equal.

**Arithmetic**

$2 \cdot 3 = 6$, so $2 \cdot 3 - 4 = 6 - \boxed{\phantom{x}}$.

**Algebra**

If $a = b$, then $a - c = b - \boxed{\phantom{x}}$.

[ ] are operations that undo each other.

## Example

**1** **Solving Equations by Subtracting** Solve $h + 9 = 14$.

Get $h$ alone on one side of the equation.

$$h \ + \ 9 \ = \ \quad 14$$
$$\underline{- \boxed{\phantom{x}} \ - \boxed{\phantom{x}}}$$

← Subtract 9 from each side to undo the [ ] and get **h** by itself.

$$h = \boxed{\phantom{x}}$$

← **Simplify.**

**Check** $h + 9 = 14$

← Check your solution in the original equation.

$$\boxed{\phantom{x}} + 9 \overset{?}{=} 14$$

← Substitute [ ] for **h**.

$$\boxed{\phantom{x}} = 14 \checkmark$$

## Quick Check

**1.** Solve $w + 4.3 = 9.1$. Check the solution.

## Example

❷ **Growth** Rita's height in first grade was 44 inches. In the fourth grade, Rita's height was 51 inches. How many inches did Rita grow between the first and fourth grades?

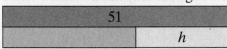

| Height in fourth grade | |
| --- | --- |
| Height in first grade | Inches grown |

Let $h$ = the number of inches grown.

| 51 | |
| --- | --- |
| | $h$ |

The equation $44 + \boxed{\phantom{x}} = 51$ models this situation.

$$44 + h = 51$$

$$44 + h - \boxed{\phantom{x}} = 51 - \boxed{\phantom{x}} \qquad \leftarrow \text{Subtract } \boxed{\phantom{x}} \text{ from both sides to undo the addition.}$$

$$h - \boxed{\phantom{x}} \qquad \leftarrow \text{Simplify.}$$

Rita grew $\boxed{\phantom{x}}$ inches.

## Quick Check

2. A cat has gained 1.8 pounds in a year. It now weighs 11.6 pounds. Write and solve an equation to find how much it weighed one year ago. Check the solution.

Name _____ Class _____ Date _____

# Lesson 3-6

**Solving Subtraction Equations**

| Lesson Objective<br>To use addition to solve equations | NAEP 2005 Strand: Algebra<br>Topic: Equations and Inequalities<br>Local Standards: _____ |

## Vocabulary and Key Concepts

**Addition Property of Equality**

If you [ ] the same value to each side of an equation, the two sides remain equal.

**Arithmetic**

$2 \cdot 3 = 6$, so $2 \cdot 3 + 4 = 6 +$ [ ].

**Algebra**

If $a = b$, then $a + c = b +$ [ ].

## Example

**①** **Solving Equations by Adding** Solve $p - 22.3 = 5.08$.

$p - 22.3 +$ [ ] $= 5.08 +$ [ ] ← **Add** [ ] **to undo the subtraction.**

$p =$ [ ] ← **Simplify.**

## Quick Check

1. Solve each equation.

a. $n - 53 = 28$

b. $x - 43 = 12$

**Example**

**2 Entertainment** The sale price of a CD is $11.49. This is $3.50 less than the regular price of the CD. What is the regular price of the CD?

**Words**  sale price is [     ] less than regular price

Let $r$ = the regular price.

**Equation**  [          ] = [    ] − [          ]

$r$ −  3.50  =  11.49  ← Write the equation.
  + [          ]  + [          ]  ← Add [     ] to each side to undo the subtraction.

$r$ = [          ]  ← Simplify.

The regular price of the CD is [          ].

**Quick Check**

2. The temperature dropped 9°F between 7 P.M. and midnight. It was 54°F at midnight. Write an equation to find the temperature at 7 P.M.

[                                                                      ]

# Lesson 3-7

**Solving Multiplication and Division Equations**

| Lesson Objective | NAEP 2005 Strand: Algebra |
|---|---|
| To use multiplication and division to solve equations | Topic: Equations and Inequalities |
| | Local Standards: _____ |

## Key Concepts

**Division Property of Equality**

If you [        ] each side of an equation by the same nonzero number, the two sides remain equal.

| **Arithmetic** | **Algebra** |
|---|---|
| $4 \times 2 = 8$, so $4 \times 2 \div 2 = 8 \div \boxed{\phantom{x}}$. | If $a = b$ and $c \neq 0$, then $a \div c = b \div \boxed{\phantom{x}}$. |

**Multiplication Property of Equality**

If you [        ] each side of an equation by the same number, the two sides remain equal.

| **Arithmetic** | **Algebra** |
|---|---|
| $6 \div 2 = 3$, so $(6 \div 2) \times 2 = 3 \times \boxed{\phantom{x}}$. | If $a = b$, then $a \cdot c = b \cdot \boxed{\phantom{x}}$. |

## Example

**❶ Solving Equations by Dividing** Solve $6x = 144$.

$$6x \div \boxed{\phantom{x}} = 144 \div \boxed{\phantom{x}}$$   ← Divide each side by $\boxed{\phantom{x}}$ to undo the multiplication and get *x* alone on one side.

$$x = \boxed{\phantom{xx}}$$   ← Simplify.

**Check**   $6x = 144$   ← Check your solution in the original equation.

$$6 \times \boxed{\phantom{x}} \stackrel{?}{=} 144$$   ← Replace *x* with $\boxed{\phantom{x}}$.

$$\boxed{\phantom{xxx}} = 144 \checkmark$$

## Quick Check

**1.** Solve $0.8p = 32$. Then check the solution.

## Examples

**❷ Entertainment** The cost of a pay-per-view concert on television is $39.95. Five friends decide to watch the concert together and split the cost equally. What amount will each friend pay?

Use a diagram to help write an equation.

| Total Cost | | | | |
|---|---|---|---|---|
| $c$ | $c$ | $c$ | $c$ | $c$ |

Let $c$ = each person's share of the cost of the concert.

The equation [＿＿＿] = 39.95 models this situation.

$$5c = 39.95 \qquad \leftarrow \textbf{Write the equation.}$$

$$5c \div \boxed{\phantom{x}} = 39.95 \div \boxed{\phantom{x}} \qquad \leftarrow \begin{array}{l}\textbf{Divide each side by } \boxed{\phantom{x}} \textbf{ to undo the} \\ \textbf{multiplication.}\end{array}$$

$$c = \boxed{\phantom{xxxx}} \qquad \leftarrow \textbf{Simplify.}$$

Each friend's share is [＿＿＿＿].

**❸ Solving an Equation by Multiplying** Solve $x \div 6.3 = 9$.

$$x \div 6.3 \times \boxed{\phantom{xx}} = 9 \times \boxed{\phantom{xx}} \qquad \leftarrow \begin{array}{l}\textbf{Multiply by 6.3 to undo the } \boxed{\phantom{xxxx}} \\ \textbf{and get } \textit{x} \textbf{ alone.}\end{array}$$

$$x = \boxed{\phantom{xxxx}} \qquad \leftarrow \textbf{Simplify.}$$

## Quick Check

**2.** A club sells greeting cards for a fundraiser. The profit for each card sold is $0.35. The club's total profit is $302.75. Use an equation to find the number of greeting cards the club sells.

**3.** Solve $w \div 1.5 = 10$. Then check the solution.

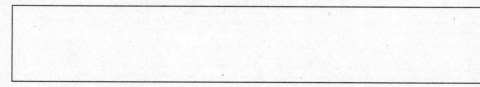

# Lesson 3-8

**The Distributive Property**

| Lesson Objective | NAEP 2005 Strand: Number Properties and Operations |
|---|---|
| To use the Distributive Property to simplify expressions in problem-solving situations | **Topics:** Number Sense; Number Operations |
| | **Local Standards:** _____ |

## Key Concepts

**The Distributive Property**

**Arithmetic**

$8 \times (4 + 6) = (8 \times 4) + (8 \times \boxed{\phantom{0}})$

$7 \times (6 - 2) = (7 \times \boxed{\phantom{0}}) - (7 \times \boxed{\phantom{0}})$

**Algebra**

$a(b + c) = ab + \boxed{\phantom{0}}$

$a(b - c) = ab - \boxed{\phantom{0}}$

## Example

❶ **Evaluating an Expression** Use the Distributive Property to simplify $5 \times 47$.

**What you think**

Think of 47 as $40 + 7$.

Then multiply by 5: $5 \times 40 = \boxed{\phantom{0}}$ and $5 \times 7 = 35$.

Now add the two products: $\boxed{\phantom{0}} + \boxed{\phantom{0}} = \boxed{\phantom{0}}$.

**Why it works**

$5 \times 47 = 5 \times (\boxed{\phantom{0}} + \boxed{\phantom{0}})$  ← Write 47 as $\boxed{\phantom{0}}$ + 7.

$= (5 \times 40) + (5 \times 7)$  ← Use the Distributive Property.

$= \boxed{\phantom{0}} + \boxed{\phantom{0}}$  ← Simplify within parentheses.

$= \boxed{\phantom{0}}$  ← Add.

## Quick Check

1. Use the Distributive Property to simplify $5 \times 68$.

## Example

❷ **Money** A student bought 4 tickets that cost $5.50. What was the total cost of the tickets?

$4 \times 5.50 = 4\left(5.00 + \boxed{\phantom{xxxx}}\right)$  ← **Write 5.5 as 5.00 +** $\boxed{\phantom{xxx}}$ **.**

$= (4 \times 5.00) + (4 \times 0.50)$  ← **Use the Distributive Property.**

$= \boxed{\phantom{xxxx}} + \boxed{\phantom{xxxx}}$  ← **Simplify within parentheses.**

$= \boxed{\phantom{xxxx}}$  ← **Add.**

The total cost was $\boxed{\phantom{xxx}}$.

## Quick Check

**2.** A local bookstore charges $2.80 for each used book. What is the charge for 5 used books?

$\boxed{\phantom{xxxxxxxxxxxxxxxxxxxxxxxxxxxxxxxxxxxxxxxxxxxxx}}$

# Lesson 4-1

**Divisibility and Mental Math**

| **Lesson Objective** | **NAEP 2005 Strand:** Number Properties and Operations |
|---|---|
| To check for divisibility using mental math and to use divisibility to solve problems | **Topic:** Properties of Number and Operations |
| | **Local Standards:** _____ |

## Vocabulary and Key Concepts

**Divisibility of Whole Numbers**

**A whole number is divisible by**

- ☐ , if the number ends in 0, 2, 4, 6, or 8.
- ☐ , if the sum of the number's digits is divisible by 3.
- ☐ , if the number ends in 0 or 5.
- ☐ , if the sum of the number's digits is divisible by 9.
- ☐ , if the number ends in 0.

One whole number is ☐ by a second whole number if the

remainder is ☐ when the first number is divided by the second number.

An even number is _____

An odd number is _____

## Example

**1** **Using Mental Math for Divisibility**

**a.** Is 46 divisible by 3?

**Think** Since $3 \times 15 = 45$

and $3 \times 16 =$ ☐ ,

46 ☐ divisible by 3.

**b.** Is 63 divisible by 7?

**Think** Since $7 \times 9 = 63$,

63 ☐ divisible by 7.

## Quick Check

**1. a.** Is 64 divisible by 6? ☐

**b.** Is 93 divisible by 3? ☐

## Examples

❷ **Divisibility by 2, 3, 5, and 10**  Test 580 for divisibility by 2, 3, 5, and 10.

2: 580 is an [_____] number. So 580 is divisible by 2.

3: Find the sum of the digits in 580.

$5 + 8 + 0 = $ [_____]

The sum of the digits is [_____], which [_____] divisible by 3.

So 580 [_____] divisible by 3.

5: 580 ends in 0. So 580 [_____] divisible by 5.

10: 580 ends in 0. So 580 [_____] divisible by 10.

❸ **Divisibility by 9**  A baker sells muffins in boxes that contain exactly 9 muffins each. Can the baker place 576 muffins in boxes of 9 with none left over?

If 576 is divisible by 9, then there will be no muffins left over.

$5 + 7 + 6 = 18$          ← Find the sum of the digits in 576.

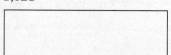

$18 \div 9 = $ [____]          ‹ The sum [_____] divisible by 9.

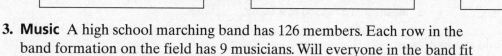

So, 576 [_____] divisible by 9. There [_____] muffins left over.

## Quick Check

2. Test each number for divisibility by 2, 3, 5, and 10.

   **a.** 150

   **b.** 1,021

   **c.** 2,112

   [_____]     [_____]     [_____]

3. **Music**  A high school marching band has 126 members. Each row in the band formation on the field has 9 musicians. Will everyone in the band fit in a nine-person row?

   [_____]

# Lesson 4-2

**Exponents**

| Lesson Objective | NAEP 2005 Strand: Algebra |
|---|---|
| To use exponents and to simplify expressions with exponents | Topic: Equations and Inequalities |
| | Local Standards: _____ |

## Vocabulary and Key Concepts

**Order of Operations**

1. Do all operations within [          ] first.

2. Do all work with exponents.

3. Multiply and divide in order from left to right.

4. [          ] and [          ] in order from left to right.

An [          ] tells you how many times a number, or base, is used as a factor.

$8 \times 8 \times 8 = 8^3$ ← [          ]

↑

[          ]

A power is _____

## Example

**1 Using Exponents** Write $5 \times 5 \times 5 \times 5$ using an exponent. Name the base and the exponent.

$5 \times 5 \times 5 \times 5 = 5^{\boxed{\phantom{x}}}$ ← $5^4$ means that 5 is used as a factor $\boxed{\phantom{x}}$ times.

The base is $\boxed{\phantom{x}}$ and the exponent is $\boxed{\phantom{x}}$.

## Quick Check

1. Write each expression using an exponent. Name the base and the exponent.
   **a.** $3.94 \times 3.94$      **b.** $7 \times 7 \times 7 \times 7$      **c.** $x \cdot x \cdot x$

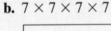

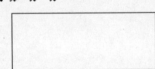

## Examples

❷ **Simplifying a Power** What is the value of $6^3$?

$6^3 = 6 \times 6 \times 6 = $ [ ] ← The base [ ] is used as a factor [ ] times.

❸ **Simplifying an Expression** Simplify $24 - (8 - 1.2 \times 5)^2$.

$24 - \left(8 - \boxed{\phantom{x}}\right)^2$ ← Simplify within parentheses. Simplify $1.2 \times 5$.

$24 - \left(\boxed{\phantom{x}}\right)^2$ ← In parentheses, simplify $8 - 6$.

$24 - \boxed{\phantom{x}}$ ← Simplify $2^2$.

$\boxed{\phantom{x}}$ ← Subtract 4 from 24.

## Quick Check

2. **Astronomy** Phobos, the largest of Mars' moons, has a diameter of $3^3$ kilometers. What is the value of $3^3$?

[ ]

3. a. Simplify $2^3 - 6 \div 3$.

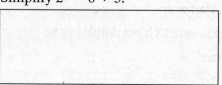

b. Simplify $5 + (2 + 1)^2$.

Name _____  Class _____  Date _____

# Lesson 4-3                                   **Prime Numbers and Prime Factorization**

| **Lesson Objective** | **NAEP 2005 Strand:** Number Properties and Operations |
| --- | --- |
| To factor numbers and to find the prime factorization of numbers | **Topic:** Properties of Number and Operations |
| | **Local Standards:** _____ |

## Vocabulary

A factor is _____

_____

A [_____] is a whole number greater than 1 with more than two factors.

A prime number is _____

_____

A [_____] is the writing of a composite number as the product of

prime numbers.

## Example

**❶ Finding Factors** List the factors of each number.

   **a.** 24

     $1 \times 24$         ← **Write each pair of factors. Start with 1.**

     $2 \times \boxed{\phantom{0}}, 3 \times \boxed{\phantom{0}}, 4 \times \boxed{\phantom{0}}$  ← **2, 3, and 4 are factors. Skip 5, since 24 is not divisible by 5.**

     $6 \times \boxed{\phantom{0}}$     ← **Stop when you repeat factors.**

     The factors of 24 are $\boxed{\phantom{0}}, \boxed{\phantom{0}}, \boxed{\phantom{0}}, \boxed{\phantom{0}}, \boxed{\phantom{0}}, \boxed{\phantom{0}}, \boxed{\phantom{0}},$ and $\boxed{\phantom{0}}$.

   **b.** 35

     $1 \times 35$  ← **Write each pair of factors. Start with 1.**

     $\boxed{\phantom{0}} \times 7$  ← **Skip 2, 3, and 4, since 35 is not divisible by 2, 3, or 4. 5 is a factor. Skip 6, since 35 is not divisible by 6.**

     $7 \times \boxed{\phantom{0}}$  ← **Stop when you repeat factors.**

     The factors of 35 are $\boxed{\phantom{0}}, \boxed{\phantom{0}}, \boxed{\phantom{0}},$ and $\boxed{\phantom{0}}$.

## Quick Check

**1.** A gift box must hold the same number of pears in each row. You have 24
pears. What arrangements can you use?

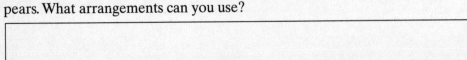

## Examples

**❷ Prime or Composite?** Is the number prime or composite? Explain.

a. 61 [        ] ; 61 has two factors, [    ] and [    ].

b. 65 [        ] ; 65 is divisible by [    ] , so it has more than two factors.

**❸ Prime Factorization** Write the prime factorization of 90 using exponents.

**Method 1** Use a division ladder

$2\overline{)90}$   ← **Divide 90 by the prime number 2. Work down.**

$3\overline{)45}$   ← **The result is 45. Divide by the prime number 3.**

$3\overline{)\boxed{\phantom{00}}}$   ← **The result is** [    ] **. Divide by 3 again.**

[    ]   ← **The prime factorization is** [  ] × [  ] × [  ] × [  ] .

**Method 2** Use a factor tree

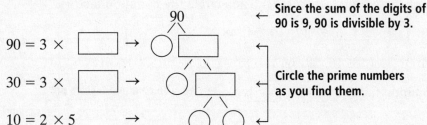

90 = 3 × [      ] →   ← **Since the sum of the digits of 90 is 9, 90 is divisible by 3.**

30 = 3 × [      ] →   ← **Circle the prime numbers as you find them.**

10 = 2 × 5   →

The prime factorization of 90 is [  ] × [  ] × [  ] × [  ] , or [  ] × [  ]² × [  ] .

## Quick Check

**2.** Is the number prime or composite? Explain.

a. 39

[                                                                ]

b. 47

[                                                                ]

c. 63

[                                                                ]

**3.** Find the prime factorization of 27.

[                                        ]

# Lesson 4-4

**Greatest Common Factor**

| **Lesson Objective**<br>To find the GCF of two or more numbers | **NAEP 2005 Strand:** Number Properties and Operations<br>**Topic:** Number Operations<br>**Local Standards:** _____ |
| --- | --- |

## Vocabulary

A _____ is a factor that two or more numbers share.

The greatest common factor (GCF) of two or more numbers is _____

_____

## Example

**❶ Using Lists of Factors** Find the greatest common factor of 48 and 64.

List the factors of 48 and the factors of 64. Then circle the common factors.

Factors of 48: 1, 2, 3, 4, 6, 8, 12, 16, 24, 48

Factors of 64: 1, 2, 4, 8, 16, 32, 64

The greatest common factor (GCF) is [ ].      ← **The common factors are**

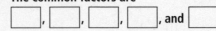

[ ] , [ ] , [ ] , [ ] , and [ ] .

## Quick Check

**1.** List the factors to find the GCF of each pair of numbers.

**a.** 6, 21    factors of 6: [ ] , [ ] , [ ] , [ ]

            factors of 21: [ ] , [ ] , [ ] , [ ]      GCF of 6 and 21: [ ]

**b.** 18, 49    factors of 18: [ ] , [ ] , [ ] , [ ] , [ ] , [ ]

             factors of 49: [ ] , [ ] , [ ]      GCF of 18 and 49: [ ]

**c.** 14, 28    factors of 14: [ ] , [ ] , [ ]

             factors of 28: [ ] , [ ] , [ ] , [ ] , [ ] , [ ]      GCF of 14 and 28: [ ]

Name _____ Class _____ Date _____

## Examples

**❷ Using a Division Ladder** Find the GCF of 84 and 90. Use a division ladder.

2) 84    90    ← **Divide by 2, a common factor of 84 and 90.**

3) [    ]  [    ]  ← **Divide by 3, a common factor of 42 and 45.**

[    ]  [    ]  ← **14 and 15 have no common factors.**

**Multiply the common factors: 2 × 3 =** [  ].

The GCF of 84 and 90 is [  ].

**❸ Using Factor Trees** Use factor trees to find the GCF of 28 and 42.

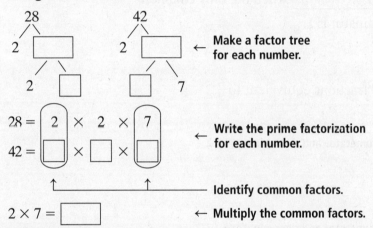

28 = ( 2 ) × 2 × ( 7 )    ← **Write the prime factorization for each number.**
42 = ( [ ] ) × [ ] × ( [ ] )

← **Make a factor tree for each number.**

← **Identify common factors.**

2 × 7 = [        ]    ← **Multiply the common factors.**

The GCF of 28 and 42 is [      ].

## Quick Check

**2.** You want to cut two ribbons into equal lengths with nothing left over. The ribbons are 18 and 42 inches long. What is the longest possible length of ribbon you can cut?

[                                                      ]

**3.** Use factor trees to find the GCF.

**a.** 48, 80, 128    **b.** 36, 60, 84

# Lesson 4-5

**Equivalent Fractions**

| Lesson Objective | NAEP 2005 Strand: Number Properties and Operations |
|---|---|
| To find equivalent forms of fractions | **Topic:** Number Operations |
| | **Local Standards:** _____ |

## Vocabulary

Equivalent fractions are _____

_____

A fraction is in [ _____ ] when the only common

factor of the numerator and denominator is 1.

## Example

❶ **Equivalent Fractions** Write three fractions equivalent to $\frac{6}{9}$.

 $\frac{6}{9} = \frac{12}{18}$  ← **Multiply the numerator and denominator by 2.**

 $\frac{6}{9} = \frac{\Box}{\Box}$  ← **Multiply the numerator and denominator by 3.**

 $\frac{6}{9} = \frac{\Box}{\Box}$  ← **Divide the numerator and denominator by 3.**

So $\frac{\Box}{\Box} = \frac{6}{9} = \frac{12}{18} = \frac{\Box}{\Box}$ .

## Quick Check

1. Write two fractions equivalent to each fraction.
   **a.** $\frac{4}{10}$            **b.** $\frac{5}{8}$

**Examples**

**❷ Simplify a Fraction Using the GCF** Write $\frac{16}{40}$ in simplest form.

16: ☐ , ☐ , ☐ , ☐ , ☐

40: ☐ , ☐ , ☐ , ☐ , ☐ , ☐ , ☐ , ☐

← List the factors for the numerator and denominator.
Find the greatest common factor.

The GCF of 16 and 40 is ☐ .

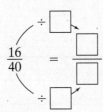

$$\frac{16}{40} = \frac{\boxed{\phantom{x}}}{\boxed{\phantom{x}}}$$

← Divide the numerator and denominator by the GCF.

The fraction $\frac{16}{40}$ written in simplest form is $\frac{\boxed{\phantom{x}}}{\boxed{\phantom{x}}}$ .

**❸ Using Prime Factorization** A store stocks 12 types of blue pens, 6 types of black pens, and 2 types of red pens. In simplest form, what fraction of the types of pens are blue?

Add to find the total number of pen types to find the denominator:

$12 + 6 + 2 =$ ☐ . Write the fraction.

$\frac{\boxed{\phantom{x}}}{\boxed{\phantom{x}}}$   ← number of types of blue pens
← total number of types of pens

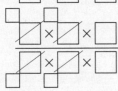

$\frac{12}{20} =$ 

← Write the prime factorization of the numerator and the denominator.
Divide the common factors.

← Divide the common factors.

So $\frac{\boxed{\phantom{x}}}{\boxed{\phantom{x}}}$ of the types of pens are blue pens.

**Quick Check**

**2.** Write $\frac{24}{32}$ in simplest form.

**3.** In simplest form, what fraction of the types of pens in Example 3 are red pens?

# Lesson 4-6

**Mixed Numbers and Improper Fractions**

| **Lesson Objective**<br>To use mixed numbers and improper fractions | **NAEP 2005 Strand:** Number Properties and Operations<br>**Topic:** Number Operations<br>**Local Standards:** _____ |
| --- | --- |

## Vocabulary

A proper fraction has _____

_____

An improper fraction has _____

_____

A mixed number shows _____

_____

## Examples

**❶ Writing an Improper Fraction** Write $4\frac{3}{5}$ as an improper fraction.

**Method 1**

$$4\frac{3}{5} = 4 + \frac{3}{5}$$

$$= \frac{\boxed{\phantom{00}}}{5} + \frac{3}{5} \qquad \leftarrow \text{ Write 4 as } \frac{20}{5}.$$

$$= \frac{\boxed{\phantom{00}}}{5} \qquad \leftarrow \text{ Add.}$$

**Method 2**

Multiply the whole number by the denominator.
(4 × 5 fifths is 20 fifths)

$$\rightarrow \quad 4\frac{3}{5} = \frac{(4 \times 5) + 3}{5} \qquad \leftarrow \begin{array}{l}\textbf{Then add the numerator.}\\ \textbf{(There are 3 more fifths.)}\end{array}$$

$$= \frac{\boxed{\phantom{00}}}{\boxed{\phantom{00}}} \qquad \leftarrow \textbf{The denominator stays the same.}$$

**❷ Cooking** A chef needs $2\frac{3}{4}$ quarts of water to make soup. How many cups will the chef need? (*Hint:* 1 cup = $\frac{1}{4}$ quart.)

Since there are 4 cups in a quart, you find the number of cups by finding the number of fourths in $2\frac{3}{4}$ quarts.

$$2\frac{3}{4} = \frac{4 \times \boxed{\phantom{0}} + \boxed{\phantom{0}}}{4} = \frac{\boxed{\phantom{0}}}{\boxed{\phantom{0}}} \qquad \leftarrow \text{ Change } 2\frac{3}{4} \text{ to an improper fraction.}$$

Since there are $\boxed{\phantom{00}}$ fourths in $2\frac{3}{4}$, the chef will need $\boxed{\phantom{00}}$ cups of water.

**Example**

❸ **Writing a Fraction as a Mixed Number** Each slice of banana bread is $\frac{1}{9}$ of a loaf. How many loaves are represented by 42 slices?

Write $\frac{42}{9}$ as a mixed number. Begin by dividing 42 by ☐ .

☐
9)$\overline{42}$    ← **The quotient represents the number of whole loaves.**
$-36$
☐    ← **The remainder represents** ☐ **slices.**

$\frac{42}{9} = 4\frac{\square}{\square}$    ← **Express the remainder as a fraction.**

$= 4\frac{\square}{\square}$    ← **Simplify.**

Forty-two slices represent ☐$\frac{\square}{\square}$ loaves.

**Quick Check**

1. Write $3\frac{4}{7}$ as an improper fraction.

2. To clean a fish tank you need $2\frac{1}{4}$ gallons of fresh water every two weeks. How many quarts do you need?

3. Write each improper fraction as a mixed number in simplest form.

a. $\frac{40}{9}$      b. $\frac{32}{6}$      c. $\frac{23}{4}$

# Lesson 4-7

**Least Common Multiple**

| Lesson Objective<br>To find the LCM of two or more numbers | NAEP 2005 Strand: Number Properties and Operations<br>Topic: Number Operations<br>Local Standards: _____ |
| --- | --- |

## Vocabulary

A multiple of a number is _____
_____

A common multiple is _____
_____

The least common multiple (LCM) of two or more numbers is _____
_____

## Examples

**❶ Finding the LCM Using Lists of Multiples** Find the least common
multiple of 6 and 9.

multiples of 6:  6,  12,  18,  24,  30,  36

multiples of 9: ☐ , ☐ , ☐ , ☐       ← List multiples of each number.
                                    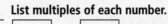 ☐ and ☐ are common multiples.

The least common multiple is ☐ .

**❷ Using Prime Factorizations** Use prime factorizations to find the LCM of
6, 9, and 15.

Write the prime factorizations for 6, 9, and 15. Then circle each different
factor where it appears the greatest number of times.

6 = 2 × ☐       ← 2 appears once.

9 = 3 × ☐       ← 3 appears the most often here (twice).

15 = 3 × ☐      ← 5 appears once. Don't circle 3 again.

☐ × ☐ × ☐ × ☐ = ☐   ← Multiply the circled factors.

The LCM of 6, 9, and 15 is ☐ .

**Quick Check**

1. List multiples to find the LCM.

    **a.** 10, 12

    multiples of 10: ☐ , ☐ , ☐ , ☐ , ☐ , ☐

    multiples of 12: ☐ , ☐ , ☐ , ☐ , ☐ , ☐

    The LCM of 10 and 12 is ☐ .

    **b.** 7, 10

2. Use prime factorizations to find the LCM of 6, 8, and 12.

# Lesson 4-8

**Comparing and Ordering Fractions**

| Lesson Objective<br>To compare and order fractions | NAEP 2005 Strand: Number Properties and Operations<br>Topic: Number Sense<br>Local Standards: _____ |
| --- | --- |

## Vocabulary

The least common denominator (LCD) of two or more fractions is _____

_____

## Examples

❶ **Comparing Fractions** Compare $\frac{5}{8}$ and $\frac{7}{10}$. Use $<$, $=$, or $>$.

First find the least common denominator. The least common multiple of

8 and 10 is ⬜ , so ⬜ is the LCD.

$$\frac{5}{8} = \frac{\boxed{\phantom{0}}}{40} \qquad \frac{7}{10} = \frac{\boxed{\phantom{0}}}{40} \quad \leftarrow \begin{array}{l}\textbf{Find equivalent fractions and}\\ \textbf{compare.}\end{array}$$

$$\frac{\boxed{\phantom{0}}}{40} \ \boxed{\phantom{0}}\ \frac{\boxed{\phantom{0}}}{40}. \text{ So, } \frac{5}{8} \ \boxed{\phantom{0}}\ \frac{7}{10}.$$

❷ **Comparing Mixed Numbers** If you need a piece of lumber that is

$4\frac{3}{16}$ feet long, is a $4\frac{1}{4}$-foot piece long enough?

Since the whole numbers are the same, compare $\frac{3}{16}$ and $\frac{1}{4}$.

$$\frac{3}{16} = \frac{3}{16} \qquad \frac{1}{4} = \frac{\boxed{\phantom{0}}}{16} \quad \leftarrow \begin{array}{l}\textbf{Find equivalent fractions.}\\ \textbf{Use the LCD 16.}\end{array}$$

$$\frac{3}{16} \ \boxed{\phantom{0}}\ \frac{4}{16}, \text{ so, } 4\frac{3}{16} \ \boxed{\phantom{0}}\ 4\frac{4}{16}. \quad \leftarrow \begin{array}{l}\textbf{Compare fractions and}\\ \textbf{mixed numbers.}\end{array}$$

The $4\frac{1}{4}$-foot piece ⬜ long enough.

## Quick Check

1. Compare $\frac{6}{8}$ and $\frac{7}{9}$. Use $<$, $=$, or $>$.

$\frac{6}{8}$ ⬜ $\frac{7}{9}$

2. In Example 2, would a $4\frac{5}{32}$-foot piece of lumber be long enough?

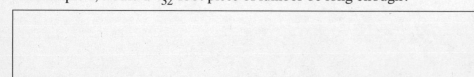

## Example

❸ **Ordering Fractions and Mixed Numbers** Order $1\frac{3}{4}$, $\frac{7}{10}$, $1\frac{11}{12}$, and $\frac{5}{8}$ from least to greatest.

**Step 1** Order the fractions. Find the LCM of 10 and 8. The LCD of the fractions is $\boxed{\phantom{xx}}$.

$$\frac{7}{10} = \frac{\boxed{\phantom{x}}}{40} \qquad \frac{5}{8} = \frac{\boxed{\phantom{x}}}{40} \qquad \leftarrow \text{ Write equivalent fractions.}$$

$$\frac{\boxed{\phantom{x}}}{\boxed{\phantom{x}}} < \frac{\boxed{\phantom{x}}}{\boxed{\phantom{x}}}. \text{ So the order of the fractions is } \frac{\boxed{\phantom{x}}}{\boxed{\phantom{x}}} < \frac{\boxed{\phantom{x}}}{\boxed{\phantom{x}}}.$$

**Step 2** Order the mixed numbers. Since the whole number parts are the same, compare $\frac{3}{4}$ and $\frac{11}{12}$.

$$\frac{3}{4} - \frac{\boxed{\phantom{x}}}{12}, \text{ so } \frac{\boxed{\phantom{x}}}{\boxed{\phantom{x}}} < \frac{\boxed{\phantom{x}}}{\boxed{\phantom{x}}}.$$

The order of the mixed numbers is $1\frac{\boxed{\phantom{x}}}{\boxed{\phantom{x}}} < 1\frac{\boxed{\phantom{x}}}{\boxed{\phantom{x}}}$.

Including the fractions first, the order is

$$\boxed{\phantom{xx}} < \boxed{\phantom{xx}} < \boxed{\phantom{xx}} < \boxed{\phantom{xx}}.$$

## Quick Check

**3.** Order $2\frac{5}{6}$, $\frac{3}{8}$, $\frac{1}{3}$, $2\frac{4}{5}$, and $1\frac{2}{3}$ from least to greatest.

# Lesson 4-9

**Fractions and Decimals**

| Lesson Objective | NAEP 2005 Strand: Number Properties and Operations |
|---|---|
| To find equivalent forms of fractions and decimals and to order fractions and decimals | **Topic:** Number Sense |
| | **Local Standards:** _____ |

## Examples

❶ **Writing a Decimal as a Fraction** Write 0.028 as a fraction in simplest form.

$0.028 = \dfrac{28}{\boxed{\phantom{000}}}$ ← Write "twenty-eight thousandths" as a fraction.

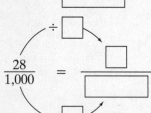

$\dfrac{28}{1{,}000} = \dfrac{\boxed{\phantom{00}}}{\boxed{\phantom{0000}}}$ ← Simplify. The GCF of 28 and 1,000 is $\boxed{\phantom{0}}$.

So, $0.028 = \boxed{\phantom{00}}$.

❷ **Writing a Fraction as a Decimal** You need at least $\frac{3}{4}$ pound of dried apricots for a recipe. You find a bag that contains 0.8 pound. Is this enough? To write $\frac{3}{4}$ as a decimal, divide 3 by 4.

**Method 1** Use pencil and paper.

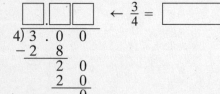

$\boxed{\phantom{0}}.\boxed{\phantom{0}}\boxed{\phantom{0}}$ ← $\frac{3}{4} = \boxed{\phantom{0000}}$

```
    .
4) 3 . 0   0
  - 2   8
      2   0
      2   0
          0
```

**Method 2** Use a calculator.

3 ÷ 4 = $\boxed{\phantom{0000}}$

Since $\boxed{\phantom{0000}}$ $\boxed{\phantom{0}}$ 0.8, there $\boxed{\phantom{0000}}$ enough in the 0.8-pound bag.

## Quick Check

1. Write 5.08 as a mixed number.

    _____

2. You answer 35 out of 40 questions correctly. Your friend answers 0.8 of the questions correctly. Who scores higher?

    _____

## Example

**❸ Ordering Numbers** Write $3.4, 2\frac{2}{3}, 3\frac{9}{20}$, and $2.6$ in order from least to greatest.

Write the two mixed numbers as decimals and compare.

$$2\frac{2}{3} = 2.\overline{6}$$   ← **Write as a decimal.**

$$3\frac{9}{20} = \boxed{\phantom{xx}}$$   ← **Write as a decimal.**

$\boxed{\phantom{xx}} < \boxed{\phantom{xx}} < \boxed{\phantom{xx}} < \boxed{\phantom{xx}}$   ← **Compare the decimals.**

The order is $\boxed{\phantom{xxx}}$ , $\boxed{\phantom{xxx}}$ , $\boxed{\phantom{xxx}}$ , $\boxed{\phantom{xxx}}$ .

## Quick Check

**3.** Write $2\frac{2}{3}, 3\frac{1}{5}, 1.8$, and $2.7$ in order from least to greatest.

# Lesson 5-1

**Estimating Sums and Differences**

| Lesson Objective | NAEP 2005 Strand: Number Properties and Operations |
|---|---|
| To estimate sums and differences with fractions and mixed numbers | **Topic:** Estimation |
| | **Local Standards:** _____ |

## Vocabulary

A benchmark is _____

_____

| Description | Examples | Benchmark |
|---|---|---|
| Numerator is very small when compared to the denominator. | $\frac{1}{8}, \frac{3}{16}, \frac{2}{25}, \frac{9}{100}$ | |
| Numerator is about one half of denominator. | $\frac{3}{8}, \frac{9}{16}, \frac{11}{25}, \frac{52}{100}$ | |
| Numerator and denominator are close to each other. | $\frac{7}{8}, \frac{14}{16}, \frac{23}{25}, \frac{95}{100}$ | |

## Example

❶ **Selecting a Fraction Benchmark** Choose a benchmark for the measurement $\frac{1}{24}$ foot.

1 is [ _____ ] compared to 24.

So choose the benchmark [ ___ ] feet.

## Quick Check

**1.** Choose a benchmark for the measurement $\frac{8}{9}$ inch.

[                                                      ]

## Examples

❷ **Estimating Sums and Differences** Estimate each sum or difference. Use the benchmarks $0, \frac{1}{2}$, and $1$.

**a.** $\frac{5}{6} + \frac{4}{7}$

$\frac{5}{6} + \frac{4}{7} \approx 1 + \boxed{\phantom{xx}}$  ← Replace each fraction with a benchmark. →

$= \boxed{\phantom{xxx}}$  ← Simplify. →

**b.** $\frac{7}{8} - \frac{1}{9}$

$\frac{7}{8} - \frac{1}{9} \approx \boxed{\phantom{x}} - \boxed{\phantom{x}}$

$= \boxed{\phantom{x}}$

❸ **Estimating With Mixed Numbers** Steven is $13\frac{11}{12}$ years old. Chloe is $9\frac{1}{4}$ years old. Estimate how many years older Steven is than Chloe.

**Estimate** $13\frac{11}{12} - 9\frac{1}{4}$.

$13\frac{11}{12} \approx \boxed{\phantom{xx}}$  ← Since $\frac{11}{12} > \frac{1}{2}$, round to 14.

$9\frac{1}{4} \approx \boxed{\phantom{x}}$  ← Since $\frac{1}{4} < \frac{1}{2}$, round to 9.

$\boxed{\phantom{xx}} - \boxed{\phantom{x}} = \boxed{\phantom{x}}$  ← Estimate by finding the difference.

Steven is about $\boxed{\phantom{x}}$ years older than Chloe.

## Quick Check

**2. a.** Estimate $\frac{5}{6} + \frac{3}{7}$.

$\frac{5}{6} + \frac{3}{7} \approx \boxed{\phantom{x}} + \boxed{\phantom{x}}$

$= \boxed{\phantom{xx}}$

**b.** Estimate $\frac{12}{13} - \frac{2}{25}$.

$\frac{12}{13} - \frac{2}{25} \approx \boxed{\phantom{x}} - \boxed{\phantom{x}}$

$= \boxed{\phantom{xx}}$

**3.** It takes $3\frac{3}{4}$ hours to drive to the beach. It takes $8\frac{1}{2}$ hours to drive to the mountains. Estimate the difference in driving times.

# Lesson 5-2

**Fractions With Like Denominators**

| **Lesson Objective** | **NAEP 2005 Strand:** Number Properties and Operations |
|---|---|
| To add and subtract fractions with like denominators | **Topic:** Number Operations |
| | **Local Standards:** _____ |

## Key Concepts

To add fractions with like denominators, add the numerators and keep the same denominator.

**Arithmetic**

$$\frac{2}{7} + \frac{3}{7} = \frac{2+3}{7} = \frac{\boxed{\phantom{0}}}{7}$$

**Algebra**

$$\frac{a}{c} + \frac{b}{c} = \frac{a+b}{c}$$

## Example

**①  Adding With Like Denominators** Find $\frac{2}{9} + \frac{4}{9}$.

$$\frac{2}{9} + \frac{4}{9} = \frac{2+4}{9}$$ ← The fractions have like denominators. Add the numerators. The denominator stays the same.

$$= \frac{\boxed{\phantom{0}}}{9}$$ ← Simplify the numerator.

$$= \frac{\boxed{\phantom{0}}}{\boxed{\phantom{0}}}$$ ← Divide the numerator and denominator by the GCF, 3.

## Quick Check

**1.**
 **a.** Add $\frac{1}{6} + \frac{1}{6}$.

**b.** Add $\frac{10}{21} + \frac{4}{21}$.

**Examples**

**❷ Sums Greater Than 1** Find $\frac{3}{4} + \frac{3}{4}$.

$\frac{3}{4} + \frac{3}{4} = \dfrac{\boxed{\phantom{0}} + \boxed{\phantom{0}}}{4}$ ← **Add the numerators. The denominator remains the same.**

$= \dfrac{\boxed{\phantom{0}}}{4}$ ← **Simplify the numerator.**

$= 1\dfrac{\boxed{\phantom{0}}}{\boxed{\phantom{0}}}$ ← **Write as a mixed number.**

$= 1\dfrac{\boxed{\phantom{0}}}{\boxed{\phantom{0}}}$ ← **Divide the numerator and denominator by the GCF, $\boxed{\phantom{0}}$.**

**❸ Subtracting With Like Denominators** Find $\frac{7}{8} - \frac{1}{8}$.

$\frac{7}{8} - \frac{1}{8} = \dfrac{\boxed{\phantom{0}} - \boxed{\phantom{0}}}{8}$ ← **Subtract the numerators. The denominator remains the same.**

$= \dfrac{\boxed{\phantom{0}}}{8}$ ← **Simplify the numerator.**

$= \dfrac{\boxed{\phantom{0}}}{\boxed{\phantom{0}}}$ ← **Write the fraction in simplest form.**

**Quick Check**

**2. a.** Find $\frac{5}{16} + \frac{13}{16}$.

**b.** Find $\frac{11}{20} + \frac{17}{20}$.

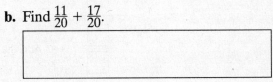

**3.** A board is $\frac{11}{12}$ foot long. You need $\frac{7}{12}$ foot of the board for a brace. How much is left after you cut off the piece you need?

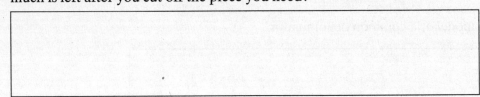

# Lesson 5-3

**Fractions With Unlike Denominators**

| Lesson Objective | NAEP 2005 Strand: Number Properties and Operations |
|---|---|
| To add and subtract fractions with unlike denominators | **Topic:** Number Operations |
| | **Local Standards:** _____ |

## Example

**1 Adding With Unlike Denominators** Find $\frac{1}{3} + \frac{1}{2}$.

**Method 1** Model $\frac{1}{3} + \frac{1}{2}$.

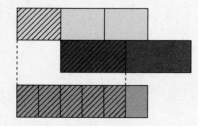

← Use the fraction model for $\frac{1}{3}$.

← Use the fraction model for $\frac{1}{2}$.

← The LCD is 6. Find a sixths fraction model with the same amount shaded.

$\frac{1}{3} + \frac{1}{2} = \dfrac{\Box}{\Box}$

**Method 2** Use a common denominator.

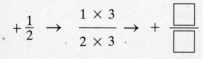

$\frac{1}{3} \rightarrow \dfrac{1 \times 2}{3 \times 2} \rightarrow \dfrac{\Box}{\Box}$

$+\frac{1}{2} \rightarrow \dfrac{1 \times 3}{2 \times 3} \rightarrow +\dfrac{\Box}{\Box}$

$\dfrac{\Box}{\Box}$

← The LCD is $\Box$. Write the fractions with the same denominator.

← Add the numerators.

## Quick Check

**1.** Find $\frac{3}{5} + \frac{1}{10}$. Use a model or a common denominator.

## Examples

**②** Sewing Nadia uses $\frac{7}{10}$ yard of blue material and $\frac{1}{6}$ yard of white material to make a pillow. How much total material did Nadia use to make the pillow?

Add $\frac{7}{10}$ and $\frac{1}{6}$ to find the total amount of material Nadia used.

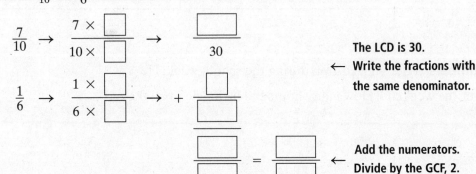

The LCD is 30.
← Write the fractions with the same denominator.

← Add the numerators.
Divide by the GCF, 2.

Nadia used ▭ yard of material.

**③** **Subtracting Fractions** If Laura skates $\frac{1}{4}$ mi more, she'll have skated $\frac{9}{10}$ mi. How far has Laura skated so far?

Subtract ▭ from ▭ to find how far Laura has skated.

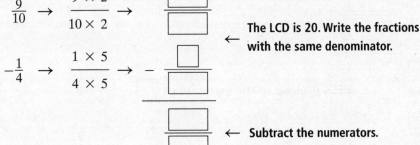

The LCD is 20. Write the fractions with the same denominator.

← Subtract the numerators.

Laura has skated ▭ mi so far.

## Quick Check

**2.** You exercise for $\frac{1}{2}$ hour on Monday and $\frac{1}{3}$ hour on Tuesday. How long did you exercise on Monday and Tuesday?

**3.** You have $\frac{2}{3}$ yard of felt. You use $\frac{1}{2}$ yard of the felt for a display. How much felt do you have left?

# Lesson 5-4

**Adding Mixed Numbers**

| Lesson Objective | NAEP 2005 Strand: Number Properties and Operations |
|---|---|
| To add mixed numbers with and without renaming | Topic: Number Operations |
| | Local Standards: _____ |

## Example

❶ **Adding Mixed Numbers** Tyler juggled $1\frac{1}{3}$ h during the school week. He juggled for $2\frac{1}{4}$ h over the weekend. How many hours did he juggle in all that week?

**Estimate** $1\frac{1}{3} + 2\frac{1}{4} \approx 1 + 2 = \boxed{\phantom{x}}$

$1\frac{1}{3} \rightarrow \quad 1 \quad \boxed{\phantom{xx}}$

$\leftarrow$ The LCD is $\boxed{\phantom{x}}$. Write the fractions with the same denominator.

$+ 2\frac{1}{4} \rightarrow + 2 \quad \boxed{\phantom{xx}}$

$\boxed{\phantom{x}} \quad \boxed{\phantom{xx}}$

$\leftarrow$ Add the whole numbers. Then add the fractions.

Tyler juggled for a total of $\boxed{\phantom{x}}\boxed{\phantom{xx}}$ hours.

**Check for Reasonableness** $\boxed{\phantom{x}}\boxed{\phantom{xx}}$ is close to the estimate of $\boxed{\phantom{x}}$.

The answer is reasonable.

## Quick Check

1. A giant tortoise traveled $2\frac{1}{3}$ yards and stopped. Then it traveled $3\frac{1}{2}$ yards. Find the total distance the giant tortoise traveled.

<br><br><br>

Daily Notetaking Guide  L1

Name _____  Class _____  Date _____

## Example

**2** **Renaming a Sum**  A mother cat weighs $14\frac{5}{8}$ lb. Her kitten weighs $1\frac{1}{2}$ lb. How much do they weigh together?

Find $14\frac{5}{8} + 1\frac{1}{2}$.

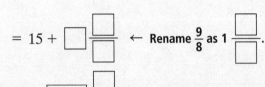

$14\frac{5}{8} \rightarrow \qquad 14 \dfrac{\boxed{\phantom{x}}}{\boxed{\phantom{x}}}$

$\qquad\qquad\qquad\qquad\qquad$ ← The LCD is 8. Write the fractions with the same denominator.

$+\ 1\frac{1}{2} \rightarrow \quad + \quad 1 \dfrac{\boxed{\phantom{x}}}{\boxed{\phantom{x}}}$

$\underline{\phantom{xxxxxx}}$

$\boxed{\phantom{xxx}}\ \dfrac{\boxed{\phantom{x}}}{\boxed{\phantom{x}}}$

← Add the whole numbers. Then add the fractions.

$= 15 + \boxed{\phantom{x}}\ \dfrac{\boxed{\phantom{x}}}{\boxed{\phantom{x}}}$

← Rename $\frac{9}{8}$ as $1\ \dfrac{\boxed{\phantom{x}}}{\boxed{\phantom{x}}}$.

$= \quad \boxed{\phantom{xxx}}\ \dfrac{\boxed{\phantom{x}}}{\boxed{\phantom{x}}}$

← Add the whole numbers.

The mother cat and kitten together weigh $\boxed{\phantom{xxx}}\ \dfrac{\boxed{\phantom{x}}}{\boxed{\phantom{x}}}$ lb.

## Quick Check

2. Find each sum.

   **a.** $3\frac{5}{6} + 5\frac{11}{12}$

   **b.** $7\frac{3}{5} + 13\frac{2}{3}$

3. **Newspapers**  One advertisement in a newspaper is $1\frac{1}{4}$ inches long. Another advertisement is $2\frac{7}{8}$ inches long. How much space is needed for both advertisements?

# Lesson 5-5

**Subtracting Mixed Numbers**

| Lesson Objectives | NAEP 2005 Strand: Number Properties and Operations |
|---|---|
| To subtract mixed numbers with and without renaming | Topic: Number Operations |
| | Local Standards: _____ |

## Examples

❶ **Subtracting Mixed Numbers** A black bear is about $5\frac{1}{4}$ ft long. An Alaskan brown bear is about $7\frac{1}{2}$ ft long. How much longer is an Alaskan brown bear than a black bear?

To calculate the difference in lengths, find $7\frac{1}{2} - 5\frac{1}{4}$.

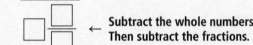

$7\frac{1}{2} \rightarrow 7\frac{\square}{\square}$   ← **The LCD is 4. Write $\frac{1}{2}$ as $\frac{\square}{4}$.**

$-5\frac{1}{4} \rightarrow -5\ \frac{1}{4}$

$\dfrac{\square\ \frac{\square}{\square}}{}$   ← **Subtract the whole numbers. Then subtract the fractions.**

An Alaskan brown bear is $\boxed{\phantom{0}}\frac{\square}{\square}$ ft longer than a black bear.

❷ **Renaming a Whole Number** Find $9 - 1\frac{2}{3}$.
Write 9 as a mixed number. Use 3 for the denominator since you must subtract $\frac{2}{3}$.

$9 \rightarrow 8\frac{\square}{\square}$   ← **Rename 9 as $8 + 1 = 8 + \frac{\square}{\square}$, or $8\frac{\square}{\square}$.**

$-1\frac{2}{3} \rightarrow -1\ \frac{2}{3}$

$\dfrac{\square\ \frac{\square}{\square}}{}$   ← **Subtract the whole numbers. Then subtract the fractions.**

## Example

**❸ Renaming a Mixed Number** A two-week-old panda bear weighed $\frac{3}{4}$ pound. At age one month, the cub weighed $2\frac{3}{10}$ pounds. How many pounds did it gain?

To answer the question, find  $-$ ▢. Since $\frac{3}{10} < \frac{3}{4}$, rename $2\frac{3}{10}$.

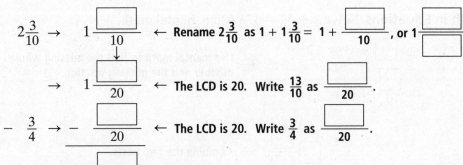

$2\frac{3}{10} \rightarrow \quad 1\dfrac{\boxed{\phantom{x}}}{10} \quad \leftarrow$ **Rename $2\frac{3}{10}$ as $1 + 1\frac{3}{10} = 1 + \dfrac{\boxed{\phantom{x}}}{10}$, or $1\dfrac{\boxed{\phantom{x}}}{\boxed{\phantom{x}}}$.**

$\rightarrow \quad 1\dfrac{\boxed{\phantom{x}}}{20} \quad \leftarrow$ **The LCD is 20. Write $\frac{13}{10}$ as $\dfrac{\boxed{\phantom{x}}}{20}$.**

$-\ \dfrac{3}{4} \rightarrow \quad -\ \dfrac{\boxed{\phantom{x}}}{20} \quad \leftarrow$ **The LCD is 20. Write $\frac{3}{4}$ as $\dfrac{\boxed{\phantom{x}}}{20}$.**

$\dfrac{\boxed{\phantom{x}}}{\boxed{\phantom{x}}} \quad \leftarrow$ **Subtract.**

The panda bear gained $\dfrac{\boxed{\phantom{x}}}{\boxed{\phantom{x}}}$ pounds.

## Quick Check

**1.** What is the difference in height between a plant that is $14\frac{13}{16}$ inches tall and a plant that is $7\frac{5}{8}$ inches tall?

**2. a.** Find $5 - 3\frac{2}{3}$

**b.** Find $10 - 4\frac{1}{4}$

**3.** A picture frame is $1\frac{3}{4}$ feet wide and $3\frac{5}{6}$ feet long. How much longer is the picture frame than it is wide?

## Lesson 5-6

**Equations With Fractions**

| Lesson Objective | NAEP 2005 Strand: Algebra |
|---|---|
| To solve equations with fractions | **Topic:** Equations and Inequalities |
| | **Local Standards:** _____ |

## Examples

**❶ Using Mental Math in Equations** Solve $x + 3\frac{4}{9} = 12\frac{7}{9}$ using mental math.

$$\boxed{\phantom{x}} + 3 = 12$$

$$\frac{\boxed{\phantom{x}}}{9} + \frac{4}{9} = \frac{7}{9}$$

← Use mental math to find the missing whole number and the missing fraction.

$$x = \boxed{\phantom{x}}\frac{\boxed{\phantom{x}}}{\boxed{\phantom{x}}}$$ ← Combine the two parts.

$$= \boxed{\phantom{x}}\frac{\boxed{\phantom{x}}}{\boxed{\phantom{x}}}$$ ← Simplify.

**❷ Solving Equations With Fractions** Solve $x - \frac{1}{8} = \frac{3}{4}$.

$$x - \frac{1}{8} + \frac{\boxed{\phantom{x}}}{\boxed{\phantom{x}}} = \frac{3}{4} + \frac{\boxed{\phantom{x}}}{\boxed{\phantom{x}}}$$ ← Add $\frac{1}{8}$ to each side.

$$x = \frac{\boxed{\phantom{x}}}{8} + \frac{1}{8}$$ ← The LCD is 8. Write $\frac{3}{4}$ as $\frac{\boxed{\phantom{x}}}{8}$.

$$x = \frac{\boxed{\phantom{x}}}{\boxed{\phantom{x}}}$$ ← Add.

## Quick Check

**1.** Solve each equation using mental math.

**a.** $x - 1\frac{3}{8} = 1\frac{3}{8}$

**b.** $14\frac{1}{4} + x = 25\frac{1}{2}$

**c.** $5\frac{5}{6} - x = 2\frac{1}{6}$

Name _____ Class _____ Date _____

## Example

**❸** An empty container weighs $\frac{1}{12}$ lb. The same container full of chopped fruit weighs $\frac{7}{8}$ lb. How much does the fruit weigh?

**Words**

| weight of empty container | + | weight of fruit | = | weight of full container |

Let $f$ = the weight of the fruit.

**Equation**

$$\frac{\square}{\square} \quad + \quad \square \quad = \quad \frac{\square}{\square}$$

$\frac{1}{12} + f - \dfrac{\square}{\boxed{\phantom{x}}} = \frac{7}{8} - \dfrac{\square}{\boxed{\phantom{x}}}$   ← Subtract $\frac{1}{12}$ from each side.

$f = \dfrac{\boxed{\phantom{xx}}}{24} - \dfrac{\boxed{\phantom{x}}}{24}$   ← The LCD is 24. Write each fraction with a denominator of 24.

$f = \dfrac{\boxed{\phantom{xx}}}{\boxed{\phantom{xx}}}$   ← Subtract.

The weight of the fruit is $\dfrac{\boxed{\phantom{xx}}}{\boxed{\phantom{xx}}}$ lb.

## Quick Check

**2. a.** Solve $n + \frac{1}{3} = \frac{11}{12}$

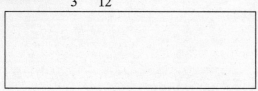

**b.** Solve $\frac{2}{5} + a = \frac{13}{20}$

**3.** You hammer a nail $2\frac{3}{8}$ inches long through a board. The nail pokes $\frac{5}{8}$ inch through the other side. How thick is the board?

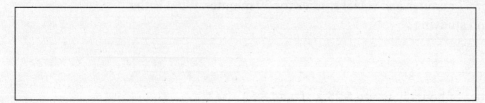

# Lesson 5-7

**Measuring Elapsed Time**

| Lesson Objective | NAEP 2005 Strand: Measurement |
|---|---|
| To add, subtract, and convert between units of time | **Topic:** Systems of Measurement |
| | **Local Standards:** _____ |

## Vocabulary

Elapsed time is _____

## Examples

**❶ Adding Units of Time** During soccer practice, the team spent 25 minutes doing drills, spent 40 minutes playing, and took a 10-minute break in the middle. How long did soccer practice last?

$25 + 40 + 10 = \boxed{\phantom{xx}}$ minutes

$\boxed{\phantom{xx}}$ minutes = 60 minutes + $\boxed{\phantom{xx}}$ minutes  ← 60 minutes equals one hour.

$= 1$ hour $\boxed{\phantom{xx}}$ minutes

Soccer practice lasted $\boxed{\phantom{xxxxxxxxxxxxxxxx}}$.

**❷ Estimating Elapsed Time** A movie begins at 7:22 P.M. and ends at 9:08 P.M. Estimate the length of the movie.

To estimate the elapsed time, round 7:22 and 9:08. Then subtract.

$7:22 \approx 7:00$  →  about $\boxed{\phantom{x}}$ hours after 12:00

$9:08 \approx \boxed{\phantom{xx}}$  →  about $\boxed{\phantom{x}}$ hours after 12:00

Since 9:00 is $\boxed{\phantom{x}}$ hours past 7:00, the movie is about $\boxed{\phantom{x}}$ hours long.

## Quick Check

**1.** You study math for 47 minutes and social studies for 39 minutes. What is the total time you spend studying?

$\boxed{\phantom{xxxxxxxxxxxxxxxxxxxxxxxxxxxxxxxxxxxxxxxxxx}}$

**2.** Estimate the number of hours between 5:25 A.M. and 8:52 A.M.

$\boxed{\phantom{xxxxxxxxxxxxxxxxxxxxxxxxxxxxxxxxxxxxxxxxxx}}$

## Examples

❸ **Calculating Elapsed Time** Find the elapsed time between 10:15 A.M. and 2:40 P.M.

Since 12:00 noon falls between the two times, you first need to find the elapsed time from 10:15 A.M. to noon.

| 12:00 → | 11 h 60 min | ← Rename 12:00 as 11 hours 60 minutes. |
| 10:15 → | − 10 h 15 min | ← Subtract the beginning time. |
| | ☐ | ← Subtract. |

You need to add the ending time to the elapsed time from 10:15 A.M. to noon.

+ 1 h 45 min

2:40 → + 2 h 40 min

☐

3 h 85 min = ☐ hours + ☐ min ← Since 85 min is more than 1 h, rename.

There are ☐ hours ☐ minutes between 10:15 A.M. and 2:40 P.M.

❹ **Reading and Using a Schedule** You arrive at the Glenmont bus stop at 8:00 A.M. and buy a ticket for the next bus.

a. How long will you wait for the next bus?

The bus runs every ☐ minutes. You arrived ☐ minutes after the 7:55 A.M. bus, so you will wait ☐ − ☐, or ☐ minutes.

| Buses Run Every 15 min Monday–Friday | |
| LEAVE | ARRIVE |
| Glenmont | Reedville |
| 7:40 A.M. | 8:15 A.M. |
| 7:55 A.M. | 8:30 A.M. |
| ... | ... |
| 9:55 A.M. | 10:30 A.M. |

b. What time will you arrive at the Reedville bus stop?

The next bus will leave at ☐ A.M. Using the first run, the elapsed time of the bus ride is ☐ A.M. − ☐ A.M., or ☐ min. So, you will arrive at 8:10 + ☐ min, or ☐ A.M.

## Quick Check

3. Find the elapsed time from 10:00 A.M. to 7:15 P.M.

4. Use the bus schedule from Example 4. It is a 5-minute walk from the bus stop in Reedville to a gym. You arrive at the Glenmont bus stop at 4:30 P.M. What time do you get to the gym?

Name _____ Class _____ Date _____

# Lesson 6-1                                    **Multiplying Fractions**

<table>
<tr><td>

**Lesson Objective**

To multiply fractions and to solve problems by multiplying fractions

</td><td>

**NAEP 2005 Strand:** Number Properties and Operations

**Topic:** Number Operations

**Local Standards:** _____

</td></tr>
</table>

## Key Concepts

**Multiplying Fractions**

| **Arithmetic** | **Algebra** |
|---|---|
| $\frac{3}{4} \times \frac{1}{2} = \frac{3 \times 1}{4 \times 2} = \frac{3}{8}$ | $\frac{a}{b} \cdot \frac{c}{d} = \frac{ac}{bd}$ , where $b$ and $d$ are not zero. |

## Example

**1** **Multiplying Two Fractions** Find $\frac{5}{6}$ of $\frac{3}{8}$.

$$\frac{5}{6} \cdot \frac{3}{8} = \frac{5 \cdot 3}{6 \cdot 8} \qquad \leftarrow \text{ Multiply the numerators.}$$
$$\qquad\qquad\qquad \leftarrow \text{ Multiply the denominators.}$$

$$= \frac{\boxed{\phantom{xx}}}{\boxed{\phantom{xx}}} \qquad \leftarrow \text{ Find the two products.}$$

$$= \frac{\boxed{\phantom{xx}}}{\boxed{\phantom{xx}}} \qquad \leftarrow \text{ Simplify.}$$

## Quick Check

**1. a.** Find $\frac{3}{5} \cdot \frac{1}{4}$.

**b.** Find $\frac{2}{9} \times \frac{5}{7}$.

## Example

**②** **Multiplying a Whole Number** There are 30 students in Shari's homeroom. Of these students, $\frac{2}{5}$ worked at the school fair. How many students in Shari's homeroom worked at the school fair?

Find the number of students by multiplying $\frac{2}{5}$ and 30.

$\frac{2}{5} \cdot 30 = \frac{2}{5} \cdot \frac{30}{1}$     ← Write 30 as $\frac{30}{1}$.

$= \dfrac{2}{\boxed{\phantom{x}} \,\cancel{5}} \cdot \dfrac{\cancel{30}^{\boxed{\phantom{x}}}}{1}$     ← Divide 30 and 5 by their GCF, 5.

$= \dfrac{\boxed{\phantom{xxx}}}{\boxed{\phantom{xxx}}}$     ← Multiply the numerators and denominators.

$= \boxed{\phantom{xxx}}$     ← Simplify.

$\boxed{\phantom{xxx}}$ students in Shari's homeroom worked at the school fair.

## Quick Check

**2.** A baby alligator is $\frac{5}{6}$ foot long. An adult alligator is 12 times as long as the baby alligator. How long is the adult alligator?

$\boxed{\phantom{xxxxxxxxxxxxxxxxxxxxxxxxxxxxxxxxxxxxxxxxxxx}}$

# Lesson 6-2

**Multiplying Mixed Numbers**

| Lesson Objective | NAEP 2005 Strand: Number Properties and Operations |
|---|---|
| To estimate and find the products of mixed numbers | Topic: Number Operations |
| | Local Standards: _____ |

## Example

**1** **Estimating Products** The pages of a book are $5\frac{1}{9}$ inches wide and $8\frac{3}{4}$ inches

long. Estimate the area of a page in square inches.

**Step 1** Round the length and width to the nearest whole numbers.

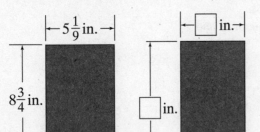

**Step 2** Multiply to estimate the area.

Area = length × width

$\approx 5 \times \boxed{\phantom{00}}$

$= \boxed{\phantom{00}}$

The area of a page is about $\boxed{\phantom{00}}$ square inches.

## Quick Check

**1. a.** Estimate $5\frac{5}{6} \times 6\frac{4}{9}$.

**b.** Estimate $7\frac{11}{16} \cdot 7\frac{1}{5}$.

## Examples

**❷ Multiplying Improper Fractions** Find the product $3\frac{3}{8} \times 1\frac{5}{9}$.

**Estimate** $3\frac{3}{8} \times 1\frac{5}{9} \approx \boxed{\phantom{0}} \times \boxed{\phantom{0}}$, or $\boxed{\phantom{0}}$.

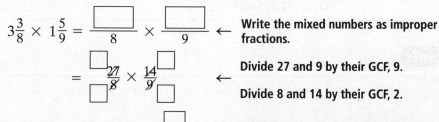

$3\frac{3}{8} \times 1\frac{5}{9} = \dfrac{\boxed{\phantom{0}}}{8} \times \dfrac{\boxed{\phantom{0}}}{9}$  ← Write the mixed numbers as improper fractions.

$= \dfrac{\boxed{\phantom{0}}}{\boxed{\phantom{0}}}\dfrac{\overset{}{\cancel{27}}}{8} \times \dfrac{\overset{}{\cancel{14}}}{\cancel{9}}\dfrac{\boxed{\phantom{0}}}{\boxed{\phantom{0}}}$  ← Divide 27 and 9 by their GCF, 9.

← Divide 8 and 14 by their GCF, 2.

$= \dfrac{21}{4}$, or $\boxed{\phantom{0}}\dfrac{\boxed{\phantom{0}}}{\boxed{\phantom{0}}}$  ← Multiply the numerators and denominators. Then write as a mixed number.

**Check for Reasonableness** $\boxed{\phantom{0}}\dfrac{\boxed{\phantom{0}}}{\boxed{\phantom{0}}}$ is near the estimate of $\boxed{\phantom{0}}$.

**❸** A gear on a machine makes $2\frac{2}{3}$ turns in one minute. How many turns does this gear make in $4\frac{1}{2}$ minutes?

$\boxed{\begin{array}{c}\text{total number}\\\text{of turns}\end{array}} = 2\frac{2}{3} \times \boxed{\text{number of minutes}}$

$= 2\frac{2}{3} \times 4\frac{1}{2}$

$= \dfrac{\boxed{\phantom{0}}}{3} \times \dfrac{\boxed{\phantom{0}}}{2}$  ← Write the mixed numbers as improper fractions.

$= \dfrac{\boxed{\phantom{0}}}{\boxed{\phantom{0}}}\dfrac{\overset{}{\cancel{8}}}{\cancel{3}} \times \dfrac{\overset{}{\cancel{9}}}{\cancel{2}}\dfrac{\boxed{\phantom{0}}}{\boxed{\phantom{0}}}$  ← Divide 8 and 2 by their GCF, 2.

← Divide 3 and 9 by their GCF, 3.

$= \dfrac{12}{\boxed{\phantom{0}}}$, or $\boxed{\phantom{0}}$  ← Multiply the numerators and denominators.

The gear makes $\boxed{\phantom{0}}$ turns in $4\frac{1}{2}$ minutes.

## Quick Check

**2. a.** Find $10\frac{1}{4} \times 2\frac{3}{4}$.

**b.** Find $7\frac{1}{3} \times 3\frac{3}{4}$.

**3.** How many turns can the gear in Example 3 make in $5\frac{1}{4}$ minutes?

# Lesson 6-3

**Dividing Fractions**

| Lesson Objective | NAEP 2005 Strand: Number Properties and Operations |
|---|---|
| To divide fractions and to solve problems by dividing fractions | Topic: Number Operations |
| | Local Standards: _____ |

## Vocabulary and Key Concepts

**Dividing Fractions**

| Arithmetic | Algebra |
|---|---|
| $\frac{3}{5} \div \frac{1}{3} = \frac{3}{5} \times \frac{3}{1}$ | $\frac{a}{b} \div \frac{c}{d} = \frac{a}{b} \times \frac{d}{c}$, where $b$, $c$, and $d$ are not 0. |

Two numbers are reciprocals if _____

## Example

**1 Writing a Reciprocal** Write the reciprocal of each number.

**a.** $\frac{4}{9}$

Since $\frac{4}{9} \times \dfrac{\boxed{\phantom{0}}}{\boxed{\phantom{0}}} = \dfrac{\boxed{\phantom{0}}}{\boxed{\phantom{0}}}$ or 1, the reciprocal is $\dfrac{\boxed{\phantom{0}}}{\boxed{\phantom{0}}}$.

**b.** 5

Write 5 as $\frac{5}{1}$.

Since $\frac{5}{1} \times \dfrac{\boxed{\phantom{0}}}{\boxed{\phantom{0}}} = \dfrac{\boxed{\phantom{0}}}{\boxed{\phantom{0}}}$ or 1, the reciprocal is $\dfrac{\boxed{\phantom{0}}}{\boxed{\phantom{0}}}$.

## Quick Check

**1. a.** Find the reciprocal of $\frac{3}{4}$.

**b.** Find the reciprocal of 7.

Name _____ Class _____ Date _____

## Examples

❷ **Dividing with Fractions** Find $\frac{3}{8} \div \frac{7}{12}$.

$\frac{3}{8} \div \frac{7}{12} = \frac{3}{8} \times \frac{12}{7}$     ← Multiply by $\frac{\boxed{\phantom{0}}}{\boxed{\phantom{0}}}$, the reciprocal of $\frac{7}{12}$.

$= \frac{3}{\underset{2}{\cancel{8}}} \times \frac{\overset{3}{\cancel{12}}}{7}$     ← Divide 8 and 12 by their GCF, $\boxed{\phantom{0}}$.

$= \frac{\boxed{\phantom{0}}}{\boxed{\phantom{0}}}$     ← Multiply.

❸ **Recipes** Chris uses $\frac{3}{4}$ cup of brown sugar in each batch of his banana muffins. He has a total of 5 cups of brown sugar. How many batches of banana muffins can Chris bake?

You want to find out how many $\frac{3}{4}$-cup portions are in 5 cups, so divide 5 by $\frac{3}{4}$.

$5 \div \frac{3}{4} = \frac{\boxed{\phantom{0}}}{\boxed{\phantom{0}}} \div \frac{3}{4}$     ← Write 5 as $\frac{5}{1}$.

$= \frac{\boxed{\phantom{0}}}{\boxed{\phantom{0}}} \times \frac{\boxed{\phantom{0}}}{\boxed{\phantom{0}}}$     ← Multiply by $\frac{\boxed{\phantom{0}}}{\boxed{\phantom{0}}}$, the reciprocal of $\frac{3}{4}$.

$= \frac{\boxed{\phantom{0}}}{\boxed{\phantom{0}}}$     ← Multiply.

$= 6\frac{\boxed{\phantom{0}}}{\boxed{\phantom{0}}}$     ← Simplify.

Chris has enough brown sugar to bake $\boxed{\phantom{0}} \frac{\boxed{\phantom{0}}}{\boxed{\phantom{0}}}$ batches of banana muffins.

## Quick Check

**2. a.** Find $\frac{9}{16} \div \frac{3}{4}$.

**b.** Find $\frac{4}{5} \div \frac{1}{3}$.

**3.** Your art teacher cuts $\frac{5}{6}$ yard of fabric into five equal pieces. How long is each piece of fabric?

# Lesson 6-4

**Dividing Mixed Numbers**

| **Lesson Objective**<br>To estimate and compute the quotient of mixed numbers | **NAEP 2005 Strand:** Number Properties and Operations<br>**Topic:** Number Operations<br>**Local Standards:** _____ |
| --- | --- |

## Examples

❶ **Estimating Quotients** Paulo wants to put a row of decorative tiles along a wall. The wall is $72\frac{3}{8}$ inches wide. Each tile is $3\frac{3}{4}$ inches wide. Estimate the number of tiles he will need. Draw a diagram to model the situation.

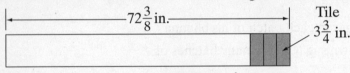

Tile
$3\frac{3}{4}$ in.

$72\frac{3}{8} \div 3\frac{3}{4}$    ← **Round each mixed number to the nearest whole number.**

☐ ÷ ☐ = 18    ← **Divide.**

Paulo needs about ☐ tiles.

❷ **Multiple Choice** Shaleen has enough oatmeal to make 5 batches of cookies. She wants to distribute $3\frac{1}{3}$ cups of raisins equally among the batches. What amount of raisins should she put into each batch?

**A.** $\frac{1}{4}$ cup      **B.** $\frac{1}{3}$ cup      **C.** $\frac{2}{3}$ cup      **D.** $\frac{3}{4}$ cup

☐ ÷ ☐    ← **Divide the number of cups by the number of batches.**

$\dfrac{☐}{☐} \div ☐ = \dfrac{10}{3} \div \dfrac{5}{1}$    ← **Substitute. Then write the numbers as improper fractions.**

$= \dfrac{10}{3} \times \dfrac{☐}{☐}$    ← **Multiply by $\frac{1}{5}$, the reciprocal of 5.**

$= \dfrac{\overset{2}{\cancel{10}}}{3} \times \dfrac{1}{\underset{1}{\cancel{5}}}$    ← **Divide 10 and 5 by their GCF, ☐.**

$= \dfrac{☐}{☐}$    ← **Multiply.**

Each batch of cookies gets $\dfrac{☐}{☐}$ cups of raisins. The correct answer is choice ☐.

**Check for Reasonableness** You can estimate $3\frac{1}{3} \div 5$. The result is $3 \div 5$ or

 $\dfrac{☐}{☐}$ , so $\dfrac{☐}{☐}$ cup is a reasonable answer.

Name _____ Class _____ Date _____

**❸ Dividing Mixed Numbers** Find $6\frac{1}{4} \div 1\frac{7}{8}$.

$$6\frac{1}{4} \div 1\frac{7}{8} = \frac{25}{4} \div \frac{15}{8}$$ ← Write the numbers as improper fractions.

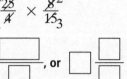 ← Multiply by $\frac{\square}{\square}$, the reciprocal of $\frac{15}{8}$.

 ← Divide 25 and 15 by their GCF, $\square$.
Divide 4 and 8 by their GCF, $\square$.

 ← Multiply and simplify.

**Quick Check**

**1. a.** Estimate $7\frac{2}{5} \div 1\frac{3}{7}$.

**b.** Estimate $14\frac{9}{16} \div 3\frac{8}{19}$.

**2.** Suppose Shaleen has $1\frac{2}{3}$ cups of raisins in Example 2. How many cups of raisins should go into each batch to make 5 batches of cookies?

**3. a.** Find $7 \div 1\frac{1}{6}$.

**b.** Find $6\frac{5}{6} \div 3\frac{1}{3}$.

# Lesson 6-5

Solving Fraction Equations by Multiplying

| Lesson Objective | NAEP 2005 Strand: Algebra |
|---|---|
| To write fraction equations and solve them by multiplying | Topic: Equations and Inequalities |
| | Local Standards: _____ |

## Examples

**❶ Solving Equations by Multiplying** Solve $\frac{c}{3} = 14$.

A. 42          B. 45          C. 47          D. 50

$$\frac{c}{3} = 14$$

$\boxed{\phantom{x}} \cdot \frac{c}{3} = \boxed{\phantom{x}} \cdot 14$  ← Multiply each side by $\boxed{\phantom{x}}$ to undo the division and get $c$ by itself.

$\frac{1\cancel{3}}{1} \cdot \frac{c}{\cancel{3}_1} = \boxed{\phantom{x}}$  ← Write 3 as $\frac{3}{1}$. Simplify.

$\dfrac{\boxed{\phantom{x}}}{1} = \boxed{\phantom{x}}$  ← Multiply the numerators and the denominators.

$c = \boxed{\phantom{x}}$  ← Simplify.

The solution is $\boxed{\phantom{x}}$. The correct answer is $\boxed{\phantom{x}}$.

**❷ Using Reciprocals to Solve Equations** Solve $\frac{3}{4}m = 24$. Check the solution.

$$\frac{3}{4}m = 24$$

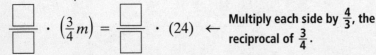

$\dfrac{\boxed{\phantom{x}}}{\boxed{\phantom{x}}} \cdot \left(\frac{3}{4}m\right) = \dfrac{\boxed{\phantom{x}}}{\boxed{\phantom{x}}} \cdot (24)$  ← Multiply each side by $\frac{4}{3}$, the reciprocal of $\frac{3}{4}$.

$\boxed{\phantom{x}} \cdot m = \boxed{\phantom{x}}$  ← Multiply.

$m = \boxed{\phantom{x}}$  ← Simplify.

**Check**     $\frac{3}{4}m = 24$  ← Start with the original equation.

$\frac{3}{4}\left(\boxed{\phantom{x}}\right) \stackrel{?}{=} 24$  ← Substitute $\boxed{\phantom{x}}$ for $m$ in the original equation.

$\boxed{\phantom{x}} = 24$ ✓  ← The solution checks.

**❸ Writing and Solving Equations** Mai Li worked $7\frac{1}{2}$ hours and earned $150. What amount did she earn per hour?

**Words** | hours worked | × | earnings per hour | = | amount earned |

Let $m$ = earnings per hour.

**Equation** ☐ × ☐ = ☐

$$7\frac{1}{2}m = 150 \qquad \leftarrow \text{Write the equation.}$$

$$\frac{\boxed{\phantom{0}}}{2}m = \frac{150}{1} \qquad \leftarrow \begin{array}{l}\text{Write } 7\frac{1}{2} \text{ as an improper fraction.}\\ \text{Write 150 as } \frac{150}{1}.\end{array}$$

$$\frac{\boxed{\phantom{0}}}{\boxed{\phantom{0}}} \cdot \left(\frac{15}{2}m\right) = \frac{\boxed{\phantom{0}}}{\boxed{\phantom{0}}} \cdot \frac{150}{1} \qquad \leftarrow \begin{array}{l}\text{Multiply each side by } \dfrac{\boxed{\phantom{0}}}{\boxed{\phantom{0}}}, \text{ the}\\ \text{reciprocal of } \dfrac{15}{2}.\end{array}$$

$$m = \frac{2}{\cancel{15}} \cdot \frac{\cancel{150}^{\boxed{\phantom{0}}}}{1} \qquad \leftarrow \text{Multiply.}$$
$$\phantom{m=\ }{}_{\boxed{\phantom{0}}}$$

$$m = \boxed{\phantom{00}} \qquad \leftarrow \text{Simplify.}$$

Mai Li earned $\boxed{\phantom{00}}$ per hour.

---

**Quick Check**

**1. a.** Solve $\frac{x}{2} = 15$.

☐

**b.** Solve $\frac{n}{6} = 12$.

☐

**2.** Solve $\frac{7}{8}x = 42$. Check the solution.

☐

**3.** Beth needs boards that are $\frac{3}{4}$ foot long. She has a board that is 8 feet long.

How many $\frac{3}{4}$-foot sections can she cut from it?

☐

# Lesson 6-6                                    **The Customary System**

| **Lesson Objective** | **NAEP 2005 Strand:** Measurement |
|---|---|
| To choose appropriate units and to estimate in the customary system | **Topic:** Systems of Measurement |
| | **Local Standards:** _____ |

## Examples

**❶ Choosing a Unit of Length** Choose an appropriate customary unit of measure to describe the length of an automobile.

The unit [_____] is too large and inches is too small.

Use [_____].

**❷ Choosing a Unit of Weight** Choose an appropriate customary unit of measure to describe the weight of a bag of popcorn.

The customary units that describe weight are [_____], pounds, and [_____].

The weight of a bag of popcorn is best described in [_____].

## Quick Check

1. Choose an appropriate unit for each length. Explain your choice.

   **a.** pencil                          **b.** adult whale

2. Choose an appropriate unit of weight for a refrigerator.

## Example

**❸ Choosing a Unit of Capacity** Choose an appropriate customary unit of measure to describe the capacity of a household bucket.

The customary units that describe capacity are fluid ounces, cups,

[_____] , [_____] , and [_____] .

The capacity of a household bucket is best described in [_____] .

## Quick Check

3. Choose an appropriate unit for each capacity. Explain your choice.

   **a.** gasoline tanker truck

   [                                                                    ]

   **b.** container of yogurt

   [                                                                    ]

Name _____ Class _____ Date _____

# Lesson 6-7

**Changing Units in the Customary System**

| **Lesson Objective** | **NAEP 2005 Strand:** Measurement |
|---|---|
| To convert between units in the customary system | **Topic:** Systems of Measurement |
| | **Local Standards:** _____ |

## Examples

**❶ Larger Units to Smaller Units** Find the number of feet in $8\frac{2}{3}$ yards.

$$8\frac{2}{3} \text{ yd} = \left(8\frac{2}{3} \times \boxed{\phantom{x}}\right) \text{ ft}$$    ← **Multiply to change to a smaller unit.**

$$= \left(\frac{\boxed{\phantom{x}}}{3} \times \frac{3}{\boxed{\phantom{x}}}\right) \text{ ft}$$    ← **Change from proper to improper fractions.**

$$= \frac{\boxed{\phantom{x}}}{\boxed{\phantom{x}}} \text{ ft, or } \boxed{\phantom{x}} \text{ ft}$$    ← **Multiply. Then simplify.**

**❷ Smaller Units to Larger Units** You need 32 inches of ribbon to wrap a package. How many feet of ribbon do you need?

An inch is smaller than a foot, so $\boxed{\phantom{xxxxxxxx}}$.

$$32 \text{ in.} = \left(32 \text{ in. } \boxed{\phantom{x}}\;\boxed{\phantom{x}}\right) \text{ ft}$$    ← $\boxed{\phantom{x}}$ **inches equal 1 foot, so divide 32 by** $\boxed{\phantom{x}}$.

$$= \left(\frac{\boxed{\phantom{x}}\;32}{1} \times \frac{1}{12\;\boxed{\phantom{x}}}\right) \text{ ft}$$    ← **Multiply by** $\frac{1}{12}$**, the reciprocal of 12.**

$$= \frac{\boxed{\phantom{x}}}{\boxed{\phantom{x}}} \text{ yd, or } 2\frac{\boxed{\phantom{x}}}{\boxed{\phantom{x}}} \text{ ft}$$    ← **Simplify.**

You need $\boxed{\phantom{x}}\frac{\boxed{\phantom{x}}}{\boxed{\phantom{x}}}$ ft of ribbon.

## Quick Check

**1.** Find the number of pounds in 2 tons.

$\boxed{\phantom{xxxxxxxxxxxxxxxxxx}}$

**2.** You need 5 cups of milk to make hot chocolate. How many quarts of milk should you buy?

$\boxed{\phantom{xxxxxxxxxxxxxxxxxx}}$

## Example

❸ **Renaming Units** A craftsperson is shipping a ceramic vase that weighs 3 lb 12 oz. The weight of the packing crate is 2 lb 6 oz. What is the total weight of the vase and the packing crate?

**A.** 5 lb 8 oz  **B.** 5 lb 15 oz  **C.** 6 lb 2 oz  **D.** 6 lb 5 oz

**Add:**

$$
\begin{array}{r}
3 \ \text{lb} \quad 12 \ \text{oz} \\
+ \ 2 \ \text{lb} \quad\ 6 \ \text{oz} \\
\hline
\boxed{\phantom{0}} \ \text{lb} \ \boxed{\phantom{00}} \ \text{oz}
\end{array}
$$

**Think:** 5 lb  18 oz = 5 lb + ☐ lb + 2 oz  ← **Rename 18 oz as 1 lb 2 oz.**

= ☐ lb ☐ oz  ← **Combine 5 lb and 1 lb.**

The total weight is ☐ lb ☐ oz. The correct answer is choice ☐.

## Quick Check

**2.** A baby weighed 6 pounds 8 ounces at birth. She has since gained 1 pound 9 ounces. How much does she weigh now?

Name _____ Class _____ Date _____

# Lesson 7-1

| Lesson Objective | NAEP 2005 Strand: Number Properties and Operations |
|---|---|
| To write ratios to compare real world quantities | Topic: Ratios and Proportional Reasoning |
| | Local Standards: _____ |

## Vocabulary

A ratio is _____

_____

Two ratios are equivalent if _____

_____

## Example

**1** **Three Ways to Write a Ratio** During a school trip, there are 3 teachers and 25 students on each bus. Write each ratio in three ways.

  **a.** teachers to students

    There are 3 teachers and [ ] students on each bus.

    teachers to students → 3 to [ ] or 3 : [ ] or $\dfrac{3}{\boxed{\phantom{0}}}$

  **b.** students to teachers

    There are [ ] students and [ ] teachers on each bus.

    students to teachers → 25 to [ ] or 25 : [ ] or $\dfrac{25}{\boxed{\phantom{0}}}$

## Quick Check

**1.** Use the recipe at the right to write each ratio in three ways.

  **a.** pretzels to cereal

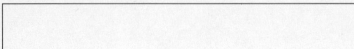

  **b.** pretzels to party mix

PARTY MIX
Makes 6 cups
4 cups  cereal
2 cups  pretzels
3 tbsp Worcestershire
    sauce

## Examples

**❷ Writing Equivalent Ratios** Write two different ratios equal to 24 : 8.

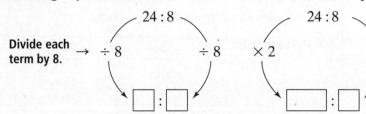

Two ratios equal to 24 : 8 are ☐ and ☐ .

**❸ Writing a Ratio in Simplest Form** Write each ratio in simplest form.

**a.** 121 to 11

**b.** 28 : 16

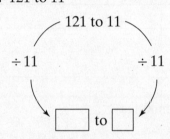   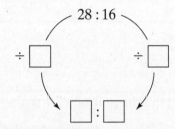

In simplest form, the ratio 121 to 11 is ☐ .

In simplest form, the ratio 28 : 16 is ☐ .

## Quick Check

2. Write two different ratios equal to each ratio.

**a.** $\frac{10}{35}$   **b.** 12 : 3   **c.** 8 to 22

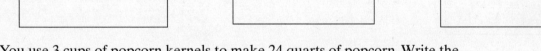

3. You use 3 cups of popcorn kernels to make 24 quarts of popcorn. Write the ratio of the amount of kernels to the amount of popcorn in simplest form.

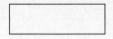

# Lesson 7-2

**Unit Rates**

| Lesson Objective | NAEP 2005 Strand: Number Properties and Operations |
|---|---|
| To find and use unit rates and unit costs | Topic: Ratios and Proportional Reasoning |
| | Local Standards: _____ |

## Vocabulary

A rate is _____

_____

A unit rate is _____

_____

A unit cost is _____

_____

## Example

❶ **Finding a Unit Rate** Find the unit rate for typing 145 words in 5 minutes.

$$\frac{145 \div 5}{5 \div 5} = \frac{29}{1}$$

← **Divide by 5 to find the number of words typed in one minute.**

The unit rate is [        ] or [      ] words per minute.

## Quick Check

**1.** Find the unit rate for $2.37 for 3 pounds of grapes.

[                    ]

## Examples

❷ **Comparing Unit Cost** The same brand of pretzels comes in two sizes: a 10-ounce bag for $.99, and an 18-ounce bag for $1.49. Which size is a better buy? Round each unit price to the nearest cent.

Divide to find the unit price of each size.

price → $.99
size → 10 oz ≈ $ [ ] per ounce

price → $1.49
size → 18 oz ≈ $ [ ] per ounce

The better buy costs less per ounce. Since [ ] is less than [ ], the [ ]-ounce bag is the better buy.

❸ **Using a Unit Rate** Apples cost $1.49 for 1 pound. How much do 5 pounds of apples cost?

**A.** $6.25        **B.** $7.45        **C.** $8.15        **D.** $8.85

Write the unit rate as a ratio. Then find an equal ratio.

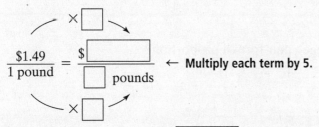

$$\frac{\$1.49}{1 \text{ pound}} = \frac{\$ \boxed{\phantom{xxx}}}{\boxed{\phantom{x}} \text{ pounds}} \quad \leftarrow \text{ Multiply each term by 5.}$$

Five pounds of apples cost [ ]. The correct answer is choice [ ].

## Quick Check

**2.** You can buy 6 ounces of yogurt for $.68 or 32 ounces of yogurt for $2.89. Find each unit price. Which is the better buy?

[ ]

**3.** Write each unit rate as a ratio. Then find an equivalent ratio.

**a.** You can earn $5.25 in 1 hour. How much do you earn in 5 hours?

[ ]

**b.** You type 25 words in 1 minute. How many words can you type in 10 minutes?

[ ]

# Lesson 7-3

| Lesson Objective | NAEP 2005 Strand: Number Properties and Operations |
| --- | --- |
| Understand proportions and determine whether two ratios are proportional | Topic: Ratios and Proportional Reasoning |
| | Local Standards: _____ |

## Vocabulary and Key Concepts

**Cross Products**

The cross products of a proportion are always equal.

**Arithmetic:** If $\frac{2}{4} = \frac{3}{6}$, then $2 \times 6 = 4 \times 3$.

**Algebra:** If $\frac{a}{b} = \frac{c}{d}$, $b \neq 0$ and $d \neq 0$, then $ad = bc$.

A proportion is _____

## Example

❶ **Identifying Proportions** Do the ratios in each pair form a proportion?

a. $\frac{6}{14}, \frac{42}{77}$

$\frac{6}{14} \overset{?}{=} \frac{42}{77}$ ← $14 \times \boxed{\phantom{0}} = 98$, not 77

$\frac{6}{14} \boxed{\phantom{0}} \frac{42}{77}$ ← Compare ratios.

b. $\frac{3}{13}, \frac{9}{39}$

$\frac{3}{13} \overset{?}{=} \frac{9}{39}$

$\frac{3}{13} \boxed{\phantom{0}} \frac{9}{39}$ ← Compare ratios.

$\frac{6}{14}$ and $\frac{42}{77}$ do *not* form a proportion.

$\frac{3}{13}$ and $\frac{9}{39}$ form a proportion.

## Quick Check

**1.** Do the ratios $\frac{8}{5}$ and $\frac{36}{20}$ form a proportion? Explain.

### Example

❷ **Using Cross Products** Are the ratios $\frac{9}{10}$ and $\frac{18}{30}$ equivalent?

$$\frac{9}{10} \overset{?}{=} \frac{18}{30} \qquad \leftarrow \textbf{Write a proportion.}$$

$9 \times \boxed{\phantom{xxxx}} \overset{?}{=} 18 \times \boxed{\phantom{xxxx}} \qquad \leftarrow$ **Write the cross products.**

$270 \boxed{\phantom{x}} 180 \qquad \leftarrow$ **Multiply.**

The ratios $\frac{9}{10}$ and $\frac{18}{30}$ $\boxed{\phantom{xxxx}}$ form a proportion.

### Quick Check

**2.** In a middle school, 1 of every 12 students has a birthday in June. In a class of 26 students, there are 3 students with a birthday in June. Are these ratios equivalent? Explain.

# Lesson 7-4

**Solving Proportions**

| Lesson Objective | NAEP 2005 Strand: Number Properties and Operations |
|---|---|
| To solve proportions using number sense and cross products | Topic: Ratios and Proportional Reasoning |
| | Local Standards: _____ |

## Example

❶ **Using a Unit Rate** Leslie biked 45 miles in 5 hours. How far could she bike in 3 hours?

Write a proportion that compares miles biked to hours.

miles → $\dfrac{45}{\boxed{\phantom{0}}}$ = $\dfrac{\blacksquare}{\boxed{\phantom{0}}}$ ← miles
hours → ← hours

Find a unit rate for 45 miles and 5 hours.

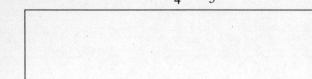

$\dfrac{45}{5} = \dfrac{\boxed{\phantom{0}}}{1}$  ← Divide each term by 5 to find the number of miles traveled in one hour.

So the unit rate is $\boxed{\phantom{0}}$ miles per hour.

$\boxed{\phantom{0}} \times 3 = \boxed{\phantom{0}}$  ← Multiply the unit rate by the number of miles.

Leslie could bike $\boxed{\phantom{0}}$ miles in 3 hours.

## Quick Check

1. Use a unit rate to solve $\dfrac{12}{4} = \dfrac{\blacksquare}{5}$.

Name _____ Class _____ Date _____

## Examples

**❷ Solving a Proportion** Solve $\frac{21}{n} = \frac{14}{26}$.

$\frac{7}{13} = \frac{21}{n}$ ← Write the ratio as a fraction in simplest form.

$\overset{\times 3}{\underset{\times 3}{\frac{7}{13} = \frac{21}{n}}}$ ← Since 7 × 3 = 21, multiply 13 × 3 to find $n$.

$13 \times 3 = \boxed{\phantom{XX}}$, so $n = \boxed{\phantom{XX}}$.

**❸ Using Cross Products** Janet earned \$31.50 for 5 hours of work. How much does she earn for 7 hours of work at the same rate of pay?

Write a proportion that compares hours of work to pay.

Let $p$ = the amount of pay.

hours → $\dfrac{5}{\boxed{\phantom{XXX}}} = \dfrac{7}{p}$ ← hours    ← Write a proportion.
pay (\$) →                         ← pay (\$)

$5 \cdot \boxed{\phantom{XX}} = \boxed{\phantom{XXX}} \cdot 7$ ← Write the cross products.

$5p = \boxed{\phantom{XXX}}$ ← Multiply.

$\dfrac{5p}{5} = \dfrac{\boxed{\phantom{XXX}}}{\boxed{\phantom{X}}}$ ← Division Property of Equality

$p = \boxed{\phantom{XXX}}$ ← Simplify.

Janet will earn \$$\boxed{\phantom{XXX}}$ for 7 hours of work.

## Quick Check

**2.**  **a.** Solve $\frac{6}{8} = \frac{n}{20}$.          **b.** Solve $\frac{9}{12} = \frac{3}{x}$.

    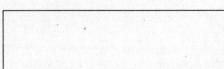

**3.** If 5 notebooks cost \$7.85, how much do 3 notebooks cost?

# Lesson 7-5

**Scale Drawings**

| **Lesson Objective**<br>To find the size of a drawing and use scales to find actual dimensions | **NAEP 2005 Strands:** Number Properties and<br>               Operations; Measurement<br><br>**Topics:** Ratios and Proportional Reasoning; Measuring<br>       Physical Attributes; Systems of Measurement<br><br>**Local Standards:** _____ |
| --- | --- |

## Vocabulary

A scale is _____

_____

## Examples

**❶ Finding the Scale of a Drawing** The length of a drawing of a kitten is 3 cm. The actual length of the kitten is 27 cm. What is the scale of the drawing?

$$\frac{\text{drawing length} \rightarrow}{\text{actual length} \rightarrow} \quad \frac{3 \text{ cm}}{\boxed{\phantom{xx}} \text{ cm}} = \frac{1}{\boxed{\phantom{x}}} \quad \leftarrow \begin{array}{l}\textbf{Divide each measure by}\\ \textbf{the GCF, 3.}\end{array}$$

The scale is $\boxed{\phantom{x}}$ cm to $\boxed{\phantom{x}}$ cm, or $\boxed{\phantom{xxx}}$ .

**❷ Finding Distances on a Map** Use a map scale of 1 in. : 20 mi to find the actual distance represented on a map by 3 in.

**Step 1** Write the scale ratio: $\dfrac{\boxed{\phantom{xxxx}}}{\boxed{\phantom{xxxx}}}$ .

**Step 2** Use a proportion.

Let $y$ = the actual distance represented by 3 in.

$$\frac{1 \text{ in.}}{\boxed{\phantom{xx}} \text{ mi}} = \frac{3 \text{ in.}}{y \text{ mi}} \quad \begin{array}{l}\leftarrow \textbf{map distances}\\ \leftarrow \textbf{actual distances}\end{array}$$

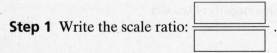

$$\frac{1}{20} = \frac{3}{y}$$

Since $20 \times 3 = \boxed{\phantom{xx}}$ , the actual distance is $\boxed{\phantom{x}}$ miles.

❸ **Models** Suppose you are making a model of an 18-meter boat. Use a scale of 1 cm : 2.5 m to find the length of your model boat.

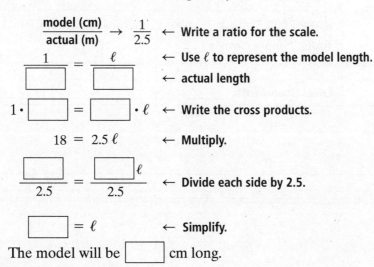

$$\frac{\text{model (cm)}}{\text{actual (m)}} \rightarrow \frac{1}{2.5} \quad \leftarrow \text{Write a ratio for the scale.}$$

$$\frac{1}{\boxed{\phantom{x}}} = \frac{\ell}{\boxed{\phantom{x}}} \quad \begin{array}{l} \leftarrow \text{Use } \ell \text{ to represent the model length.} \\ \leftarrow \text{actual length} \end{array}$$

$$1 \cdot \boxed{\phantom{x}} = \boxed{\phantom{x}} \cdot \ell \quad \leftarrow \text{Write the cross products.}$$

$$18 = 2.5\,\ell \quad \leftarrow \text{Multiply.}$$

$$\frac{\boxed{\phantom{x}}}{2.5} = \frac{\boxed{\phantom{x}}\ell}{2.5} \quad \leftarrow \text{Divide each side by 2.5.}$$

$$\boxed{\phantom{x}} = \ell \quad \leftarrow \text{Simplify.}$$

The model will be $\boxed{\phantom{x}}$ cm long.

**Quick Check**

1. The length of a drawing of an object is 6 inches. The length of the actual object is 84 inches. What is the scale of the drawing?

2. Use the map and scale to find the approximate distance from Winfield to Montgomery. Use a ruler to estimate the map distance.

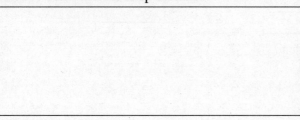

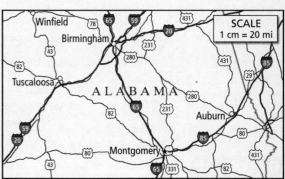

3. Suppose the boat in Example 3 is 1.5 meters tall. How tall will the model be?

Name _____ Class _____ Date _____

# Lesson 7-6                                    Percents, Fractions, and Decimals

| Lesson Objective | NAEP 2005 Strand: Number Properties and Operations |
|---|---|
| To find equivalent forms of fractions, decimals, and percents | Topic: Number Sense |
| | Local Standards: _____ |

## Vocabulary

A percent is _____

_____

## Examples

**1** **Representing Percents** Write 4% as a fraction. Write your answer in simplest form.

$4\% = \dfrac{4}{\boxed{\phantom{000}}}$ ← **Write the percent as a fraction with a denominator of 100.**

$= \dfrac{\boxed{\phantom{00}}}{\boxed{\phantom{000}}}$ ← **Write the fraction in simplest form.**

**2** **Writing a Percent as a Decimal** Write each percent as a decimal.

**a.** 87%                                          **b.** 9%

$87\% = \dfrac{87}{\boxed{\phantom{000}}}$ ← **Write each percent as a fraction with a denominator of** $\boxed{\phantom{000}}$ . → $9\% = \dfrac{9}{\boxed{\phantom{000}}}$

$= \boxed{\phantom{000}}$ ← **Write each fraction as a decimal.** → $= \boxed{\phantom{000}}$

## Quick Check

**1. a.** Write 55% as a fraction.

<br><br>

**b.** Write 4% as a fraction.

<br><br>

**2. a.** Write 25% as a decimal.

<br><br>

**b.** Write 2% as a decimal.

<br><br>

## Examples

❸ **Writing a Decimal as a Percent** Write 0.16 decimal as a percent.

$$0.16 = \dfrac{\boxed{\phantom{0}}}{100} = \boxed{\phantom{000}}\%$$ ← Write the decimal as a fraction with a denominator of 100.

❹ **Writing a Fraction as a Percent** Write $\frac{7}{20}$ as a percent.

$$\dfrac{7}{20} = \dfrac{x}{100}$$ ← Write a proportion. Percents have 100 in the denominator.

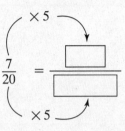

← Find the fraction with a denominator of $\boxed{\phantom{00000}}$ equal to $\dfrac{7}{20}$ .

$$\dfrac{7}{20} - \dfrac{35}{100} = \boxed{\phantom{000}}\%$$ ← Write using a percent symbol.

## Quick Check

**3.** Write each decimal as a percent.

**a.** 0.52        **b.** 0.05        **c.** 0.5

**4.** According to a news article, 1 of every 20 neurosurgeons in the United States is a woman. Write the fraction $\frac{1}{20}$ as a percent.

# Lesson 7-7

**Finding the Percent of a Number**

| **Lesson Objective**<br>To use percents to find part of a whole | **NAEP 2005 Strand:** Number Properties and Operations<br>**Topic:** Ratios and Proportional Reasoning<br>**Local Standards:** _____ |
| --- | --- |

## Examples

**①  Using a Proportion**  Find 60% of 45.

Let *n* represent the number you want to find.

$$\frac{n}{\boxed{\phantom{xx}}} = \frac{60}{100} \quad \leftarrow \text{part}$$
$$\leftarrow \text{whole}$$

$$\boxed{\phantom{xxx}} \times n = 60 \times \boxed{\phantom{xx}} \quad \leftarrow \textbf{Write the cross products.}$$

$$100n = 2{,}700 \quad \leftarrow \textbf{Multiply.}$$

$$n = \boxed{\phantom{xx}} \quad \leftarrow \textbf{Divide each side by 100.}$$

60% of 45 is $\boxed{\phantom{xx}}$ .

**②  Using a Decimal**  Find 88% of 250.

$$88\% = \boxed{\phantom{xxxx}} \quad \leftarrow \textbf{Write 88\% as a decimal.}$$

$$\boxed{\phantom{xxx}} \times 250 = \boxed{\phantom{xxx}} \quad \leftarrow \textbf{Multiply.}$$

So, 88% of 250 is $\boxed{\phantom{xx}}$ .

## Quick Check

**1.** You buy a $40 shirt on sale at 20% off. Find 20% of $40.

**2. a.** Find 12% of 91.

**b.** Find 18% of 121.

Name _____ Class _____ Date _____

## Example

❸ **Using Mental Math** Use mental math to find 75% of 84.

**What you think**

$75\% = \frac{3}{4}$          $\frac{3}{4} \times 84 = \boxed{\phantom{xx}}$.          75% of 84 is $\boxed{\phantom{xx}}$.

**Why it works**

$$75\% = \frac{75}{100}$$

$$= \frac{\boxed{\phantom{x}}}{\boxed{\phantom{x}}} \qquad \leftarrow \text{ **Write 75% as a fraction in simplest form.**}$$

$$\frac{3}{4} \times 84 = \frac{3}{4} \times \frac{\boxed{\phantom{xx}}}{\boxed{\phantom{x}}} \qquad \leftarrow \text{ **Multiply } \frac{3}{4} \text{ by 84. Rewrite 84 as** } \frac{\boxed{\phantom{xx}}}{\boxed{\phantom{x}}}.$$

$$= \frac{\boxed{\phantom{xxx}}}{\boxed{\phantom{x}}} \qquad \leftarrow \text{ **Simplify.**}$$

$$= \boxed{\phantom{xx}} \qquad \leftarrow \text{ **Divide.**}$$

## Quick Check

**3.** Use mental math to find 75% of 12.

# Lesson 7-8

| Lesson Objective | NAEP 2005 Strand: Data Analysis and Probability |
|---|---|
| To read and make circle graphs to represent real world data | **Topic:** Data Representation |
| | **Local Standards:** _____ |

## Vocabulary

A circle graph is _____

_____

## Example

**① Reading a Circle Graph** Use the circle graph to the right.

a. What brand of jacket sold 43%?

Brand [  ] sold 43%.

b. What percent of Brand C were sold?

[  ]% of Brand C were sold.

c. Describe the amount of jackets sold that were Brand A.

A little less than [        ] of the circle corresponds to Brand A. Almost [        ] of the jackets sold were Brand A jackets.

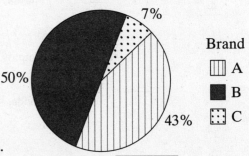

**Brands of Jackets Sold**

7%

50%

43%

Brand

A

B

C

## Quick Check

**1. a.** According to the graph in Example 1, what brand of jackets sold 50%?

**b.** Which brands account for 93% of the jackets sold?

**c.** Were more Brand A jacketrs or Brand B jackets sold?

## Example

❷ **Sketching a Circle Graph**  Make a circle graph of the data in the table.

First, use a calculator to change the data to percents of the total.

$56 + $33 + $18 + $24 = $131

Round to the nearest percent.

| Weekly Budget | |
|---|---|
| Savings | $56 |
| Hobbies | $33 |
| Food | $18 |
| Other | $24 |

$\frac{56}{131} \approx$ [    ]%     $\frac{33}{131} \approx$ [    ]%

$\frac{18}{131} \approx$ [    ]%     $\frac{24}{131} \approx$ [    ]%

Use number sense to divide the circle.

43% is slightly less than [          ] the circle.

$25\% = \dfrac{\Box}{\Box}$

18% is slightly less than $\frac{1}{5}$ of the circle.

[          ]% is the percent left.

**Weekly Budget**

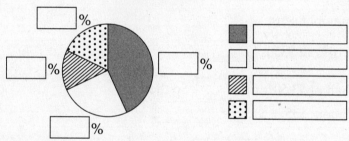

## Quick Check

2. Of 50 students surveyed, 13 bought a hot lunch, 9 packed a lunch, 6 bought a salad, and 22 bought a sandwich. Sketch a circle graph of the data.

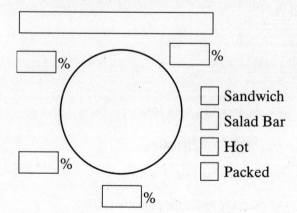

Sandwich
Salad Bar
Hot
Packed

# Lesson 7-9

**Estimating With Percents**

| **Lesson Objective**<br>To use mental math and estimation<br>with percents | **NAEP 2005 Strand:** Number Properties and Operations<br>**Topic:** Ratios and Proportional Reasoning<br>**Local Standards:** _____ |
|---|---|

## Examples

**① Estimating Cost** Using a 5% sales tax, estimate the sales tax and the total cost for a pair of sneakers that costs $34.99.

**Method 1** Estimate the cost and multiply.

Round the cost of the sneakers to $35.

$$5\% \text{ of } 35 = \boxed{\phantom{xxx}} \times 35 \quad \leftarrow \text{ Write 5\% as a decimal.}$$

$$= \boxed{\phantom{xxx}} \quad \leftarrow \text{ Multiply to find the tax.}$$

$$35 + \boxed{\phantom{xxx}} = \boxed{\phantom{xxx}} \quad \leftarrow \begin{array}{l}\text{Find the sum of the price}\\\text{and the tax.}\end{array}$$

The cost of the sneakers, including tax, is about $\boxed{\phantom{xxx}}$.

**Method 2** Estimtae the cost and use number sense.

Round the cost of the sneakers to $35. 10% of $35 is $\boxed{\phantom{xxx}}$.

Since 5% is half of 10%, 5% of $35 is half of $3.50, or $\boxed{\phantom{xxx}}$. So the tax is about $\boxed{\phantom{xxx}}$. The total cost is about $35 + $1.75 = $\boxed{\phantom{xxx}}$.

The total cost of the sneakers, including tax, is about $\boxed{\phantom{xxx}}$.

**② Estimating a Tip** Estimate a 15% tip for a bill of $29.34.

**What you think**

The bill is about $29. I can break apart 15% into 10% and 5%.

Since 10% of $29 is $2.90, 5% is half of $2.90, or $\boxed{\phantom{xxx}}$.

A 15% tip is about $\boxed{\phantom{xxx}} + \boxed{\phantom{xxx}}$, or $\boxed{\phantom{xxx}}$.

**Why it works**

$$15\% \times \$29 = (10\% + 5\%) \times \$29 \quad \leftarrow \text{ Replace 15\% with 10\% + }\boxed{\phantom{x}}\text{\%.}$$

$$= 10\% \times \boxed{\phantom{xx}} + 5\% \times \boxed{\phantom{xx}} \quad \leftarrow \text{ Distributive Property}$$

$$= \$2.90 + \left(\tfrac{1}{2} \times 10\% \times \$29\right) \quad \leftarrow \text{ Replace 5\% with }\tfrac{1}{2} \times 10\%.$$

$$= \$2.90 + \boxed{\phantom{xxx}} \quad \leftarrow \text{ Simplify inside the parentheses.}$$

$$= \boxed{\phantom{xxx}} \quad \leftarrow \text{ Add.}$$

**❸ Estimating a Sale Price** A jacket is on sale for 20% off the regular price of $49.95. Estimate the sale price of the jacket.

### What you think

The regular price of the jacket is about $50.

If the price is 20% off, you pay 100% − 20%, or [ ] of the regular price.

80% of $50 = [ ].

The sale price is [ ].

### Why it works

The sale price is 20% off the regular cost.

20% × $50 = [ ] × $50    ← **Write 20% as a decimal.**

= [ ]    ← **Simplify.**

Subtract the amount saved from the regular price.

$50 − [ ] = [ ]. The sale price is about [ ].

---

**Quick Check**

1. Use a 6% tax rate to estimate the total cost for a hat that costs $9.99.

2. Estimate a 15% tip for a bill of $41.63.

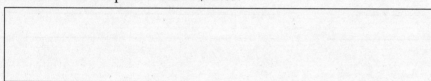

3. Estimate the sale price of a $40.19 baseball glove at 40% off.

# Lesson 8-1

**Points, Lines, Segments, and Rays**

| **Lesson Objective** | **NAEP 2005 Strand:** Geometry |
|---|---|
| To identify and work with points, lines, segments, and rays | **Topic:** Relationships Among Geometric Figures |
| | **Local Standards:** _____ |

## Vocabulary

Points $A$, $B$, and $C$

A point is _____

_____

_____

$\overleftrightarrow{DE}$ or $\overleftrightarrow{ED}$

A line is _____

_____

_____

$\overline{DE}$ or $\overline{ED}$

A segment is _____

_____

_____

_____

$\overrightarrow{DE}$

A ray is _____

_____

_____

_____

A plane is _____

_____

Intersecting lines have _____

Parallel lines _____

Skew lines are _____

_____

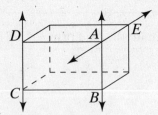

Plane $ABCD$

$\overleftrightarrow{AB}$ is [＿＿＿＿＿] to $\overleftrightarrow{DC}$.

$\overleftrightarrow{AE}$ [＿＿＿＿＿] $\overleftrightarrow{AB}$.

$\overleftrightarrow{AE}$ and $\overleftrightarrow{DC}$ are [＿＿＿＿＿].

Name _____ Class _____ Date _____

## Examples

**❶ Naming Lines, Segments, and Rays** Name each line, segment, or ray.

a.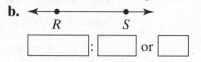

b.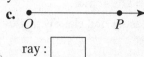

c.

$\boxed{\phantom{XXXX}}$ : $\overline{BA}$ or $\boxed{\phantom{XX}}$          $\boxed{\phantom{XXX}}$ : $\boxed{\phantom{XX}}$ or $\boxed{\phantom{XX}}$          ray : $\boxed{\phantom{XX}}$

**❷ Identify Line Relationships** Name each of the following.

a. two parallel lines

$\overleftrightarrow{XY}$ and $\overleftrightarrow{WU}$ are parallel. $\overleftrightarrow{XW}$ and $\boxed{\phantom{XX}}$ are also parallel.

b. two skew lines

$\overleftrightarrow{WX}$ and $\overleftrightarrow{ZU}$ are skew. $\overleftrightarrow{WX}$ and $\boxed{\phantom{XX}}$, $\overleftrightarrow{YZ}$ and $\boxed{\phantom{XX}}$, or

$\overleftrightarrow{ZU}$ and $\boxed{\phantom{XX}}$ are also pairs of skew lines.

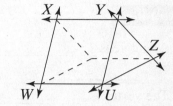

## Quick Check

**1.** Use the figure at the right.

a. Give two names for the line. $\boxed{\phantom{XXXXXXXXXXXXXXXXXX}}$

b. Name three segments. $\boxed{\phantom{XXXXXXXXXXXXXXXX}}$

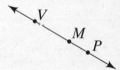

**2. a.** Name two streets on the map that are parallel.

$\boxed{\phantom{XXXXXXXXXXXXXXXXXXXXXXXXXXXXX}}$

b. Name two streets on the map that intersect.

$\boxed{\phantom{XXXXXXXXXXXXXXXXXXXXXXXXXXXXXXXXXX}}$

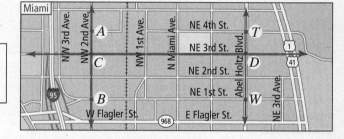

# Lesson 8-2

**Angles**

| **Lesson Objective** | **NAEP 2005 Strand:** Geometry |
|---|---|
| To measure and classify angles | **Topic:** Dimension and Shape |
| | **Local Standards:** _____ |

## Vocabulary

An angle is _____

_____

The vertex is _____

_____

Degrees are _____

_____

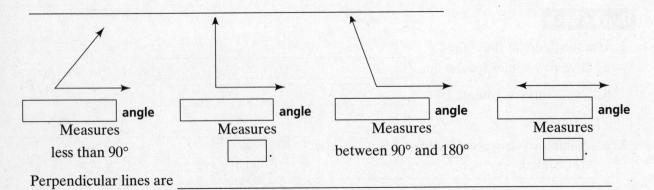

| | angle | | angle | | angle | | angle |
|---|---|---|---|---|---|---|---|
| Measures | | Measures | | Measures | | Measures | |
| less than 90° | | ☐ . | | between 90° and 180° | | ☐ . | |

Perpendicular lines are _____

_____

## Examples

❶ Use a protractor to measure the angle.

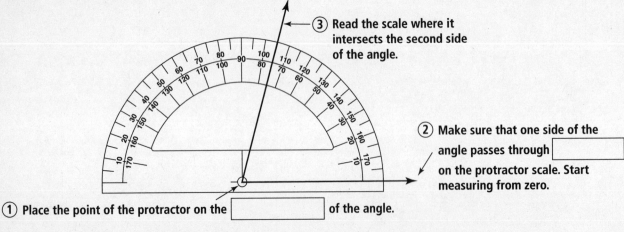

③ Read the scale where it intersects the second side of the angle.

② Make sure that one side of the angle passes through ☐ on the protractor scale. Start measuring from zero.

① Place the point of the protractor on the ☐ of the angle.

The angle measure is ☐ .

Name _____ Class _____ Date _____

❷ **Classifying Angles** Classify each angle as *acute, right, obtuse,* or *straight.*

a. 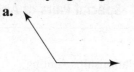      b. 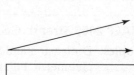      c.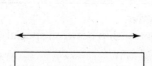

```
[          ]        [          ]        [          ]
```

❸ **Multiple Choice** Quadrilateral *WXYZ* has different types of angles. Which angle is acute?

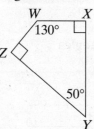

**A.** ∠W      **B.** ∠X      **C.** ∠Y      **D.** ∠Z

∠X and ∠Z are [＿＿] angles. ∠W measures [＿＿] 90°. ∠Y is
[＿＿], because it measures between 0° and 90°.

The correct answer is choice [＿＿].

**Quick Check**

**1.** Use a protractor to measure the angle.   [＿＿]

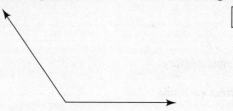

**2.** Estimate the measure of the angle. Classify the angle as *acute, right, obtuse,* or *straight.*

```
[                                        ]
```

**3.** Classify the angles in quadrilateral *WXYZ* in Example 3 as *acute, right, obtuse,* or *straight.*

a. ∠W      b. ∠X      c. ∠Z

```
[          ]        [          ]        [          ]
```

# Lesson 8-3

**Special Pairs of Angles**

| Lesson Objective | NAEP 2005 Strand: Geometry |
|---|---|
| To use the relationship between special pairs of angles | **Topics:** Dimension and Shape; Relationships Among Geometric Figures |
| | **Local Standards:** _____ |

## Vocabulary

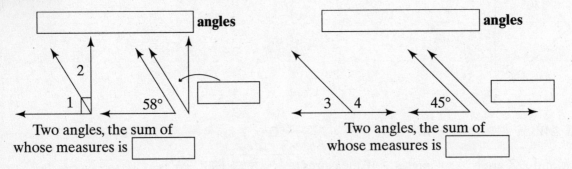

_____ **angles**       _____ **angles**

Two angles, the sum of whose measures is [ ]

Two angles, the sum of whose measures is [ ]

Vertical angles are _____

Congruent angles have _____

## Example

❶ **Finding the Complement of an Angle** Find the complement of a 66°
angle.

Let $x$ = the measure of the angle's complement.

$x + 66° = \boxed{\phantom{00}}$    ← **The angles are complementary.**

$x + 66° - \boxed{\phantom{0}} = 90° - \boxed{\phantom{0}}$    ← **Subtract** $\boxed{\phantom{0}}$ **from each side.**

$x = \boxed{\phantom{0}}$    ← **Simplify.**

The complement of a 66° angle measures 24°.

## Quick Check

**1.** Find the value of $x$.

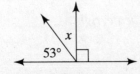

## Examples

❷ **Using Supplementary Angles** Find the value of $x$.

$$x + 125° = \boxed{\phantom{xxx}}$$ ← The angles are supplementary.

$$x + 125° - \boxed{\phantom{xxx}} = 180° - \boxed{\phantom{xxx}}$$ ← Subtract 125° from each side.

$$x = \boxed{\phantom{xxx}}$$ ← Simplify.

❸ **Vertical Angles** Use the diagram to identify each of the following.

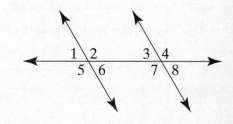

**a.** a pair of obtuse vertical angles

∠2 and ∠5, ∠4 and ∠7

**b.** a pair of acute vertical angles

∠1 and $\boxed{\phantom{xxx}}$ , ∠3 and $\boxed{\phantom{xxx}}$

## Quick Check

**2.** Find the value of $x$.

$\boxed{\phantom{xxx}}$

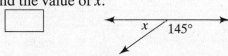

**3.** The measure of ∠5 in the photo is 142°. Find the measures of ∠6 and ∠7.

# Lesson 8-4

**Classifying Triangles**

| **Lesson Objective**<br>To classify triangles by their angles and by their sides | **NAEP 2005 Strand:** Geometry<br>**Topics:** Dimension and Shape; Relationships Between Geometric Figures<br><br>**Local Standards:** _____ |
| --- | --- |

## Vocabulary

A triangle is _____

_____

The sum of the angle measures is [          ].

Congruent segments are _____

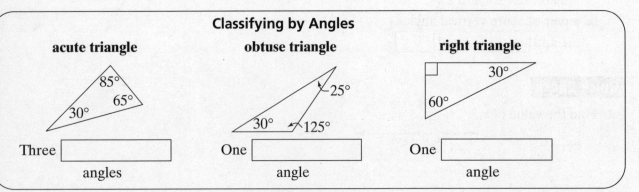

### Classifying by Angles

**acute triangle**

85°
65°
30°

Three [          ] angles

**obtuse triangle**

25°
30° 125°

One [          ] angle

**right triangle**

30°
60°

One [          ] angle

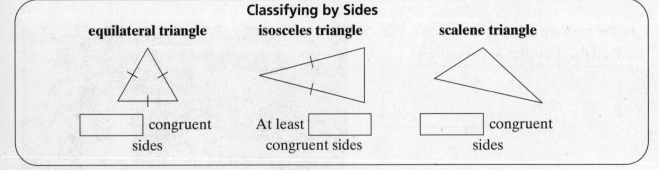

### Classifying by Sides

**equilateral triangle**

[          ] congruent sides

**isosceles triangle**

At least [          ] congruent sides

**scalene triangle**

[          ] congruent sides

## Examples

**❶ Classifying Triangles by Angles** Classify each triangle by its angles.

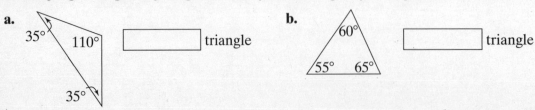

**a.**

35° 110°

35°

[          ] triangle

**b.**

60°

55° 65°

[          ] triangle

**②** **Finding an Angle's Measure** Two angles of a triangle measure 48° and 90°. What is the measure of the third angle?

Write and solve an equation to find the measure of the third angle.

$x + 48° + 90° =$ ⬜ ← The sum of the angle measures is ⬜.

$x +$ ⬜ $= 180°$ ← Add 48° and 90°.

$x + 138° -$ ⬜ $= 180° -$ ⬜ ← Subtract 138° from each side.

$x =$ ⬜ ← Simplify.

The third angle measures ⬜.

**③** **Classifying Triangles by Sides** Classify each triangle by its sides.

a.
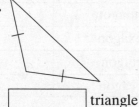

⬜ triangle

b.
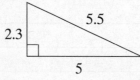
2.3   5.5   5

⬜ triangle

## Quick Check

1. Classify the triangle at the right by its angles. ⬜

25°
65°

2. The angles of a triangle measure 58°, 72°, and $x$. Find $x$.

⬜

3. Classify the triangle at the right by its sides. Explain your reasoning.

⬜

Name _____ Class _____ Date _____

# Lesson 8-5

**Exploring and Classifying Polygons**

| Lesson Objective | NAEP 2005 Strand: Geometry |
|---|---|
| To identify regular polygons and to classify quadrilaterals | **Topics:** Dimension and Shape; Relationships Among Geometric Figures |
| | **Local Standards:** _____ |

## Vocabulary

A polygon is _____

_____

A regular polygon is _____

_____

An irregular polygon is _____

_____

A quadrilateral is _____

| Polygon | Number of Sides |
|---|---|
| Triangle | |
| Quadrilateral | |
| Pentagon | |
| Hexagon | |
| Octagon | |
| Decagon | |

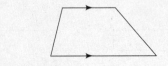

A trapezoid has _____

_____

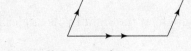

A parallelogram has _____

_____

A rectangle is _____

_____

_____

A rhombus is _____

_____

_____

A square is _____

_____

_____

## Examples

**①  Identifying Polygons** Identify each polygon according to the number of sides it has.

a.  [        ]

b. 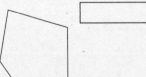 [        ]

**❷ Identifying Regular Polygons** Determine whether each polygon is *regular* or *irregular*.

**a.**

In the figure, all sides are [          ] and all angles are congruent,
so the figure is [          ].

**b.**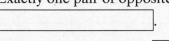

In the figure, all sides are congruent and all angles are [          ],
so the figure is [          ].

**❸ Classifying Quadrilaterals** Write all the possible names for the quadrilateral.

Which is the best name?

Exactly one pair of opposite sides is

[          ].

Its only possible name is [          ].

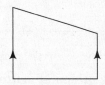

## Quick Check

**1.** Identify each polygon according to the number of sides it has.

**a.**     **b.**     **c.**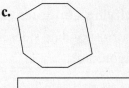

[          ]    [          ]    [          ]

**2.** Determine whether each polygon is *regular* or *irregular*.

**a.** 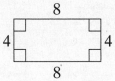    [          ]

**b.**     [          ]

**3.** Write all of the names for the quadrilateral at the right.
Which is the best name? Explain.

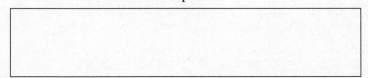    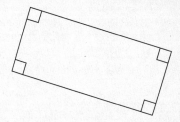

# Lesson 8-6

**Congruent and Similar Figures**

| Lesson Objective | NAEP 2005 Strand: Geometry |
|---|---|
| To identify congruent and similar figures | Topic: Transformation of Shapes and Preservation of Properties |
| | Local Standards: _____ |

## Vocabulary

Congruent figures have _____

_____

Corresponding sides of congruent figures are [          ], and

corresponding angles of congruent figures are [          ].

Similar figures have _____

_____

Corresponding angles of similar figures are [          ], and

ratios of corresponding sides of similar figures are [          ].

## Example

**❶ Identifying Congruent Figures** Are the pentagons congruent?
The corresponding sides and angles are [          ], so the
pentagons are [          ].

## Quick Check

1. Tell whether each trapezoid is congruent to the first given trapezoid.

a. 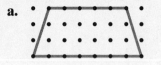     b.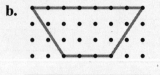

[          ]          [          ]

### Examples

❷ **Identifying Similar Figures** Show that these triangles are similar.

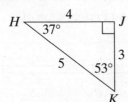 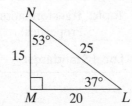

The measures of ∠H and ∠L are [ _____ ].

The measures of ∠J and ∠M are [ _____ ].

The measures of ∠K and ∠N are [ _____ ].

$\frac{3}{15} = \frac{1}{5}, \frac{4}{20} = \frac{\square}{\square}, \frac{5}{25} = \frac{\square}{\square}$

The measures of corresponding angles are equal. The lengths of corresponding sides form equal ratios. The triangles are [ _____ ].

❸ Triangles *VWX* and *XYZ* are similar. The measure of ∠V is 65°.

The measure of ∠W is 45°. What is the measure of ∠Z? Explain.

The measure of ∠X is [ _____ ], since the sum of the angles

in a triangle equals [ _____ ]. ∠X and ∠Z are corresponding

angles. So the measure of ∠Z is [ _____ ].

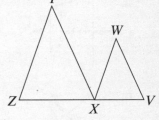

### Quick Check

**2.** Is the given triangle similar to △*KJH* in Example 2?

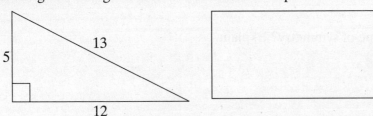

**3.** In Example 3, the measure of $\overline{VW}$ is 4 units, the measure of $\overline{WX}$ is 5 units, and the measure of $\overline{XY}$ is 12 units. Find the measure of $\overline{YZ}$.

Name _____ Class _____ Date _____

# Lesson 8-7

**Line Symmetry**

| Lesson Objective<br>To find lines of symmetry | NAEP 2005 Strand: Geometry<br>Topic: Transformation of Shapes and Preservation of<br>Properties<br>Local Standards: _____ |
|---|---|

## Vocabulary

A figure has line symmetry if _____

_____

This dividing line is called a [          ].

## Example

**1** **Testing for Line Symmetry**  For each figure, is the dashed line a line of
symmetry? Explain.

a. [          ] : if you fold the figure along the line, the two parts match.

b. [          ] : if you fold the figure along the line, the two parts do not match.

## Quick Check

**1.** Is the dashed line in the figure a line of symmetry? Explain.

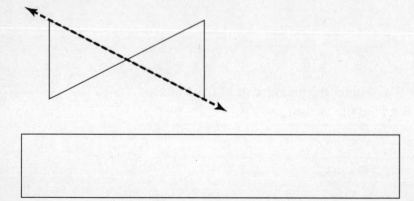

[                                        ]

## Example

**2** How many lines of symmetry does each figure have? Draw the lines of symmetry.

**a.** [rectangle]    The rectangle has [   ] lines of symmetry.

**b.** [hexagon]    The hexagon has [   ] lines of symmetry.

## Quick Check

**2.** How many lines of symmetry does each figure have? Draw the lines of symmetry.

**a.**     [   ]

**b.** 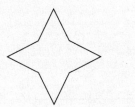    [   ]

# Lesson 8-8

**Transformations**

| **Lesson Objective**<br>To identify and draw translations,<br>reflections, and rotations | **NAEP 2005 Strand:** Geometry<br>**Topic:** Transformation of Shapes and Preservation<br>of Properties<br><br>**Local Standards:** _____ |
| --- | --- |

## Vocabulary

A transformation of a figure is _____

_____

The new figure is the [ ] of the original.

A translation, or [ ], is _____

_____

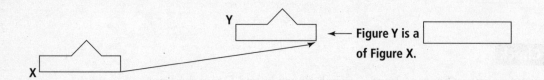

Figure Y is a [ ] of Figure X.

A reflection, or [ ], is _____

_____

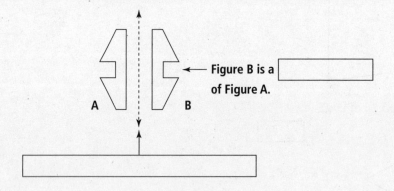

Figure B is a [ ] of Figure A.

A rotation, or [ ], is _____

[ ] of rotation

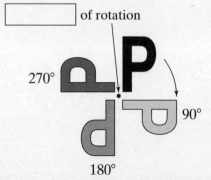

## Examples

**1** **Identifying Translations** Is the second figure a translation of the first figure?

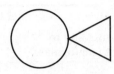
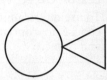

**2** **Drawing Reflections** Draw the reflection of the figure over the given line of reflection.

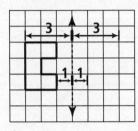

← Use the grid to locate the vertices equidistant from the line of reflection. Then connect the vertices.

**3** Tell whether each figure is a rotation of the shape at right. If so, give the angle of rotation.

**a.**

**b.**

**c.**

## Quick Check

**1.** Is the second figure a translation of the first figure?

**2.** Draw the reflection of the figure over the given line of reflection.

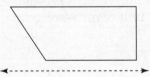

**3.** Tell whether each figure is a rotation of the shape at the right.

**a.**

**b.**

**c.**

# Lesson 9-1

| **Lesson Objective** | **NAEP 2005 Strand:** Measurement |
|---|---|
| To use metric units of measure and to choose appropriate units of length, mass, and capacity | **Topic:** Systems of Measurement |
| | **Local Standards:** _____ |

## Vocabulary

The metric system is _____

A meter (m) is _____

Mass is _____

A gram (g) is _____

Capacity is _____

A liter (L) is _____

## Examples

**❶ Choosing a Unit of Length** Choose an appropriate metric unit of length for a classroom.

A classroom is much shorter than a [          ] but longer than a
[          ]. The most appropriate unit of measure is [          ].

**❷ Choosing a Unit of Mass** Choose an appropriate metric unit of mass.

**a.** a sewing needle

The mass of a sewing needle is much less than the mass of a paperclip. An appropriate unit of measure is [          ].

**b.** a compact disc

The mass of a compact disc is much greater than the mass of an eyelash. An appropriate unit of measure is [          ].

**❸ Choosing a Unit of Capacity** Choose an appropriate metric unit of capacity.

**a.** a kitchen sink

The capacity of a kitchen sink is much less than the capacity of 2 or 3 bathtubs. An appropriate unit of measure is [          ].

**b.** a shampoo bottle

The capacity of a shampoo bottle is less than the capacity of a bottle of juice. An appropriate unit of measure is [          ].

Name _____ Class _____ Date _____

## Quick Check

1. Choose an appropriate metric unit of length for a city block.

   [ ]

2. Choose an appropriate metric unit of mass.

   **a.** a car

   [ ]

   **b.** a desk

   [ ]

   **c.** a robin's feather

   [ ]

3. Choose an appropriate metric unit of capacity.

   **a.** a car's fuel tank

   [ ]

   **b.** a pond

   [ ]

   **c.** a test tube

   [ ]

# Lesson 9-2

**Converting Units
in the Metric System**

| Lesson Objective<br>To convert between metric measurements | NAEP 2005 Strand: Measurement<br>Topic: Systems of Measurement<br>Local Standards: _____ |
|---|---|

## Examples

**❶ Converting to Smaller Units** Convert 41 centimeters to millimeters.

The centimeter is a larger unit than the millimeter. To convert centimeters to millimeters, [＿＿＿＿] by [＿＿＿＿].

$41 \times 10 = 41.0$ ← **To multiply by** [＿＿＿＿] **, move the decimal point 1 place to the right.**

$41 \text{ cm} =$ [＿＿＿＿] mm

**❷ Converting to Larger Units** Convert each measurement.

**a.** 4,201 meters to kilometers

The meter is a smaller unit than the kilometer. To convert meters to kilometers, [＿＿＿＿] by [＿＿＿＿].

$4,201 \div 1,000 = 4.201$ ← **To divide by** [＿＿＿＿] **, move the decimal point 3 places to the left.**

$4,201 \text{ m} =$ [＿＿＿＿] km

**b.** 195 centimeters to meters

The centimeter is a smaller unit than the meter. To convert centimeters to meters, [＿＿＿＿] by [＿＿＿＿].

$195 \div 100 = 1.95$ ← **To divide by** [＿＿＿＿] **, move the decimal point 2 places to the left.**

$195 \text{ cm} =$ [＿＿＿＿] m

**❸ Converting Units of Mass or Capacity** Complete each statement.

**a.** 125 g = ▨ kg

To convert grams to kilograms, divide by ⬚ .

$125 \div 1{,}000 = 0.125$ ← To divide by ⬚ , move the decimal point ⬚ place(s) to the left.

125 g = ⬚ kg

**b.** 8.4 L = ▨ mL

To convert liters to milliliters, multiply by ⬚ .

$8.4 \times 1{,}000 = 8{,}400$ ← To multiply by ⬚ , move the decimal point ⬚ place(s) to the right.

8.4 L = ⬚ mL

## Quick Check

**1.** Convert each measurement.

    **a.** 15 centimeters to millimeters     **b.** 837 kilometers to meters

**2.** A sprinter runs 60,000 meters each week. How many kilometers does the sprinter run each week?

**3.** Complete each statement.

    **a.** 15 mg = ⬚ g     **b.** 386 L = ⬚ kL     **c.** 8.2 cg = ⬚ g

# Lesson 9-3

**Perimeters and Areas of Rectangles**

| Lesson Objective | NAEP 2005 Strand: Measurement |
|---|---|
| To solve problems involving perimeters and areas of rectangles | **Topic:** Measuring Physical Attributes |
| | **Local Standards:** _____ |

## Vocabulary and Key Concepts

**Perimeter and Area of a Rectangle**

$P = 2\left(\boxed{\phantom{x}} + \boxed{\phantom{x}}\right)$

$A = \boxed{\phantom{x}} \times \boxed{\phantom{x}}$

**Perimeter and Area of a Square**

$P = \boxed{\phantom{x}}\, s$

$A = s^{\boxed{\phantom{x}}}$

Perimeter is _____

Area is _____

## Examples

**1** **Finding Perimeter and Area** To renovate their bedroom, the Novaks are carpeting the floor and pasting a wallpaper border along the top of each wall. Find the perimeter and area of their bedroom.

14 ft | bedroom

12 ft

The length is $\boxed{\phantom{xx}}$ ft. The width is $\boxed{\phantom{xx}}$ ft. →

$P = 2(\ell + w)$  ← Use the formula for perimeter.

$\quad = 2(12 + 14)$  ← Substitute $\boxed{\phantom{xx}}$ for $\ell$ and $\boxed{\phantom{xx}}$ for $w$.

$\quad = 2 \times \boxed{\phantom{xx}}$  ← Add.

$\quad = \boxed{\phantom{xx}}$  ← Multiply.

$A = \ell \times w$  ← Use the formula for area.

$\quad = 12 \times 14$  ← Substitute $\boxed{\phantom{xx}}$ for $\ell$ and $\boxed{\phantom{xx}}$ for $w$.

$\quad = \boxed{\phantom{xx}}$  ← Multiply.

The perimeter is $\boxed{\phantom{xxx}}$ feet. The area is $\boxed{\phantom{xxx}}$ square feet.

**❷ Finding the Area of a Square** The perimeter of a square is 28 meters.
Find its area.

**A.** 35 m$^2$       **B.** 39 m$^2$       **C.** 47 m$^2$       **D.** 49 m$^2$

Use the perimeter formula.            Use the area formula.

$$P = 4s$$

$$\boxed{\phantom{xxx}} = 4s$$

$$\frac{\boxed{\phantom{xxx}}}{4} = \frac{4s}{4}$$

$$\boxed{\phantom{xx}} = s$$

$$A = s^2$$

$$= \boxed{\phantom{x}}^2$$

$$= \boxed{\phantom{xxx}}$$

The area of the square is $\boxed{\phantom{xxxxxxx}}$ square meters or $\boxed{\phantom{xxxxxx}}$.

The correct answer is choice $\boxed{\phantom{x}}$.

## Quick Check

1. Find the perimeter and area of a rectangle with a length of 8 feet and
   a width of 5 feet.

<br><br><br>

2. Find the area of a square given $s = 11$ inches.

<br><br>

# Lesson 9-4

**Areas of Parallelograms and Triangles**

| Lesson Objective | NAEP 2005 Strand: Measurement |
|---|---|
| To solve problems involving areas of parallelograms, triangles, and complex figures | **Topic:** Measuring Physical Attributes |
| | **Local Standards:** _____ |

## Vocabulary and Key Concepts

**Area of a Parallelogram**

$A = \square \times \square$

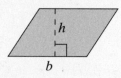 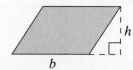

**Area of a Triangle**

$A = \frac{1}{2}\square \times \square$

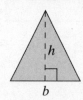 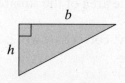

The $\boxed{\phantom{xxx}}$ of a parallelogram can be any side of a parallelogram.

The height of a parallelogram is _____

Any side of a triangle can be the $\boxed{\phantom{xxx}}$ of a triangle.

The height of a triangle is _____

_____

## Example

**❶ Finding the Area of a Parallelogram** Find the area of the parallelogram.

$A = b \times h$    ← **Use the formula for the area of a parallelogram.**

$= \boxed{\phantom{x}} \times \boxed{\phantom{xxx}}$    ← **Substitute** $\boxed{\phantom{x}}$ **for b and** $\boxed{\phantom{xx}}$ **for h.**

$= \boxed{\phantom{xxx}}$    ← **Simplify.**

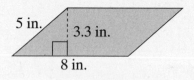

The area of the parallelogram is $\boxed{\phantom{xxx}}$ square inches.

## Quick Check

**1.** Find the area of a parallelogram with $b = 14$ m and $h = 5$ m.

$\boxed{\phantom{xxxxxxxxxxxxxxx}}$

Name _____ Class _____ Date _____

**Examples**

❷ **Finding the Area of a Triangle** A park is a triangular plot of land. The triangle has a base of 214 m and a height of 70 m. Find its area.

$A = \frac{1}{2}\boxed{\phantom{x}} \times \boxed{\phantom{x}}$   ← Use the formula for the area of a triangle.

$= \frac{1}{2} \times \boxed{\phantom{xxxx}} \times \boxed{\phantom{xxxx}}$   ← Substitute $\boxed{\phantom{xx}}$ for *b* and $\boxed{\phantom{xx}}$ for *h*.

$= \boxed{\phantom{xxxx}}$   ← Simplify.

The area of the triangle is $\boxed{\phantom{xxxx}}$ square meters.

❸ **Finding the Area of a Complex Figure** Find the area of the figure.

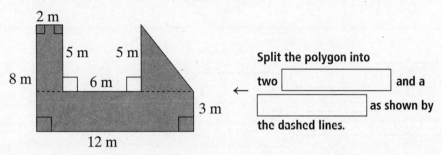

Split the polygon into
two $\boxed{\phantom{xxxx}}$ and a
$\boxed{\phantom{xxxx}}$ as shown by
the dashed lines.

Area of the smaller rectangle: $2 \times 5 = \boxed{\phantom{x}}$, or $\boxed{\phantom{x}}$ m$^2$

Area of the larger rectangle: $3 \times 12 = \boxed{\phantom{x}}$, or $\boxed{\phantom{x}}$ m$^2$   ← Find the area of each polygon.

Area of the triangle: $\frac{1}{2}(5 \times 4) = \frac{1}{2}(\boxed{\phantom{x}})$, or $\boxed{\phantom{x}}$ m$^2$

The total area is $\boxed{\phantom{x}} + \boxed{\phantom{x}} + \boxed{\phantom{x}}$, or $\boxed{\phantom{x}}$ square meters.

**Quick Check**

2. A triangle has a base of 30 meters and a height of 17.3 meters. Find its area.

3. Find the area of the complex figure below.

# Lesson 9-5

**Circles and Circumference**

| **Lesson Objective**<br>To identify the parts of a circle and find radius, diameter, and circumference | **NAEP 2005 Strand:** Measurement<br>**Topic:** Measuring Physical Attributes<br>**Local Standards:** _____ |
| --- | --- |

## Vocabulary and Key Concepts

**Circumference of a Circle**

$C = \pi d$

$C = 2\pi r$

A circle is _____

_____

_____

A radius is _____

_____

_____

A chord is _____

_____

A diameter is _____

_____

Circumference is _____

_____

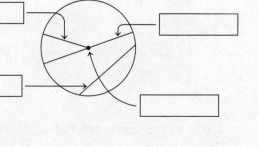

## Example

**1 Identifying Parts of a Circle**

a. List the radii shown in circle $R$.

The radii are ⬚ , ⬚ , and ⬚ .

b. List the chords shown in circle $R$.

The chords are ⬚ , ⬚ , and ⬚ .

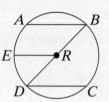

## Quick Check

1. Write the diameter shown in circle $R$. ⬚

## Examples

**❷ Finding the Radius and Diameter** On July 22, 2002, the world's largest wooden nickel was unveiled in San Antonio, Texas. The radius of the wooden nickel is 80 inches. What is its diameter?

$d =$ ⬚      ← **The diameter is twice the radius.**

   $=$ ⬚ $\times$ ⬚      ← **Substitute.**

   $=$ ⬚      ← **Simplify.**

The diameter is ⬚ inches.

**❸ Finding Circumference** The surface of one type of trampoline is bounded by a circular frame with a 7-foot radius. Find the circumference of the frame to the nearest foot.

   **A.** 40 feet      **B.** 44 feet      **C.** 49 feet      **D.** 51 feet

$C = \pi d$      ← **Use the formula for the circumference of a circle.**

   $\approx$ ⬚ $\times$ ⬚      ← **Substitute** ⬚ $\times$ ⬚ **for $d$ and 3.14 for $\pi$.**

   $=$ ⬚      ← **Multiply.**

The circumference of the trampoline frame is about ⬚ feet.

The correct answer is choice ⬚.

## Quick Check

**2.** Find the radius when $d = 6$ cm.

**3.** A circle has a radius of 11 m. What expression describes the circumference of the circle in meters?

# Lesson 9-6

**Area of a Circle**

| Lesson Objective<br>To find the area of a circle | NAEP 2005 Strand: Measurement |
| --- | --- |
| | Topic: Measuring Physical Attributes |
| | Local Standards: _____ |

## Key Concepts

**Area of a Circle**

$A = \pi r^2$

## Example

**1** **Finding the Area of a Circle** Find the area of a circle with diameter 18 inches. Use 3.14 for $\pi$.

The radius is half the diameter, or ☐ inches.

**Estimate** Use 3 for $\pi$. So, $A \approx 3 \times 9^2$, or ☐ square inches.

$A = \pi r^2$  ← **Use the formula for the area of a circle.**

$\approx$ ☐ $\times$ ☐$^2$  ← **Substitute** ☐ **for** $r$ **and** ☐ **for** $\pi$.

$=$ ☐  ← **Multiply.**

The area is about ☐ square inches.

## Quick Check

**1.** Find the area of each circle. Use 3.14 for $\pi$.

**a.**

**b.**

**c.**

## Example

❷ **Gardening** Find the area of a circular flower bed with radius 7 feet. Use $\frac{22}{7}$ for $\pi$.

$A = \pi r^2$        ← **Use the formula for the area of a circle.**

$\approx \dfrac{\boxed{\phantom{xx}}}{\boxed{\phantom{xx}}} \times \boxed{\phantom{x}}^2$   ← **Use** $\dfrac{\boxed{\phantom{xx}}}{\boxed{\phantom{xx}}}$ **for $\pi$ and** $\boxed{\phantom{x}}$ **for $r$.**

$= \dfrac{22}{\cancel{7}} \times \cancel{49}^{\;\boxed{\phantom{x}}}$   ← **Divide 7 and 49 by their GCF, 7.**
$\phantom{xxx}\boxed{\phantom{x}}$

$= \boxed{\phantom{xxxxx}}$   ← **Multiply.**

The area of the flower bed is about $\boxed{\phantom{xxxx}}$ square feet.

## Quick Check

2. Find the area of a pizza with a 14-in. diameter. Use $\frac{22}{7}$ for $\pi$.

<br>
<br>
<br>
<br>

# Lesson 9-7

| Lesson Objective<br>To identify three-dimensional figures | **NAEP 2005 Strand:** Geometry<br>**Topic:** Dimension and Shape<br>**Local Standards:** _____ |
| --- | --- |

## Vocabulary

A three-dimensional figure is _____

_____

A prism is _____

_____

A cube is _____

_____

 A pyramid is _____

_____

A cylinder is _____

_____

 A cone is _____

_____

A sphere is _____

_____

The flat surfaces of a three-dimensional
figure are called [      ].

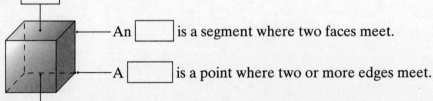

An [      ] is a segment where two faces meet.

A [      ] is a point where two or more edges meet.

When you draw three-dimensional figures, use dashed lines to indicate "hidden" edges.

Name _____ Class _____ Date _____

## Examples

**❶ Naming Prisms** Name the prism.

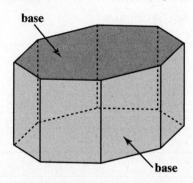

base

base

Each base is an [_____]. The figure is an [_____] prism.

**❷ Identifying Three-Dimensional Figures** Name the three-dimensional figure shown.

The figure is a [_____] with a [_____]

for a base. The figure is a [_____].

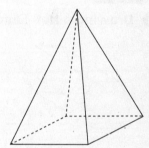

## Quick Check

**1.** Name each prism.

a.

b.

c.

**2.** Name the three-dimensional figures below.

⸳⸳⸳⸳⸳⸳⸳⸳⸳⸳⸳⸳⸳⸳⸳⸳⸳⸳⸳⸳⸳⸳⸳⸳⸳⸳⸳⸳⸳⸳⸳⸳⸳⸳⸳⸳⸳⸳⸳⸳⸳⸳⸳⸳⸳⸳⸳⸳⸳⸳⸳⸳⸳⸳⸳⸳⸳

# Lesson 9-8

**Surface Areas of Prisms**

| **Lesson Objective**<br>To use nets and find the surface of rectangular prisms | **NAEP 2005 Strand:** Measurement<br>**Topic:** Measuring Physical Attributes<br>**Local Standards:** _____ |
|---|---|

## Vocabulary

A net is _____

_____

Surface area is _____

_____

## Example

❶ **Drawing a Net** Draw a net for the hexagonal prism.

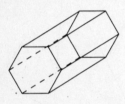

**Step 1** Draw one [    ]. ⟶

**Step 2** Draw one [    ] that connects the two bases.

**Step 3** Draw the other [    ]. ⟶

**Step 4** Draw the remaining [    ].

## Quick Check

**1.** Draw a net for a cube.

Name _____ Class _____ Date _____

### Example

❷ **Finding the Surface Area of a Prism**  Find the surface area of the pizza box.

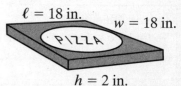

$\ell = 18$ in.
$w = 18$ in.
$h = 2$ in.

**Step 1**  Draw and label a net for the prism.

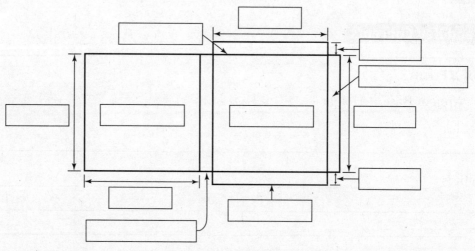

**Step 2**  Find and add the areas of all the rectangles.

| Back | Top | Left | Bottom | Right | Front |
|------|-----|------|--------|-------|-------|
| $18 \times 2$ | $+\ 18 \times 18$ | $+\ \square \times \square$ | $+\ \square \times \square$ | $+\ \square \times \square$ | $+\ \square \times \square$ |
| $=\quad 36$ | $+\quad 324$ | $+\ \boxed{\phantom{xx}}$ | $+\ \boxed{\phantom{xx}}$ | $+\ \boxed{\phantom{xx}}$ | $+\ \boxed{\phantom{xx}} = \boxed{\phantom{xxx}}$ |

The surface area of the pizza box is $\boxed{\phantom{xxx}}$ square inches.

### Quick Check

**2.** Find the surface area of the prism.

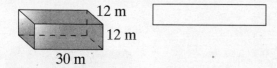

12 m
12 m
30 m

$\boxed{\phantom{xxxxxxxxx}}$

# Lesson 9-9

**Volumes of Rectangular Prisms**

| **Lesson Objective**<br>To find the volume of rectangular prisms | **NAEP 2005 Strand:** Measurement<br>**Topic:** Measuring Physical Attributes<br>**Local Standards:** _____ |
|---|---|

## Vocabulary and Key Concepts

**Volume of a Prism**

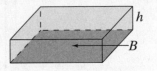

Volume = Area of Base × Height

$V = \boxed{\phantom{x}} \times \boxed{\phantom{x}}$

A cubic unit is _____

_____

Volume is _____

_____

## Example

**1** **Counting Cubes to Find Volume** Find the volume of the rectangular prism shown.

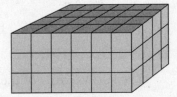

Each layer of the prism is 4 cubes by 6 cubes. This equals
$\boxed{\phantom{x}} \times \boxed{\phantom{x}}$, or $\boxed{\phantom{xx}}$ cubes. The prism is 3 layers tall. The
prism has a total of $\boxed{\phantom{x}} \times \boxed{\phantom{xx}}$, or $\boxed{\phantom{xx}}$ cubes.

The volume of the prism is $\boxed{\phantom{xx}}$ cubic units.

## Quick Check

**1.** Find the volume of the rectangular prism at the right.

$\boxed{\phantom{xxxxxxxxxxxxxxxxxxxxxxxxx}}$

## Example

**❷ Finding the Volume of a Prism** Find the volume of the storage container shown.

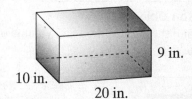

$V = \ell \times w \times h$  ← Use the formula for the volume of a rectangular prism.

$= \boxed{\phantom{xx}} \times \boxed{\phantom{xx}} \times \boxed{\phantom{xx}}$  ← Substitute 20 for $\ell$, 10 for $w$, and 9 for $h$.

$= \boxed{\phantom{xxxx}}$  ← Multiply.

The volume is about $\boxed{\phantom{xxxxx}}$ cubic inches, or $\boxed{\phantom{xxxxx}}$ in.$^3$.

## Quick Check

**2.** Find the volume of a rectangular prism with a length of 8 meters, a width of 7 meters, and a height of 10 meters.

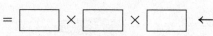

# Lesson 9-10

**Surface Areas and Volumes of Cylinders**

| Lesson Objective | NAEP 2005 Strand: Measurement |
|---|---|
| To find the surface area and volume of cylinders | Topic: Measuring Physical Attributes |
| | Local Standards: _____ |

## Examples

**❶ Finding the Surface Area of a Cylinder** Find the surface area of the cylinder. Use 3.14 for $\pi$.

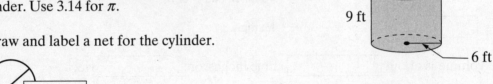

9 ft

6 ft

**Step 1** Draw and label a net for the cylinder.

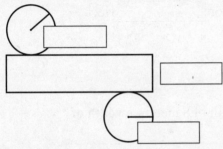

**Step 2** Find the area of one circle.

$A = \pi r^2$  ← Use the formula for the area of a circle.

$\approx \boxed{\phantom{xxx}} \times \boxed{\phantom{x}}^2$  ← Substitute 6 for $r$ and 3.14 for $\pi$.

$= \boxed{\phantom{xxxxx}}$  ← Multiply.

$= \boxed{\phantom{xxxxx}}$  ← Round to the nearest tenth.

**Step 3** Find the area of the rectangle.

$A = \ell \times w$  ← Use the formula.

$= \boxed{\phantom{xxx}} \times h$  ← The length of the rectangle is the circumference of the circle. The width of the rectangle is the height of the cylinder.

$\approx \boxed{\phantom{xxx}}(\boxed{\phantom{xx}}) \times \boxed{\phantom{x}}$  ← Substitute 12 for $d$, 9 for $h$, and 3.14 for $\pi$.

$= \boxed{\phantom{xxxxx}}$  ← Multiply.

$= \boxed{\phantom{xxxxx}}$  ← Round to the nearest tenth.

**Step 4** Add the areas of the rectangle and the two circles.

$\boxed{\phantom{xxxx}} + \boxed{\phantom{xxxx}} + \boxed{\phantom{xxxx}} = \boxed{\phantom{xxxx}}$

The surface area of the cylinder is about $\boxed{\phantom{xxxx}}$ square feet.

❷ **Finding the Volume of a Cylinder** Find the volume of the can of tuna. Use 3.14 for $\pi$.

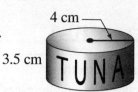

4 cm
3.5 cm
TUNA

**Step 1** Find the area of the base.

$$\text{Area of Base} = \pi \times r^2$$

$$\approx 3.14 \times \boxed{\phantom{x}}^2 \quad \leftarrow \quad \text{Substitute } \boxed{\phantom{x}} \text{ for } r \text{ and 3.14 for } \pi.$$

$$= \boxed{\phantom{xxxxx}} \quad \leftarrow \quad \text{Multiply.}$$

**Step 2** Find the volume.

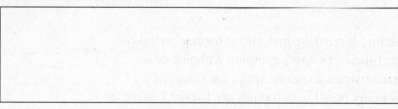

$$\text{Volume} = B \times h$$

$$\approx \boxed{\phantom{xxxx}} \times \boxed{\phantom{xx}} \quad \leftarrow \quad \text{Substitute } \boxed{\phantom{xxxx}} \text{ for } B \text{ and } \boxed{\phantom{xxxx}} \text{ for } h.$$

$$\approx \boxed{\phantom{xxxx}} \quad \leftarrow \quad \text{Multiply.}$$

The volume is about $\boxed{\phantom{xxxxx}}$ cubic centimeters, or $\boxed{\phantom{xxxxx}}$ cm$^3$.

**Quick Check**

1. Find the surface area of the cylinder at the right. Use 3.14 for $\pi$. Round to the nearest tenth.

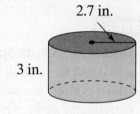

2.7 in.
3 in.

2. Find the volume of a cylinder with a radius of 4 inches and a height of 9 inches. Round to the nearest cubic inch.

# Lesson 10-1

| Lesson Objective | NAEP 2005 Strand: Data Analysis and Probability |
|---|---|
| To construct sample spaces for events and to use the counting principle | Topic: Probability |
| | Local Standards: _____ |

## Vocabulary and Key Concepts

**Counting Principle**

There are $m$ ways of making one choice and $n$ ways of making a second choice. Then there are ☐ × ☐ ways to make the first choice followed by the second choice.

An outcome is _____

An event is _____

A sample space is _____

A tree diagram is _____

_____

## Example

**❶ Finding a Sample Space** Madeline is creating invitations for her birthday party. She has a choice of green, blue, or yellow paper and a choice of a clown border or a cake border. Construct a sample space for selecting a paper color and a border. How many possible outcomes are there? List all of the possible combinations.

☐ paper and clown border

☐ paper and cake border

☐ paper and clown border

☐ paper and cake border

☐ paper and clown border

☐ paper and cake border

The number of possible outcomes is ☐ .

## Quick Check

**1.** A bicycle comes in 3 models and 3 colors. Construct the sample space to find how many bicycle choices you have. How many possible outcomes are there?

## Examples

❷ **Using a Tree Diagram** You spin a spinner with 5 equal-sized sections numbered 1 through 5. You then toss a coin. Make a tree diagram to find all possible outcomes. How many are there?

Look at the tree diagram at the right.

The diagram shows [ ] equally likely outcomes.

| Spinner | Coin | Outcome |
|---------|------|---------|
| 1 | H | 1H |
|   | T | 1T |
| 2 | H | 2H |
|   | T | 2T |
| 3 | H | 3H |
|   | T | 3T |
| 4 | H | 4H |
|   | T | 4T |
| 5 | H | 5H |
|   | T | 5T |

❸ **Using the Counting Principle** Flight attendants can wear one of four shirts, three pants, and two jackets. How many different combinations of uniforms are possible?

**A.** 24          **B.** 26          **C.** 28          **D.** 32

Use the counting principle to find the total number of uniforms.

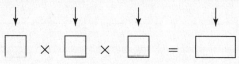

Shirts   Pants   Jackets   Uniforms

[ ] × [ ] × [ ] = [ ]

There are [ ] different uniform combinations. The correct answer is choice [ ].

## Quick Check

2. You can choose blue or khaki pants and a red, yellow, or green shirt. Construct the sample space using a tree diagram. How many outfits are possible?

3. In the menu to the right, add cherry ripple ice cream as a flavor and fudge as a topping. Find the new number of different desserts.

**Ice Cream Menu**

**Flavors**
Vanilla
Chocolate
Strawberry
Banana
Peach

**Toppings**
Nuts
Sprinkles
Cherries

**Cones**
Waffle
Sugar

# Lesson 10-2

**Probability**

| Lesson Objective | NAEP 2005 Strand: Data Analysis and Probability |
|---|---|
| To find the probability of an event and its complement | Topic: Probability |
| | Local Standards: _____ |

## Vocabulary and Key Concepts

**Probability of an Event**

For equally likely outcomes:

the probability of an event = $\dfrac{\boxed{\phantom{xxxxxxxxxxxxxxx}}}{\boxed{\phantom{xxxxxxxxxxxxxxx}}}$

Equally likely outcomes are _____

The probability of an event is _____

_____

The complement of an event is _____

## Examples

**❶ Probability of an Event** A spinner is divided into 8 equal sections numbered 1 through 8. Find each probability for one spin of the spinner.

**a.** $P(6)$

There is $\boxed{\phantom{x}}$ outcome for the event "6" out of 8 equally likely outcomes.

$P(6) = \dfrac{\boxed{\phantom{x}}}{\boxed{\phantom{x}}}$ ← outcomes with event "6"

← total number of outcomes

The probability of spinning a 6 is $\dfrac{\boxed{\phantom{x}}}{\boxed{\phantom{x}}}$ .

**b.** $P(2 \text{ or } 3)$

There is 1 outcome for the event "2" and 1 outcome for the event "3"

out of $\boxed{\phantom{x}}$ equally likely outcomes.

$P(2 \text{ or } 3) = \dfrac{\boxed{\phantom{x}}}{\boxed{\phantom{x}}}$ ← outcomes with event "2" or event "3"

← total number of outcomes

$= \dfrac{\boxed{\phantom{x}}}{\boxed{\phantom{x}}}$ ← Simplify.

❷ **Complement of an Event** In Mr. Ching's class of 25 students, 4 students have birthdays in November. Mr. Ching selects a student at random. What is $P$(November birthday)? What is $P$(not November birthday)?

$P$(November) = $\dfrac{\boxed{\phantom{00}}}{\boxed{\phantom{00}}}$     ← **number of students with November birthdays**
   ← **total number of students**

The event "not November birthday" is the complement of the event "November birthday." The sum of the probabilities of an event and its complement is 1.

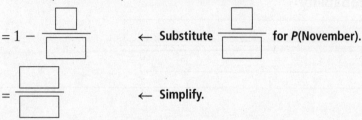

$P$(not November) = $1 - P$(November)   ← **Write the formula.**

$= 1 - \dfrac{\boxed{\phantom{00}}}{\boxed{\phantom{00}}}$   ← **Substitute** $\dfrac{\boxed{\phantom{00}}}{\boxed{\phantom{00}}}$ **for** $P$(November).

$= \dfrac{\boxed{\phantom{00}}}{\boxed{\phantom{00}}}$   ← **Simplify.**

$P$(November) is $\boxed{\phantom{000}}$ . $P$(not November) is $\boxed{\phantom{000}}$ .

❸ **Finding Probability** The 6th grade class made 73 of the 100 posters made by the school.

**a.** Find the probability that a randomly selected poster was made by the 6th grade class. Write your answer as a fraction, a decimal, and a percent.

$P$(6th grade poster) = $\dfrac{\boxed{\phantom{00}}}{\boxed{\phantom{00}}}$   ← **number of 6th grade posters**
   ← **total number of posters**

$= \boxed{\phantom{0000}}$ , or $\boxed{\phantom{000}}$ %

**b.** State whether the above event is *impossible*, *unlikely*, *equally likely*, *likely*, or *certain*.

The probability is between $\boxed{\phantom{00}}$ and $\boxed{\phantom{00}}$ , so the event is $\boxed{\phantom{0000}}$ .

## Quick Check

**1.** You roll a number cube once. Find $P$(4 or 6).

$\boxed{\phantom{00000000000000000000000000000000000000}}$

**2.** You roll a number cube once. Find $P$(not 6).

$\boxed{\phantom{00000000000000000000000000000000000000}}$

**3.** In a bag of mixed nuts, 6 of 10 nuts are pecans. What is the probability that a randomly selected nut is a pecan? Write your answer as a decimal.

$\boxed{\phantom{00000000000000000000000000000000000000}}$

# Lesson 10-3

**Experimental Probability**

| Lesson Objective<br>To find experimental probability | NAEP 2005 Strand: Data Analysis and Probability<br>Topic: Probability<br>Local Standards: _____ |
|---|---|

## Key Concepts

**Experimental Probability**

$$P(\text{event}) = \frac{\boxed{\phantom{xxxxxxxxxxxxxxxxxxxxxxx}}}{\boxed{\phantom{xxxxxxxxxxxxxxxx}}}$$

## Example

❶ **Experimental Probability** In 30 times at bat, Jan struck out 14 times. What is the experimental probability that Jan will strike out at her next at-bat?

$$P(\text{strike-out}) = \frac{\boxed{\phantom{xx}}}{\boxed{\phantom{xx}}}$$  ← **number of strike-outs**
    ← **total number of at-bats**

$$= \frac{\boxed{\phantom{xx}}}{\boxed{\phantom{xx}}}$$  ← **Simplify.**

The experimental probability of a strike-out is $\dfrac{\boxed{\phantom{xx}}}{\boxed{\phantom{xx}}}$.

## Quick Check

1. In 20 tennis matches against Jennie, Ai-Ling wins 9 times. What is the experimental probability that Jennie wins a match?

   $\boxed{\phantom{xxxxxxxxxxxxxxxxxxxxxxxxxxxxx}}$

## Example

❷ **Analyzing Experimental Probability** You and your friend want to play a game with a spinner. The table at right shows the results of 120 spins. Which of the following games seems fair? Explain.

| Red | Yellow | Blue |
|-----|--------|------|
| 58 | 23 | 39 |

**a.** You win with yellow and your friend wins with blue.

The experimental probability of spinning a yellow is $\dfrac{\boxed{\phantom{00}}}{\boxed{\phantom{00}}}$.

The experimental probability of spinning a blue is $\dfrac{\boxed{\phantom{00}}}{\boxed{\phantom{00}}}$.

Since the spinner favors blue, the game seems to be $\boxed{\phantom{00000}}$.

**b.** You win with red and your friend wins with blue or yellow.

$39 + 23 = \boxed{\phantom{00}}$ ← **Add to find the number of trials for blue or yellow.**

So $P(\text{red}) = \dfrac{\boxed{\phantom{00}}}{\boxed{\phantom{00}}}$ and $P(\text{blue or yellow}) = \dfrac{\boxed{\phantom{00}}}{\boxed{\phantom{00}}}$.

Since the probabilities are about the same, the game seems to be $\boxed{\phantom{0000}}$.

## Quick Check

2. In Example 2, suppose you win with red or blue and your friend wins with red or yellow. Does the game seem fair? Explain.

# Lesson 10-4

**Making Predictions From Data**

| Lesson Objective | NAEP 2005 Strand: Data Analysis and Probability |
|---|---|
| To make predictions using probabilities and samples | Topic: Probability |
| | Local Standards: _____ |

## Vocabulary

A population is _____

_____

A sample is _____

_____

## Example

❶ **Making a Prediction** Kiko bought 35 raffle tickets. Each ticket has a 20% probability of winning a prize. How many prizes should he expect to win?

$$\boxed{\begin{array}{c}\text{number of tickets}\\\text{that win a prize}\end{array}} \times \boxed{\text{number of tickets}} = \boxed{P(\text{prize})}$$

$$\dfrac{\boxed{\phantom{0}}}{\boxed{\phantom{0}}} \times \boxed{\phantom{00}} = \boxed{\phantom{0}} \quad \leftarrow \begin{array}{l}\text{Write 20\% as } \frac{1}{5}.\\ \text{Then multiply.}\end{array}$$

He can predict that about ☐ tickets will win a prize.

## Quick Check

1. At an arcade, Juanita plays a game 20 times. She has a 30% probability of winning. How many times can she expect to win?

## Example

❷ **Quality Control** A random sample shows that 6 wallets out of 400 are defective. Predict how many wallets out of 15,000 will be defective.

**Words** $\longrightarrow$

$$\boxed{\dfrac{\text{number defective in sample}}{\text{total number in sample}}} = \boxed{\dfrac{\text{total number defective}}{\text{total number}}}$$

Let $n = \boxed{\begin{array}{c}\text{the number of defective wallets}\\ \text{in the population}\end{array}}$.

**Proportion**

$$\dfrac{\boxed{\phantom{xx}}}{\boxed{\phantom{xxxx}}} = \dfrac{\boxed{\phantom{xx}}}{\boxed{\phantom{xxxx}}}$$

$$\dfrac{\boxed{\phantom{xx}}}{\boxed{\phantom{xxxx}}} = \dfrac{\boxed{\phantom{xx}}}{\boxed{\phantom{xxxx}}}$$

$400\boxed{\phantom{xx}} = 6 \cdot \boxed{\phantom{xxxx}}$  ← **Write the cross products.**

$400n = \boxed{\phantom{xxxxx}}$  ← **Simplify.**

$\dfrac{400n}{\boxed{\phantom{xx}}} = \dfrac{\boxed{\phantom{xxxx}}}{\boxed{\phantom{xx}}}$  ← **Divide each side by 400.**

$n = \boxed{\phantom{xxxx}}$  ← **Simplify.**

It is likely that about $\boxed{\phantom{xxx}}$ wallets are defective.

## Quick Check

2. Suppose 1,000 toy robots are selected at random from 20,000 robots, and 54 robots are found faulty. Predict how many of the 20,000 robots are likely to be faulty.

# Lesson 10-5                                    **Independent Events**

| **Lesson Objective** | **NAEP 2005 Strand:** Data Analysis and Probability |
|---|---|
| To find probabilities of independent events | **Topic:** Probability |
| | **Local Standards:** _____ |

## Vocabulary and Key Concepts

**Probability of Independent Events**

If $A$ and $B$ are independent events, then

$$P(A, \text{then } B) = \boxed{\phantom{xxx}} \times \boxed{\phantom{xxx}}$$

If the occurrence of one event does not affect the probability of another

event, the two are $\boxed{\phantom{xxxxxxxxxxxxx}}$.

$\boxed{\phantom{xxxxxxxxxxx}}$ consists of two or more separate events.

## Example

❶ **Identifying Independent Events** Decide whether or not events in each
group are independent. Explain.

**a.** You toss a coin and get heads. You then toss the same coin again and get
tails.

The events are $\boxed{\phantom{xxxxxxxxxx}}$. The first coin toss has

$\boxed{\phantom{xxxxx}}$ on the occurrence of the second coin toss.

**b.** You have a bowl of 4 green marbles and 7 orange marbles. You draw one
of the marbles from the bowl. Without replacing it, you draw another
marble from the bowl.

The events are $\boxed{\phantom{xxxxxxxxxx}}$. After you draw the first

marble, there will be one less marble in the bowl. The first selection

$\boxed{\phantom{xxxxx}}$ the second selection.

## Quick Check

**1.** You select a card from a deck of cards. Without replacing it, you select
another card. Are the events independent? Explain.

$\boxed{\phantom{xxxxxxxxxxxxxxxxxxxxxxxxxxxxxxxxxxxxxxxxxxxxxxxx}}$

### Examples

❷ **Probability of an Independent Event** There are six cubes in a bag. Four cubes are red and two cubes are yellow. You draw a cube and put it back in the bag. You repeat this process two more times. Find the probability that you draw red cubes all three times.

The events are independent. The probability of drawing a red cube is

$\dfrac{4}{6}$, or $\dfrac{\square}{\square}$.

$P(\text{red, then red, then red}) = \dfrac{\square}{\square} \times \dfrac{\square}{\square} \times \dfrac{\square}{\square}$  ← **Use the formula.**

$= \dfrac{\square}{\square}$  ← **Multiply.**

The probability of drawing three red cubes is $\dfrac{\square}{\square}$.

❸ **Alarm System** Two neighbors have the same alarm system. Each alarm has 600 possible codes. What is the probability that the neighbors have the same code?

One neighbor has one of the 600 codes. The probability that the other

neighbor has the same code is $\dfrac{\square}{\square}$.

### Quick Check

2. For the situation in Example 2, find $P(\text{yellow, then yellow})$.

$P(\text{yellow, then yellow}) = \dfrac{2}{\square} \cdot \dfrac{2}{\square} = \dfrac{\square}{\square} = \dfrac{\square}{\square}$

3. You guess at random the answers of four true-or-false questions. What is the probability that all four answers are correct?

# Lesson 11-1

**Exploring Integers**

| Lesson Objective | NAEP 2005 Strand: Number Properties and Operations |
|---|---|
| To use integers, opposites, and absolute values to represent real-life situations | **Topic:** Number Sense |
| | **Local Standards:** _____ |

## Vocabulary

Two numbers are opposites if _____

_____

Integers are _____

_____

The absolute value of a number is _____

_____

## Examples

❶ **Representing Situations with Integers** You are six spaces behind your opponent in a board game. What integer represents your situation?

☐   ← **An integer less than 0 is represented as** ☐.

❷ **Identifying Opposites** Write the opposite of 6.

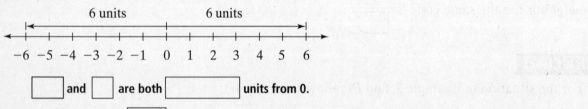

☐ **and** ☐ **are both** ☐ **units from 0.**

The opposite of 6 is ☐.

## Quick Check

**1.** The elevation of New Orleans, Louisiana, is 8 feet below sea level. Use an integer to represent this elevation.

_____

**2.** Write the opposite of −5.

Name _____ Class _____ Date _____

## Example

❸ **Finding Absolute Value**  Find |−19|.

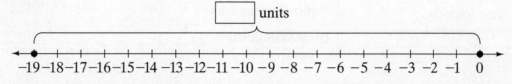

units

−19 −18 −17 −16 −15 −14 −13 −12 −11 −10 −9 −8 −7 −6 −5 −4 −3 −2 −1  0

Since −19 is ⬚ units from 0, |−19| = 19.

## Quick Check

**3. a.** Find |−1|.

**b.** Find |7|.

# Lesson 11-2

**Comparing and Ordering Integers**

| Lesson Objective | NAEP 2005 Strand: Number Properties and Operations |
|---|---|
| To compare and order integers | **Topic:** Number Sense |
| | **Local Standards:** _____ |

## Examples

**❶ Comparing Integers**

   **a.** Compare −12 and −10.

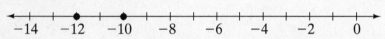

   ← Graph −12 and −10 on the same number line.

   Since −12 is to the left of −10 on the number line, −12 ☐ −10, or −10 ☐ −12.

   **b.** Compare 3 and −5.

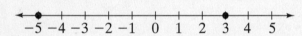

   ← Graph 3 and −5 on the same number line.

   Since 3 is to the ☐ of −5 on the number line, 3 ☐ −5, or −5 ☐ 3.

**❷ Ordering Integers**

   **a.** Order from least to greatest: 16, −2, −35, 68, −10. Use five as the number line interval.

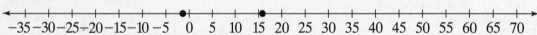

   In order from least to greatest, the numbers are

   ☐ , ☐ , ☐ , ☐ , ☐ .

   **b.** Order from least to greatest: 4, 0, −3, 1, −2.
   Use one as the number line interval.

   In order from least to greatest, the numbers are

   ☐ , ☐ , ☐ , ☐ , ☐ .

## Quick Check

1. Compare using < or >.

    a. 5 ☐ −3

    b. −12 ☐ 9

2. Order these scores from least to greatest: −25, 100, −50, 75.

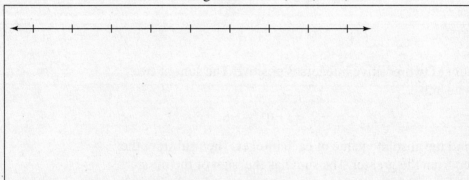

# Lesson 11-3                                          Adding Integers

| Lesson Objective | NAEP 2005 Strand: Number Properties and Operations |
|---|---|
| To add integers and to solve problems by adding integers | Topic: Number Operations |
| | Local Standards: _____ |

## Key Concepts

**Adding Integers**

**Same Signs** The sum of two positive integers is positive. The sum of two negative integers is negative.

**Examples:** $2 + 6 = 8$          $-2 + (-6) = -8$

**Different Signs** Find the absolute value of each integer. Then subtract the lesser absolute value from the greater. The sum has the sign of the integer with the greater absolute value.

**Examples:** $3 + (-7) = -4$          $-3 + 7 = 4$

## Examples

❶ **Using a Number Line to Add Integers** Use a number line to find $-3 + (-5)$.

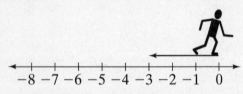

Start at ☐ . Face the positive direction.

Move ☐ 3 units for −3.

So, $-3 + (-5) = $ ☐ .

Then move ☐ 5 units for ☐ .

You stop at ☐ .

❷ **Sports** A football team loses 4 yards on one play. On the next play, the team gains 7 yards. Find $-4 + 7$. Use a number line to find the sum.

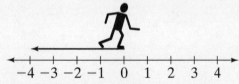

Start at ☐ , and face the positive direction.

Move backward ☐ units for −4.

The result is a gain of ☐ yards.

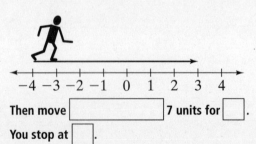

Then move ☐ 7 units for ☐ .

You stop at ☐ .

**❸ Adding Integers** Find $-6 + (-10)$.

$$-6 + (-10) = \boxed{\phantom{000}}$$

↑

The sum of two negative

numbers is $\boxed{\phantom{000}}$.

**❹ Adding Integers** Find each sum.

**a.** $8 + (-10)$  **b.** $-4 + 16$

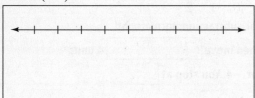  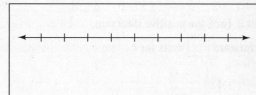

$|8| = \boxed{\phantom{00}}$  ← Find the absolute →  $|-4| = \boxed{\phantom{00}}$

$|-10| = \boxed{\phantom{00}}$  value of each integer.  $|16| = \boxed{\phantom{00}}$

$10 - 8 = \boxed{\phantom{00}}$  ← Subtract the →  $16 - 4 = \boxed{\phantom{00}}$
absolute values.

$8 + (-10) = \boxed{\phantom{00}}$  The sum has the sign  $-4 + 16 = \boxed{\phantom{00}}$
← of the integer with the →
greater absolute value.

## Quick Check

**1.** Use a number line to find each sum.

  **a.** $-1 + (-3)$  **b.** $4 + (-1)$

**2.** Find $-4 + 1$.

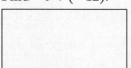

**3.** Find $-9 + (-12)$.

**4.** Find $-11 + 4$.

# Lesson 11-4

**Subtracting Integers**

| Lesson Objective | NAEP 2005 Strand: Number Properties and Operations |
|---|---|
| To subtract integers and to solve problems by subtracting integers | **Topic:** Number Operations |
| | **Local Standards:** _____ |

## Key Concepts

**Subtracting Integers** You subtract an integer by adding its opposite.

**Examples:**

$10 - 6 = 10 + \boxed{\phantom{00}}$ $\qquad 10 - (-6) = 10 + \boxed{\phantom{00}}$

$-10 - 6 = -10 + \boxed{\phantom{00}}$ $\qquad -10 - (-6) = -10 + \boxed{\phantom{00}}$

## Examples

❶ **Using a Number Line to Subtract** Use a number line to find $4 - (-4)$.

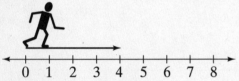 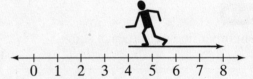

Start at 0. Face the positive direction.

Move forward $\boxed{\phantom{0}}$ units for 4.

So $4 - (-4) = \boxed{\phantom{0}}$.

For subtraction, turn around.

Then move $\boxed{\phantom{000000}}$ 4 units

for −4. You stop at $\boxed{\phantom{0}}$.

❷ **Subtracting Integers** Find each difference.

**a.** $-5 - (-7)$

$-5 - (-7) = -5 + \boxed{\phantom{0}}$ ← **To subtract −7, add its opposite, 7.**

$\quad\quad\quad = \boxed{\phantom{0}}$ ← **Simplify.**

**b.** $-9 - 6$

$-9 - 6 = -9 + \left(\boxed{\phantom{00}}\right)$ ← **To subtract 6, add its opposite, −6.**

$\quad\quad\quad = \boxed{\phantom{00}}$ ← **Simplify.**

**❸** Juan owes his sister $14. She told him to subtract $8 of what he owes if he feeds the dog. Write an integer to show how much money Juan will owe if he feeds the dog.

Find $-14 - (-8)$.

$-14 - (-8) = -14 + \boxed{\phantom{00}}$   ← **To subtract −8, add its opposite.**

$= \boxed{\phantom{00}}$   ← **Simplify.**

The integer $\boxed{\phantom{00}}$ shows that Juan will owe his sister $\boxed{\phantom{00}}$.

## Quick Check

**1. a.** Find $5 - (-1)$.

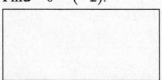

**b.** Find $-3 - 3$.

**2.** Find $-6 - (-2)$.

**3.** The research submarine *Alvin* moved from 1,872 feet below sea level to a position 1,250 feet below sea level. How far did *Alvin* move? Did it finish closer to sea level or farther from sea level?

# Lesson 11-5

**Multiplying Integers**

| Lesson Objective | NAEP 2005 Strand: Number Properties and Operations |
|---|---|
| To multiply integers and to solve problems by multiplying integers | **Topic:** Number Operations |
| | **Local Standards:** _____ |

## Key Concepts

**Multiplying Integers**

The product of two integers with the same sign is [        ].

The product of two integers with different signs is [        ].

**Examples:**

$4 \times 5 =$ [        ]          $4 \times (-5) =$ [        ]

$-4 \times (-5) =$ [        ]          $-4 \times 5 =$ [        ]

## Example

❶ **Using a Model to Multiply Integers**  Use a number line to find $5 \times (-2)$.

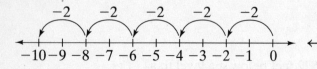

Start at 0.

Show [  ] groups

of [  ] on the number line.

The sum of 5 groups of $-2$ is [        ]. So $5 \times (-2) =$ [        ].

## Quick Check

**1. a.** Find $3 \times (-4) =$ [        ].

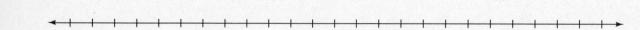

**b.** Find $-3 \times (-4) =$ [        ].

### Examples

**❷ Multiplying Integers** Find each product.

**a.** $-2 \times (-6)$     $-2 \times (-6) =$ [ ]  ← [ ] **same signs, product**

**b.** $-7 \times 2$     $-7 \times 2 =$ [ ]  ← [ ] **different signs, product**

**❸** The value of a telephone calling card decreases 20¢ for each minute used. Write an integer to express the change in the card's value for a 4-minute call.

([ ]) $\times 4 =$ [ ]  ← **Use a negative number to represent the card losing value.**

The amount, [ ] ¢, expresses the change in the card's value.

### Quick Check

**2. a.** Find $-9 \times (-3)$.

**b.** Find $5 \times (-3)$.

**3.** The temperature drops 5°F each hour for four hours. Use an integer to express the total drop in temperature.

# Lesson 11-6

**Dividing Integers**

| Lesson Objective | NAEP 2005 Strand: Number Properties and Operations |
|---|---|
| To divide integers and to solve problems by dividing integers | Topic: Number Operations |
| | Local Standards: _____ |

## Key Concepts

**Dividing Integers**

The quotient of two integers with the same sign is [ ] .

The quotient of two integers with different signs is [ ] .

**Examples:**

$20 \div 4 =$ [ ]    $20 \div (-4) =$ [ ]

$-20 \div (-4) =$ [ ]    $-20 \div 4 =$ [ ]

## Example

**❶ Dividing Integers** Find each quotient.

   **a.** $-33 \div (-3)$

same signs,

$-33 \div (-3) =$ [ ]  ← [ ] **quotient**

   **b.** $24 \div (-6)$

different signs,

$24 \div (-6) =$ [ ]  ← [ ] **quotient**

## Quick Check

**1.** Find each quotient.

   **a.** $-24 \div 6$           **b.** $-36 \div (-2)$           **c.** $48 \div (-12)$

## Example

**②** **Wind Speed** In a 2-hour period, the wind speed decreased from 28 mi/h to 18 mi/h. If the speed decreased the same amount each hour, how much did the wind speed change each hour?

**A.** 3      **B.** −3      **C.** 5      **D.** −5

Let ☐ = the average change per hour.

☐ ÷ ☐ = ☐   ← **Different signs,** ☐ **quotient.**

☐ = r   ← **Simplify.**

The wind speed changed an average of ☐ mi/h each hour. The correct answer is choice ☐.

## Quick Check

**2.** The value of one share of stock decreased $20 over the last five days. Find the average rate of change in dollars per day.

☐

# Lesson 11-7

**Solving Equations With Integers**

| Lesson Objective | NAEP 2005 Strand: Number Properties and Operations |
|---|---|
| To solve equations containing integers | **Topic:** Number Operations |
| | **Local Standards:** _____ |

## Examples

**❶ Solving Equations with Integers** Solve each equation. Check the solution.

**a.** $x + 8 = 5$

$x + 8 - \boxed{\phantom{0}} = 5 - \boxed{\phantom{0}}$    ← **Subtract** $\boxed{\phantom{0}}$ **from each side.**

$x = 5 + \left(\boxed{\phantom{0}}\right)$    ← **To subtract 8, add its opposite.**

$x = \boxed{\phantom{0}}$    ← **Simplify.**

**Check** $\boxed{\phantom{0}} + 8 = \boxed{\phantom{0}}$    ← **Check by replacing** $x$ **with** $\boxed{\phantom{0}}$.

**b.** $y - 11 = -1$

$y - 11 + \boxed{\phantom{0}} = -1 + \boxed{\phantom{0}}$    ← **Add** $\boxed{\phantom{0}}$ **to each side.**

$y = \boxed{\phantom{0}}$    ← **Simplify.**

**Check** $\boxed{\phantom{0}} - 11 = \boxed{\phantom{0}}$    ← **Check by replacing** $y$ **with** $\boxed{\phantom{0}}$.

**❷ Budget** You earn $777 doing yard work during the summer and fall and deposit it into a new savings account. You withdraw $21 on the first day of each month, starting in January. For how many months can you withdraw $21?

| **Words** | monthly withdrawals | times | number of months | equals | total of all withdrawals |
|---|---|---|---|---|---|

Let $z$ = the number of months.

**Equation**    $-21$      $\times$      $z$      $=$      $-777$

$\boxed{\phantom{000}} = \boxed{\phantom{000}}$    ← **Write the equation.**

$-21z \div \boxed{\phantom{00}} = \boxed{\phantom{00}} \div \boxed{\phantom{00}}$    ← **Divide each side by** $\boxed{\phantom{0}}$.

$z = \boxed{\phantom{0}}$    ← **Simplify.**

You can withdraw $21 per month for $\boxed{\phantom{000}}$.

**Quick Check**

1. Solve each equation. Check the solution.

   **a.** $c - 15 = -5$

   **b.** $k \div -7 = -4$

   **c.** $-6z = 36$

2. **Budget** Use Example 2. If you make 10 monthly withdrawals instead, how much can you withdraw each month?

# Lesson 11-8

**Graphing in the Coordinate Plane**

| Lesson Objective | NAEP 2005 Strand: Algebra |
|---|---|
| To name and graph points on a coordinate plane | Topic: Algebraic Representations |
| | Local Standards: _____ |

## Vocabulary

The coordinate plane is _____

_____

The plane is divided into four regions, called [  ].

The origin is _____

_____

An ordered pair is _____

_____

_____

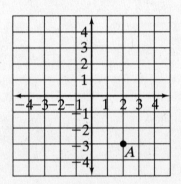

Quadrant [  ]   Quadrant [  ]

[  ]-axis

[  ]-axis

Quadrant [  ]   Quadrant [  ]

## Example

**1 Naming Coordinates** Find the coordinates of point A.

Point A is [  ] units to the right of the y-axis. The x-coordinate is [  ].

Point A is [  ] units below the x-axis. The y-coordinate is [  ].

The coordinates of point A are [        ].

## Quick Check

1. Find the coordinates of each point in the coordinate plane.

   a. B [        ]

   b. D [        ]

   c. E [        ]

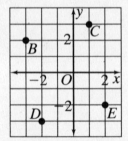

Name _____ Class _____ Date _____

## Examples

**❷ Graphing Ordered Pairs** Graph point $X(-1, -3)$ on a coordinate plane.

**Step 1**
Start at the
☐ .

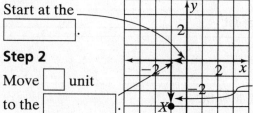

**Step 2**
Move ☐ unit
to the ☐ .

**Step 3**
Move ☐
units ☐ .

**❸ Using Map Coordinates** Use the coordinate grid. If you travel 2 units down and 3 units right from $B$, what are the coordinates of your location?

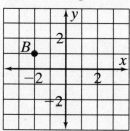

You are at ☐ .

## Quick Check

2. Graph these points on the coordinate plane:
   **a.** $A(1, 3)$
   **b.** $B(-3, 2)$
   **c.** $C(-4, -4)$

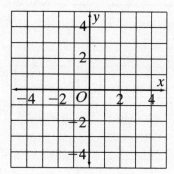

3. Use the map at the right. Suppose you leave the library and walk 2 blocks south and then 5 blocks east.

   **a.** At which building do you arrive?

   ☐

   **b.** What are the coordinates of the building?

   ☐

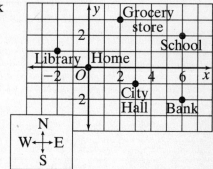

# Lesson 11-9

**Applications of Integers**

| Lesson Objective | NAEP 2005 Strand: Algebra |
|---|---|
| To apply integers to profit and loss situations | **Topic:** Algebraic Representations |
| | **Local Standards:** _____ |

## Examples

**1** **Finding Profit or Loss** Find the profit or loss for each month.

| Month | Income | Expenses |
|---|---|---|
| Sept. | $1,250 | −$1,250 |
| Oct. | $3,200 | −$2,550 |
| Nov. | $4,250 | −$3,570 |
| Dec. | $2,530 | −$2,840 |

**a.** September

$1250 + (−$1250) = $0  ← Add income and expenses for September.

There was no profit or loss for September.

**b.** October

[   ] + ( [   ] ) = [   ]  ← Add income and expenses for October.

There was a [   ] of [   ] for October.

**c.** November

[   ] + ( [   ] ) = [   ]  ← Add income and expenses for November.

There was a [   ] of [   ] for November.

**d.** December

[   ] + ( [   ] ) = [   ]  ← Add income and expenses for December.

There was a [   ] of [   ] for December.

Name _____ Class _____ Date _____

**❷ Drawing and Interpreting Graphs** Draw a line graph based on your answers to Example 1a–d. In which month did the greatest loss occur?

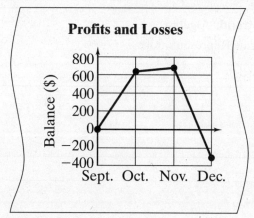

**Profits and Losses**

The balances vary from ⬚ to ⬚. So make a scale from −$400 to $800. Use intervals of $200.

The greatest loss was in ⬚.

**Quick Check**

1. Find the profit or loss for Flower Mania for January and for March.

| Income and Expenses for Flower Mania | | |
|---|---|---|
| **Month** | **Income** | **Expenses** |
| Jan. | $11,917 | −$14,803 |
| Feb. | $12,739 | −$9,482 |
| Mar. | $11,775 | −$10,954 |
| Apr. | $13,620 | −$15,149 |

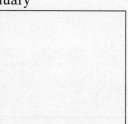

January

March

2. Use the data from the graph in Example 2. In which months did the company show profit?

# Lesson 11-10

**Graphing Functions**

| Lesson Objective | NAEP 2005 Strand: Algebra |
|---|---|
| To make a function table and to graph a function | Topic: Algebraic Representations |
| | Local Standards: _____ |

## Vocabulary

A function is _____

_____

## Examples

**❶ Completing a Function Table** Complete the function table if the rule is Output = Input ÷ (−3).

| Input | Output |
|---|---|
| −9 | 3 |
| −3 | 1 |
| 12 | |
| 15 | |

← Divide −9 by −3. Place 3 in the Output column.

← Divide −3 by −3. Place 1 in the Output column.

← Divide 12 by −3. Place [   ] in the Output column.

← Divide 15 by −3. Place [   ] in the Output column.

**❷ Graphing a Function** Make a table and graph the function $y = -2x$.

| Input (x) | Output (y) |
|---|---|
| −2 | 4 |
| −1 | 2 |
| 0 | |
| 1 | |
| 2 | −4 |

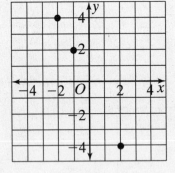

Daily Notetaking Guide L1

**❸** Henry receives $8.00 per hour for babysitting two children. The function
$e = 8h$ shows how the earnings $e$ relate to the number of hours $h$ that
Henry babysits. Make a table and graph the function.

| Hours | Earnings ($) |
|-------|--------------|
| 1 | 8 |
| 2 | |
| 3 | |
| 4 | |

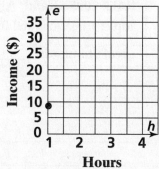

**Quick Check**

**1.** Complete the function table for each rule.

   **a.** Rule: Output = Input ÷ 4

| Input | Output |
|-------|--------|
| 16 | |
| −24 | |
| 36 | |

   **b.** Rule: Output = Input − 8

| Input | Output |
|-------|--------|
| −6 | |
| −1 | |
| 4 | |

**2.** Make a table and graph the function $y = x - 3$.

| Input (x) | Output (y) |
|-----------|------------|
| | |
| | |
| | |
| | |

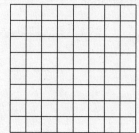

**3.** A car is driven at a steady rate of 45 miles per hour. The function $d = 45t$ shows
how time $t$ relates to distance $d$. Make a table and graph the function.

| Time (hours) | Distance (miles) |
|--------------|------------------|
| 0 | |
| 1 | |
| 2 | |
| 3 | |
| 4 | |
| 5 | |

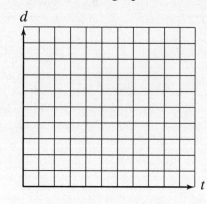

# Lesson 12-1

**Solving Two-Step Equations**

| Lesson Objective | NAEP 2005 Strand: Algebra |
|---|---|
| To solve two-step equations and to use two-step equations to solve problems | **Topic:** Equations and Inequalities |
| | **Local Standards:** _____ |

## Vocabulary

A two-step equation is _____

_____

## Example

**1** **Solving a Two-Step Equation**  Solve $6x - 14 = 16$.

**A.** 3          **B.** 4          **C.** 5          **D.** 6

$$6x - 14 = 16$$

$$6x - 14 + \boxed{\phantom{0}} = 16 + \boxed{\phantom{0}} \quad \leftarrow \textbf{Add } \boxed{\phantom{0}} \textbf{ to each side to undo the subtraction.}$$

$$6x = 30 \quad \leftarrow \textbf{Simplify.}$$

$$\frac{6x}{\boxed{\phantom{0}}} = \frac{30}{\boxed{\phantom{0}}} \quad \leftarrow \textbf{Divide each side by } \boxed{\phantom{0}} \textbf{ to undo the multiplication.}$$

$$x = \boxed{\phantom{0}} \quad \leftarrow \textbf{Simplify.}$$

The correct answer is choice $\boxed{\phantom{0}}$.

## Quick Check

**1.** Solve each equation. Check the solution.

**a.** $5x + 3 = 18$

**b.** $3x - 4 = 23$

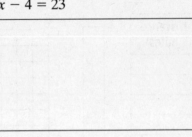

## Example

❷ The Science Club sells birdfeeders for $8 each. The club spends $32 in building materials. The club's profit is $128. How many birdfeeders did the club sell? Use $b$ to represent the number of birdfeeders. Use the equation $8b - 32 = 128$.

$$8b - 32 = 128$$

$$8b - 32 + \boxed{\phantom{xx}} = 128 + \boxed{\phantom{xx}} \quad \leftarrow \quad \text{Add } \boxed{\phantom{xx}} \text{ to each side to undo the } \boxed{\phantom{xxxxxx}}.$$

$$8b = 160 \quad \leftarrow \quad \text{Simplify.}$$

$$\frac{8b}{\boxed{\phantom{x}}} = \frac{160}{\boxed{\phantom{x}}} \quad \leftarrow \quad \text{Divide each side by } \boxed{\phantom{x}} \text{ to undo the } \boxed{\phantom{xxxxxx}}.$$

$$b = \boxed{\phantom{xxx}} \quad \leftarrow \quad \text{Simplify.}$$

The club sold $\boxed{\phantom{xx}}$ birdfeeders.

## Quick Check

2. You and a friend split the cost of a moped rental. Your friend pays the bill. You owe your friend only $12, because your friend owed you $9 from yesterday. How much was the total bill? Let $m$ represent the cost of the moped rental. Solve the equation $\frac{m}{2} - 9 = 12$.

# Lesson 12-2

**Inequalities**

| **Lesson Objective** | **NAEP 2005 Strand:** Algebra |
|---|---|
| To express and identify solutions of inequalities | **Topic:** Equations and Inequalities |
| | **Local Standards:** _____ |

## Vocabulary

An inequality is _____

_____

| Symbol | Meaning | | | |
|---|---|---|---|---|
| $<$ | is [          ] than | | | |
| $>$ | is [          ] than | | | |
| $\leq$ | is [          ] than or [          ] to | | | |
| $\geq$ | is [          ] than or [          ] to | | | |
| $\neq$ | is [          ] equal to | | | |

The graph of an inequality shows _____

_____

A solution of an inequality is _____

_____

## Example

**1** **Writing an Inequality** Maria threw the softball more than 90 feet.
Write an inequality that represents the distance.

**Words**  → | distance Maria threw the softball | | is more than | | 90 feet |

Let $m$ = the distance Maria threw the softball.

**Inequality**      $m$      [          ]      [          ]

The inequality is [          ].

## Quick Check

**1.** Skydivers jump from an altitude of 14,500 feet or less. Write an inequality to express the altitude from which skydivers jump.

[                                                                      ]

## Examples

❷ **Graphing Inequalities** Everyone in our class is 10 years old or older. Write the inequality for the situation. Then graph the inequality.

Let $a$ = the age of a person in our class, $a$ ⬚ 10.

Use a ⬚ circle to show
← that the ages include 10 years old. Include all
the numbers greater than 10.

0  5  10  15  20

❸ **Identifying Solutions of an Inequality** In order to get a bulk discount, a company must order at least 15 computers. Company X ordered 17 new computers. Do they qualify for the discounted rate?

**Words**    | order |   | is at least |   | 15 computers |

Let $c$ = computers in the order.

**Inequality**    $c$    ⬚    15

Decide whether the inequality is true or false for Company X.

$17 \geq 15$ ⬚

Company X ⬚ qualify for the discounted rate.

## Quick Check

2. You spend at least 2 hours studying. Write the inequality for the situation. Then graph the inequality.

3. You must be at least 48 inches tall to ride a certain roller coaster. Ian is 3 ft 11 in. tall. Is Ian tall enough to ride the roller coaster?

# Lesson 12-3

**Solving One-Step Inequalities**

| **Lesson Objective** | **NAEP 2005 Strand:** Algebra |
|---|---|
| To solve one-step inequalities by adding or subtracting | **Topic:** Equations and Inequalities |
| | **Local Standards:** _____ |

## Examples

❶ **Solving Inequalities** Solve $f - 4 \geq 8$.

$$f - 4 \geq 8$$

$f - 4 + \boxed{\phantom{x}} \geq 8 + \boxed{\phantom{x}}$ ← Add $\boxed{\phantom{x}}$ to each side to undo the subtraction.

$f \geq \boxed{\phantom{xx}}$ ← Simplify.

❷ **Solving Inequalities** Solve $p + 16 < 34$.

$$p + 16 < 34$$

$p + 16 - \boxed{\phantom{xx}} < 34 - \boxed{\phantom{xx}}$ ← Subtract $\boxed{\phantom{xx}}$ from each side to undo the $\boxed{\phantom{xxxxx}}$.

$p < \boxed{\phantom{xx}}$ ← Simplify.

## Quick Check

**1.** Solve $u - 6 \leq 3$.

**2.** Solve $z + 15 > 24$.

**Example**

❸ **Saving Money** Missy wants to save at least $150 this month. She has saved $112 so far. Write and solve an inequality to find how much more money she would like to save this month.

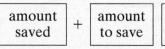

**Words**

| amount saved | + | amount to save | is at least | $150 |

Let $d$ = the amount Missy still needs to save.

**Inequality**

☐ + ☐ ☐ ☐

$$112 + d \geq 150$$

$$112 - \boxed{\phantom{000}} + d \geq 150 - \boxed{\phantom{000}}$$ ← **Subtract 112 from each side.**

$$d \geq \boxed{\phantom{000}}$$ ← **Simplify.**

Missy would like to save at least ☐ more this month.

**Quick Check**

3. A restaurant can serve a maximum of 115 people. There are now 97 people dining in the restaurant. Write and solve an inequality to find how many more people can be served.

# Lesson 12-4

**Exploring Square Roots and Rational Numbers**

| **Lesson Objective** | **NAEP 2005 Strand:** Number Properties and Operations |
|---|---|
| To find square roots and to identify rational numbers | **Topic:** Equations and Inequalities |
| | **Local Standards:** _____ |

## Vocabulary

A square root of a given number is _____

_____

A perfect square is _____

_____

A rational number is _____

_____

## Examples

**1** **Finding Square Roots** Find $\sqrt{25}$.

Since $\boxed{\phantom{0}} \times \boxed{\phantom{0}} = 25$, $\sqrt{25} = \boxed{\phantom{0}}$.

**2** **Using a Calculator** Use a calculator to find $\sqrt{20}$ to the nearest tenth.

$\sqrt{20} \approx$ [_____]  ← **On a calculator, press** **2nd** **$x^2$** **20** **=** .

$\approx$ [_____]  ← **Round to the nearest tenth.**

## Quick Check

**1.** Find $\sqrt{100}$.

**2.** Find $\sqrt{10}$ to the nearest tenth.

## Example

**❸ Identifying Rational Numbers** Tell whether each number is rational.

**a.** 1.5        1.5 is a terminating decimal. It is [＿＿＿＿＿] .

**b.** 1.42443444...    This decimal does not repeat or terminate. It is [＿＿＿＿＿] .

## Quick Check

**3.** Is 1.112111211112... a rational number? Explain.

```
┌─────────────────────────────────────────────────────────┐
│                                                           │
│                                                           │
│                                                           │
│                                                           │
└─────────────────────────────────────────────────────────┘
```

Name _____ Class _____ Date _____

# Lesson 12-5

**Introducing the Pythagorean Theorem**

| Lesson Objective | NAEP 2005 Strand: Geometry |
|---|---|
| To solve problems using the Pythagorean Theorem | **Topics:** Relationships Between Geometric Figures |
| | **Local Standards:** _____ |

## Vocabulary and Key Concepts

**Pythagorean Theorem**

In any right triangle, the sum of the squares of the lengths of the [___]

($a$ and $b$) is equal to the square of the length of the [_____] ($c$).

**Arithmetic**

$3^2 + 4^2 = $ [___]

**Algebra**

$a^2 + b^2 = $ [___]

The legs of a right triangle are _____

_____

The hypotenuse of a right triangle is _____

_____

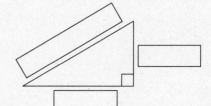

## Examples

❶ **Finding the Length of a Hypotenuse** Two legs of a right triangle measure 20 and 21 units long. Find the length of the hypotenuse.

**A.** 20 units          **B.** 29 units          **C.** 41 units          **D.** 541 units

$$a^2 + b^2 = c^2 \qquad \leftarrow \text{Write the Pythagorean Theorem.}$$

$$20^2 + 21^2 = c^2 \qquad \leftarrow \text{Substitute 20 for } a \text{ and 21 for } b.$$

$$[\quad] + [\quad] = c^2 \qquad \leftarrow \text{Square 20 and 21.}$$

$$[\quad] = c^2 \qquad \leftarrow \text{Add.}$$

$$\sqrt{[\quad]} = \sqrt{c^2} \qquad \leftarrow \text{Find the square root of each side.}$$

$$[\quad] = c \qquad \leftarrow \text{Simplify.}$$

The length of the hypotenuse is [___] units. The correct answer is choice [___].

**❷ Finding the Length of a Leg** On a map, the towns of Shake, Rattle, and Roll form a right triangle. Shake is 5 miles due north of Rattle. Roll is directly east of Rattle. Shake and Roll are 15 miles apart. How far apart are Rattle and Roll?

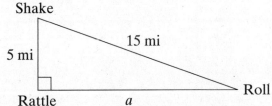

The three towns form a ⬚ triangle. One leg has length

⬚ miles. The hypotenuse has length ⬚ miles.

$$a^2 + b^2 = c^2 \qquad \leftarrow \text{Write the Pythagorean Theorem.}$$

$$a^2 + 5^2 = 15^2 \qquad \leftarrow \text{Substitute 5 for } \boxed{\phantom{x}} \text{ and 15 for } \boxed{\phantom{x}}.$$

$$a^2 + \boxed{\phantom{x}} = \boxed{\phantom{x}} \qquad \leftarrow \text{Square 5 and 15.}$$

$$a^2 + 25 - \boxed{\phantom{x}} = 225 - 25 \qquad \leftarrow \text{Subtract 25 from each side.}$$

$$a^2 = \boxed{\phantom{x}} \qquad \leftarrow \text{Simplify.}$$

$$\sqrt{a^2} = \sqrt{\boxed{\phantom{x}}} \qquad \leftarrow \text{Find the square root of each side.}$$

$$a \approx \boxed{\phantom{x}} \qquad \leftarrow \text{Simplify.}$$

Rattle is about ⬚ miles from Roll.

## Quick Check

**1.** Find the length of the hypotenuse of a triangle with legs that have lengths of 12 inches and 16 inches.

**2.** A ramp leading into a truck forms a right triangle with the ground. One leg is 10 feet long. The hypotenuse is 11 feet long. How high is the top of the ramp? Round to the nearest tenth.

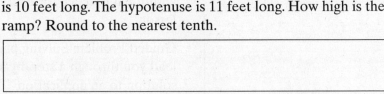

## A Note to the Student:

This section of your workbook contains a series of pages that support your mathematics understandings for each chapter and lesson presented in your student edition.

- Practice pages provide additional practice for every lesson.

- Guided Problem Solving pages lead you through a step-by-step solution to an application problem in each lesson.

- Vocabulary pages contain a variety of activities to increase your reading and math understanding, ranging from graphic organizers to vocabulary review puzzles.

Practice • Guided Problem Solving • Vocabulary

# Practice 1-1

**Write each number in words.**

**1.** 1,760

**2.** 84,505

_____

_____

**Write each number in standard form.**

**3.** three thousand forty

_____

**4.** one hundred ten

_____

**5.** 750 thousand, 33

_____

**Use < or > to make each sentence true.**

**6.** 12,680 ☐ 12,519

**7.** 25,345 ☐ 25,391

**8.** 7,657 ☐ 7,650

**9.** 101,321 ☐ 141,321

**Write the value of the digit 6 in each number.**

**10.** 46,051

**11.** 816,548

_____

_____

**12.** 42,916

**13.** 1,063,251

**Write in order from least to greatest.**

**14.** 12; 152; 12,512

**15.** 10; 10,113; 113

_____

_____

**16.** 149; 49; 14

**17.** 1,422; 142; 247

_____

_____

# 1-1 • Guided Problem Solving

**GPS** **Student Page 7, Exercise 27:**

**Apples** Order the apple types by number of cartons from least to greatest.

**Yearly Apple Production in the United States**

| Type of Apple | Cartons |
|---|---|
| Ida Red | 2,753,000 |
| Empire | 2,739,000 |
| Braeburn | 2,198,000 |
| McIntosh | 3,304,000 |
| York | 3,212,000 |

## Understand

1. Where is the information you need to do the exercise?

   _____

2. How do you determine which number is the least?

   _____

   _____

   _____

   _____

## Plan and Carry Out

3. Which apple type has the least number of cartons? _____

4. Which apple type has the greatest number of cartons? _____

5. Which apple type has the second greatest number of cartons? _____

6. Which apple type has the second least number of cartons? _____

7. Order the apple types from least to greatest by name.

   _____

8. Order the apple types from least to greatest by number of cartons.

   _____

## Check

9. Explain another way to do this problem.

   _____

   _____

## Solve Another Problem

10. Order the cities by population from least to greatest.

| Philadelphia | New York City | Chicago | Los Angeles | San Francisco |
|---|---|---|---|---|
| 1,470,151 | 8,104,079 | 2,862,244 | 3,845,541 | 744,230 |

   _____

   _____

# Practice 1-2

Estimating with Whole Numbers

**Estimate by first rounding to the nearest whole number.**

**1.** 13 + 29

_____

**2.** 348 − 22

_____

**3.** 2,983 + 523

_____

**4.** 795 − 323

_____

**5.** 2 + 23 + 48

_____

**6.** 577 − 124 − 39

_____

**Estimate using compatible numbers.**

**7.** 24 × 8

_____

**8.** 593 ÷ 6

_____

**9.** 5,974 ÷ 3

_____

**10.** 283 ÷ 105

_____

**Solve.**

**11.** With a length of about 458 meters, the *Jahre Viking* is one of the world's largest ships. Football fields have a length of about 91 meters. About how many football fields could fit alongside the *Jahre Viking?*

_____

_____

**12.** There are 407 seventh graders at Washington Middle School. If there are 18 seventh grade classrooms, about how many students are there per class?

_____

_____

# 1-2 • Guided Problem Solving

**GPS** Student Page 11, Exercise 32:

There are three small piñatas and two large piñatas at a festival. Each small piñata contains 85 prizes. Each large piñata contains 178 prizes. Estimate the total number of prizes.

## Understand

1. What are you being asked to do?

   _____

2. What numbers will you have to round to estimate the total number of prizes?

   _____

3. Does the problem tell what place to round to? If not, what place do you plan to round to?

   _____

   _____

## Plan and Carry Out

4. About how many prizes are in a small piñata? _____

5. About how many prizes are in 3 small piñatas? _____

6. About how many prizes are in a large piñata? _____

7. About how many prizes are in 2 large piñatas? _____

8. About how many prizes are there in 3 small piñatas and 2 large

   piñatas? _____

## Check

9. Should your answer be greater than or less than the numbers in the word problem?

   _____

   _____

## Solve Another Problem

10. Chelsea has 4 large piles and 3 smaller piles of pennies. The large piles each have 312 pennies, and the smaller piles each have 193 pennies. About how many pennies does Chelsea have?

    _____

    _____

# Practice 1-3

**Name each property of addition or multiplication used below.**

**1.** $(6 + 3) + 21 = 6 + (3 + 21)$

_____

_____

**2.** $13 \times 1 = 13$

_____

_____

**3.** $8 + 20 + 12 = 8 + 12 + 20$

_____

_____

**4.** $5 \times 2 \times 11 = 2 \times 11 \times 5$

_____

_____

**Use mental math to find each sum or product.**

**5.** $53 + 12 + 7$

_____

**6.** $2 \times 53 \times 5$

_____

**7.** $8 + 0 + 6$

_____

**8.** $(19 + 22) + 8$

_____

**9.** $5 \times (13 \times 20)$

_____

**10.** $4 + 23 + 6$

_____

**11.** $25 + (13 + 5)$

_____

**12.** $7 \times 25 \times (1 \times 8)$

_____

**Solve.**

**13.** Mrs. Gauthier plans to take her class on 2 field trips this year. There are 23 students in her class, and each field trip will cost $5 per student. Use mental math to find the total cost for both field trips.

_____

_____

**14.** Roshonda's garden produced 25 carrots, 127 blackberries, and 5 pumpkins. What was the total number of fruits and vegetables produced by Roshonda's garden? Use mental math to find the solution.

_____

_____

# 1-3 • Guided Problem Solving

**GPS** Student Page 15, Exercise 32:

**Art Class**  In a student art contest there are 14 drawings, 22 sculptures, and some paintings. There are 18 more paintings than sculptures. What is the total number of art pieces?

## Understand

1. What are you being asked to do?

   _____

2. Circle the information you will need to solve this problem.

3. Estimate what you expect the answer to be.

   _____

## Plan and Carry Out

4. How many drawings are there? _____

5. How many sculptures are there? _____

6. How many more paintings are there than sculptures? _____

7. What will you have to do to find the number of paintings?

   _____

8. How many paintings are there? _____

9. What is the total number of art pieces in the contest?

   _____

## Check

10. Is your answer close to your original estimate? Why or why not?

    _____

## Solve Another Problem

11. Janelle has 10 marbles. Ralph has 13 marbles, and Jennifer has 17 more marbles than Ralph has. What is the total number of marbles Janelle, Ralph, and Jennifer have?

    _____

# Practice 1-4

**Which operation would you perform first in each expression?**

1. $4 + 6 \times 9$

2. $(7 - 5) \times 3$

_____

3. $18 - 5 + 3$

4. $5 \times 2 + 6$

_____

**Find the value of each expression.**

5. $8 - 3 \times 1 + 5$

6. $(43 - 16) \times 5$

7. $14 \times 6 \div 3$

_____     _____     _____

8. $15 - (5 + 7)$

9. $9 \times (3 \times 5)$

10. $7 \times (8 + 6)$

_____     _____     _____

**Write the value of the digit 6 in each number.**

11. 42,916

12. 1,063,251

13. 816,548

_____     _____     _____

**Use <, =, or > to complete each statement.**

14. $5 - 3 \times 1 \ \boxed{\phantom{x}} \ (5 - 3) \times 1$

15. $(4 + 8) \times 3 \ \boxed{\phantom{x}} \ 4 + 8 \times 3$

16. $3 \times (8 - 2) \ \boxed{\phantom{x}} \ 3 \times 8 - 2$

17. $(7 + 2) \times 4 \ \boxed{\phantom{x}} \ 7 + 2 \times 4$

**Insert parentheses to make each statement true.**

18. $6 + 7 \times 4 = 34$

19. $14 - 5 \div 3 = 3$

_____     _____

**Write a mathematical expression and solve.**

20. Haircuts for boys cost $7. Haircuts for men cost $10. If 20 boys and 20 men went to the barber yesterday, how much did the barber earn?

_____

# 1-4 • Guided Problem Solving

**GPS** **Student Page 19, Exercise 32:**

**Coins** There are 300 coins of the same type in two stacks. One stack is 380 millimeters tall. The other is 220 millimeters tall. Find the thickness of one coin.

## Understand

1. What are you being asked to find?

    _____

2. What will you need to know to find this information?

    _____

3. What operations will you have to perform to answer the question?

    _____

## Plan and Carry Out

4. How will you find the total height of the 300 coins?

    _____

5. What is the total height of the 300 coins? _____

6. Will you have to multiply or divide to find the height of one coin?

    _____

7. How thick is one coin? _____

## Check

8. Based on your answer, how tall is a stack of 300 coins?

    _____

9. Does this match the height given in the problem? _____

## Solve Another Problem

10. Georgia walks 325 meters to an intersection, and then another 125 meters to the store. If she spends a total of 9 minutes walking, how many meters does she walk in one minute?

    _____

# Practice 1-5

**Write each decimal in words.**

1. 12.873                2. 8.0552                3. 0.00065

_____    _____    _____

_____    _____    _____

_____    _____    _____

**Write each decimal in standard form.**

4. three tenths          5. fifty-two hundredths          6. $30 + 4 + 0.9 + 0.02$

_____    _____    _____

**Write each decimal in expanded form.**

7. 213.23

_____

8. 5.625

_____

9. 19.01

_____

**What is the value of the digit 7 in each number?**

10. 0.7                11. 4.00712                12. 2.179

_____    _____    _____

**Round each decimal to the underlined place.**

13. 467.0<u>8</u>9          14. 8.<u>9</u>29          15. 72.<u>1</u>4

_____    _____    _____

# 1-5 • Guided Problem Solving

**GPS Student Page 25, Exercise 43:**

**Heights** Artists use a ratio called the Golden Mean to describe a person's height. Your height from the floor to your waist is usually six hundred eighteen thousandths of your total height. Round this number to the nearest hundredth.

## Understand

1. Is the number more or less than 1? Explain.

   _____

   _____

2. The word *thousandths* represents how many decimal places to the right of the decimal point?

   _____

## Plan and Carry Out

3. Write six hundred eighteen thousandths in standard form.

   _____

4. What digit is in the hundredths place?

   _____

5. What digit is to the right of the hundredths place?

   _____

6. Based on the number above, should you round up or down?

   _____

7. Round this number to the nearest hundredth.

   _____

## Check

8. Did you round up or down? Why?

   _____

   _____

## Solve Another Problem

9. Liz has a height of five feet and two and forty-five hundredths of an inch. Round Liz's height to the nearest inch.

   _____

# Practice 1-6

**Comparing and Ordering Decimals**

**Use <, =, or > to complete each statement.**

**1.** 0.62 ☐ 0.618

**2.** 9.8 ☐ 9.80

**3.** 1.006 ☐ 1.02

**4.** 41.3 ☐ 41.03

**5.** 2.01 ☐ 2.011

**6.** 1.400 ☐ 1.40

**7.** 5.079 ☐ 5.08

**8.** 12.96 ☐ 12.967

**9.** 15.8 ☐ 15.800

**Order each set of decimals on a number line.**

**10.** 0.2, 0.6, 0.5

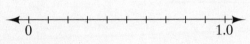

12.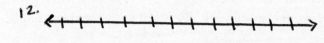

**11.** 0.26, 0.3, 0.5

**12.** Draw a number line. Use 11 tick marks. Label the first tick mark 0.6 and the eleventh tick mark 0.7. Graph 0.67 and 0.675.

  **a.** Which is greater, 0.67 or 0.675? _____

  **b.** How does the number line show which number is greater?

  _____

**13.** Models for three decimals are shown below.

  **a.** Write the decimal that each model represents.

  _____

  **b.** Order the decimals from least to greatest.

  _____

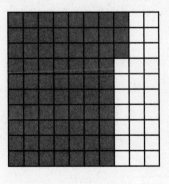 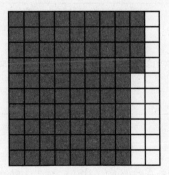 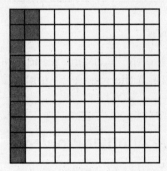

13a _____     13b _____     13c. _____

# 1-6 • Guided Problem Solving

**GPS** **Student Page 30, Exercise 27:**

**Population** About 11.4 million people live in Jakarta, Indonesia.
Roughly 13.0 million people live in Delhi, India. About 10.4 million
people live in Karachi, Pakistan. Order the cities from least to greatest
population.

## Understand

1. How many cities are discussed in the problem? _____

2. What are you asked to do?

   _____

3. Circle the populations that you need to order.

## Plan and Carry Out

4. Use placeholders to write the three numbers with the same number
   of decimal places.

   _____

5. Which number is the least?

   _____

6. Which number is the greatest?

   _____

7. Write the numbers in order from least to greatest.

   _____

8. Order the cities from least to greatest population.

   _____

## Check

9. Do the least and middle populations have smaller decimal values
   than the greatest number?

   _____

## Solve Another Problem

10. Jessie ran 3 miles in 20.53 minutes. Anne ran the same distance in
    20.02 minutes. Kara ran the same distance in 20.96 minutes. Order
    the runners from fastest to slowest.

    _____

Name _____ Class _____ Date _____

# Practice 1-7

**Adding and Subtracting Decimals**

**First estimate. Then find each sum or difference.**

**1.** 0.6 + 5.8    $\begin{array}{r} 0.6 \\ +5.8 \\ \hline \end{array}$

**2.** 2.1 + 3.4    $\begin{array}{r} 2.1 \\ +3.4 \\ \hline \end{array}$

**3.** 3.4 − 0.972    $\begin{array}{r} 3.4 \\ -0.972 \\ \hline \end{array}$

_____

**4.** 3.1 − 2.076    $\begin{array}{r} 3.1 \\ -2.076 \\ \hline \end{array}$

**5.** 8.13 − 2.716    $\begin{array}{r} 8.13 \\ -2.716 \\ \hline \end{array}$

**6.** 5.91 + 2.38    $\begin{array}{r} 5.91 \\ +2.38 \\ \hline \end{array}$

_____

**7.** 3.086 + 6.152    $\begin{array}{r} 3.086 \\ +6.152 \\ \hline \end{array}$

**8.** 4.7 − 1.9    $\begin{array}{r} 4.7 \\ -1.9 \\ \hline \end{array}$

**9.** 9.3 − 3.9    $\begin{array}{r} 9.3 \\ -3.9 \\ \hline \end{array}$

_____

**Use front-end estimation to estimate each sum.**

**10.** 12 + 0.25 + 4.75

**11.** 18.5 + 0.25 + 0.25

**12.** 11.3 + 5.7

_____

**13.** 50.6 + 10.4 + 20

**14.** 2.1 + 0.6 + 0.3

**15.** 14.3 + 16

_____

**Use the table at the right for Exercises 16–17.**

**16.** Find the sum of the decimals given in the chart.
What is the meaning of this sum?

$\begin{array}{r} (+) \\ 0.23 \\ 0.53 \\ 0.22 \\ +0.02 \\ \hline \end{array}$

_____

_____

**17.** What part of the hourly work force is aged <u>45 or older</u>?

_____

### Ages of Workers Earning Hourly Pay

| Age of Workers | Part of Work Force |
| --- | --- |
| 16–24 | 0.23 |
| 25–44 | 0.53 |
| 45–64 | 0.22 |
| 65 & over | 0.02 |

# 1-7 • Guided Problem Solving

**GPS** Student Page 35, Exercise 33:

**Population** In 2000, the New England states had a total population of about 13.92 million. Find the population of Maine.

| State | Population |
|---|---|
| Connecticut | 3.42 million |
| Maine | ? |
| Massachusetts | 6.35 million |
| New Hampshire | 1.24 million |
| Rhode Island | 1.05 million |
| Vermont | 0.61 million |

## Understand

1. What are you being asked to do?

   _____

2. How will you use the total population of the New England states to answer the question?

   _____

## Plan and Carry Out

3. Find the sum of the populations of the other states.

   _____

4. What is the total population of all the New England states?

   _____

5. Write an expression to find the population of Maine.

   _____

6. Evaluate the expression to find the population of Maine.

   _____

7. Find the population of Maine.

   _____

## Check

8. How can you check your answer?

   _____

   _____

## Solve Another Problem

9. You and a friend calculate your grade for a class. You have an 83.5 and your friend has an 85.65. Who has the higher grade? How much higher is it?

   _____

# Practice 1-8

~~Problem Solving~~ **Multiplying Decimals**

**Place the decimal point in each product.**

**1.** $4.3 \times 2.9 = 1247$

**2.** $0.279 \times 53 = 14787$

_____

**3.** $5.90 \times 6.3 = 3717$

**4.** $0.74 \times 83 = 6142$

_____

**Find each product.**

**5.** $43.59 \times 0.1$   43.59 .01

**6.** $246 \times 0.01$   .246 × .01

**7.** $726 \times 0.1$   726 × .1

_____

**8.**   0.19
     × 0.05

**9.**   6.4
     × 0.09

**10.**   240
      × 0.02

_____

**Write a multiplication statement you could use for each situation.**   1 dozen = 12    12 × .59

**11.** A pen costs $.59. How much would a dozen pens cost?

_____

**12.** A mint costs $.02. How much would a roll of 10 mints cost?

_____

**Find each product. Tell whether you would use mental math, paper and pencil, or a calculator.**

**13.** 19(0.35)

**14.** $30 \times 0.1$

_____

# 1-8 • Guided Problem Solving

**GPS** **Student Page 41, Exercise 36:**

**Nutrition** There is 0.2 gram of calcium in 1 serving of cheddar cheese. How much calcium is in 3.25 servings of cheddar cheese?

## Understand

1. What is being compared in the exercise?

   _____

   _____

   _____

2. What are you being asked to do?

   _____

   _____

3. Will you multiply or divide to determine the answer? Explain.

   _____

   _____

   _____

   _____

## Plan and Carry Out

4. How much calcium is in one serving? _____

5. How many servings do you want? _____

6. Write an expression to answer the exercise. _____

7. How many grams of calcium are in 3.25 servings of cheddar

   cheese? _____

## Check

8. Should there be more or less than 0.2 gram of calcium in 3.25 servings of cheddar cheese? Explain.

   _____

## Solve Another Problem

9. There is 0.5 gram of fat in one serving of a breakfast cereal. How many grams of fat are in 4.25 servings?

   _____

Name _____ Class _____ Date _____

# Practice 1-9 • • • • • • • • • • • • • • • • • • • • • • • • • • • • • • • • • • • • • • **Dividing Decimals**

**Draw a model to find each quotient.**

**1.** $0.4 \div 0.08$ _____

**2.** $0.8 \div 0.4$ _____

**Find each quotient.**

**3.** $1.8 \div 6$

**4.** $16 \overline{)3.2}$

**5.** $17 \overline{)5.1}$

**6.** $15 \overline{)123}$

**7.** $108 \div 5$

**8.** $50 \overline{)17.5}$

**Solve.**

**9.** A package of 25 mechanical pencils costs $5.75. How much does each pencil cost?

_____

**10.** The salt content in the Caspian Sea is 0.13 kg for every liter of water. How many kg of salt are in 70 liters?

_____

**Find each quotient.**

**11.** $0.4 \div 0.02$

**12.** $3.9 \div 0.05$

**13.** $0.2 \overline{)26}$

**14.** $0.4 \overline{)1.08}$

**15.** $0.68 \div 0.2$

**16.** $0.02 \overline{)0.06}$

# 1-9 • Guided Problem Solving

**GPS** **Student Page 46, Exercise 23:**

**School Supplies** A stack of paper measures 0.9 centimeter thick. Each piece of paper is 0.01 centimeter thick.

a. How many pieces of paper are in the stack?

b. Could each of 25 students get three pieces of paper?

## Understand

1. Circle the information you will need to solve.

2. What are you being asked to do in part (a)?

_____

3. What are you being asked to do in part (b)?

_____

_____

## Plan and Carry Out

4. How thick is one piece of paper? _____

5. How thick is the stack of paper? _____

6. Do you multiply or divide to answer part (a)? _____

7. Write an expression to answer part (a). _____

8. How many pieces of paper are in the stack? _____

9. How many pieces of paper are needed for each of 25 students to get three pieces of paper?

_____

10. Is there enough paper? _____

## Check

11. Why is the number of pieces of paper 100 times more than the height of the stack of paper?

_____

_____

## Solve Another Problem

12. A stack of baseball cards measures 5.4 centimeters thick. Each baseball card is 0.1 centimeter thick. How many baseball cards are in the stack?

_____

# 1A: Graphic Organizer

**Study Skill** As you read over the material in the chapter, keep a paper and pencil handy to write down notes and questions that you have. As with any new textbook, take a few minutes to explore the general contents of the book.

**Write your answers.**

1. How many chapters are in the text? _____

2. Where is the index located? _____

3. How many lessons are there in Chapter 1? _____

4. What is the topic of the Test-Taking Strategies page in Chapter 1?

   _____

5. Complete the graphic organizer below as you work through the chapter.

   • In the center, write the title of the chapter.

   • When you begin a lesson, write the lesson name in a rectangle.

   • When you complete a lesson, write a skill or key concept in a circle linked to that lesson block.

   • When you complete the chapter, use this graphic organizer to help you review.

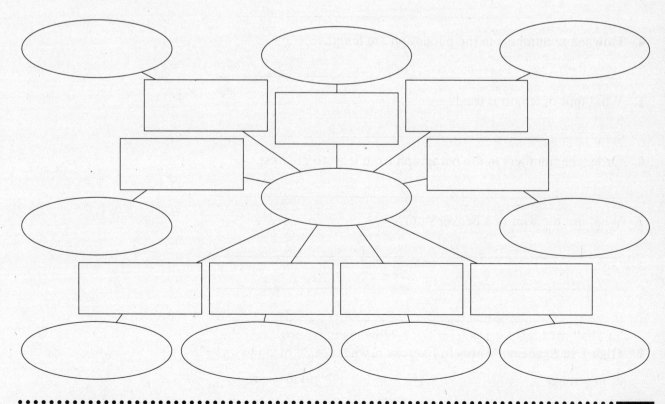

# 1B: Reading Comprehension

**For use after Lesson 1-2**

**Study Skill** Write assignments down; do not rely on your memory.

**Read the paragraph and answer the questions that follow.**

> A beaver can grow to be up to 30 inches long and stand 12 inches high. Beavers have large, flat tails that average about 10 inches long and have several uses. The tail can serve as a warning signal when slapped against the water. A beaver also uses its tail to navigate through the water while swimming or to stand on its hind legs. Beavers also have two front teeth on their upper and lower jaw. These teeth are primarily used for cutting down trees to build dams. Typically, a beaver cuts down trees between 2 and 8 inches in diameter, but has been known to cut down trees as large as 30 inches in diameter.

1. What is the paragraph about?

   _____

2. How large can a beaver grow?

   _____

3. How long is the average beaver's tail?

   _____

4. How many numbers in the paragraph are lengths?

   _____

5. What unit of length is used?

   _____

6. Order the numbers in the paragraph from least to greatest.

   _____

7. What are the uses of a beaver's tail?

   _____

   _____

   _____

8. **High-Use Academic Words** In Exercise 6, what does it mean to *order*?

   a. to arrange                    b. to measure

# 1C: Reading/Writing Math Symbols

**Study Skill** When you take notes, it helps if you learn to use abbreviations and symbols to represent words. For instance, @ means *at,* # means *number,* w/ means *with* and = means *equal.*

**Match the symbol in Column A with its meaning in Column B.**

Column A

1. <
2. =
3. $
4. >
5. )‾
6. ≈

Column B

A. dollar
B. is less than
C. is greater than
D. divided by
E. is equal to
F. is approximately equal to

**Write each mathematical statement in word form.**

7. 3.1 ≈ 3 _____

8. 4 + 7 = 11 _____

9. 5 ÷ 2 = 2.5 _____

10. 4 > 2 _____

11. 3 < 10 _____

12. 6 − 1 = 5 _____

**Write a mathematical statement for each word description.**

13. Four is less than eleven. _____

14. Seven plus six equals thirteen. _____

15. Fourteen minus eight equals six. _____

16. Eight divided by four equals two. _____

17. Twenty is greater than ten. _____

18. The product of four and five is twenty. _____

# 1D: Visual Vocabulary Practice

**For use after Lesson 1-6**

**Study Skill** When learning a new word, it helps to know if it is a name or action.

## Concept List

Commutative Property of Addition

Associative Property of Addition

Commutative Property of Multiplication

Associative Property of Multiplication

order of operations

Identity Property of Addition

Identity Property of Multiplication

standard form

expanded form

**Write the concept that best describes each exercise. Choose from the concept list above.**

| | | |
|---|---|---|
| **1.** $70 + 5 + 0.2 + 0.04$ | **2.** $0 + 2a = 2a$ | **3.** $2^3 + 4 = 4 + 2^3$ |
| _____ | _____ | _____ |
| **4.** $(3 + 2) \times 1 = (3 + 2)$ | **5.** $4^2 + 12 \div (8 - 2)$ $= 4^2 + 12 \div 6$ $= 16 + 12 \div 6$ $= 16 + 2$ $= 18$ | **6.** $(2x + y) + 5y = 2x + (y + 5y)$ |
| _____ | _____ | _____ |
| **7.** $(15 - 3)\frac{1}{4} = \frac{1}{4}(15 - 3)$ | **8.** $75.24$ | **9.** $2 \times (3 \times b) = (2 \times 3) \times b$ |
| _____ | _____ | _____ |

# 1E: Vocabulary Check

**Study Skill** Strengthen your vocabulary. Use these pages and add cues and summaries by applying the Cornell Notetaking style.

**Write the definition for each word or term at the right. To check your work, fold the paper back along the dotted line to see the correct answers.**

Associative Property of Addition

Commutative Property of Addition

expression

Commutative Property of Multiplication

Identity Property of Multiplication

# 1E: Vocabulary Check (continued)

Write the vocabulary word or term for each definition. To check your work, fold the paper forward along the dotted line to see the correct answers.

Changing the grouping of the addends does not change the sum.

_____

Changing the order of the addends does not change the sum.

_____

a mathematical phrase containing numbers and operation symbols

_____

Changing the order of the factors does not change the product.

_____

The product of 1 and *a* is *a*.

_____

# 1F: Vocabulary Review

**For use with the Chapter Review**

**Study Skill** Review your class notes as soon as possible. This will help you identify any concepts in which you need additional explanation.

**Match the term in Column A with its definition or example in Column B.**

**Column A**

1. Identity Property of Multiplication

2. place value

3. compatible numbers

4. equivalent decimals

5. Associative Property of Addition

6. Commutative Property of Addition

**Column B**

A. decimals that represent the same amount

B. $7 + (3 + 9) = (7 + 3) + 9$

C. numbers that are easy to compute mentally

D. $6 + 8 = 8 + 6$

E. $8.3 \times 1 = 8.3$

F. value of a digit based on its location in a particular number

**Match the term in Column A with its definition or example in Column B.**

**Column A**

7. Identity Property of Addition

8. Associative Property of Multiplication

9. Commutative Property of Multiplication

10. expanded form

11. standard form

12. expression

**Column B**

G. $8 \cdot 4 = 4 \cdot 8$

H. sum that shows the place and value of each digit

I. a number written using digits

J. mathematical phrase containing numbers and operations

K. $8(7 \cdot 9) = (8 \cdot 7)9$

L. $4 + 0 = 4$

Name _____  Class _____  Date _____

# Practice 2-1 
**Mean**

Find the (mean) of each data set. *(handwritten: Average + then ÷)*

1. 4, 5, 7, 5, 6, 3 = *(handwritten: 84 ÷ 6 = 14)*

2. 72, 76, 73, 74, 75

3. 85, 91, 76, 85, 93

4. 2.1, 3.2, 1.6, 2.4

**For each set of data, identify any outliers. Then determine the effect that the outlier has on the mean.**

5. 64, 65, 62, 69, 59, 23, 61, 67 _____

6. 8.1, 8.3, 7.8, 7.9, 8.4, 6.8, 8.0 _____

7. 1230, 1225, 1228, 1232, 1233, 1321, 1229, 1231 _____

**Use the table for Exercises 8–10.**

| Name | Hourly Wage |
|------|-------------|
| Julia | $8.75 |
| Ron | $7.50 |
| Miguel | $25.00 |
| Natasha | $11.00 |
| Robert | $10.50 |

8. Whose wage is an outlier in the data set?

9. Find the mean hourly wage with and without the outlier. *(handwritten: Without outlier)*

   *(handwritten: With outlier)*

10. What effect does the outlier have on the mean?

**Fill in the blanks to find the mean of each data set.**

11. 4, 6, 2, 8, 5: $\dfrac{25}{\Box} = \Box$

12. 10, 4, 2, 12, 6, 8: $\dfrac{\Box}{6} = \Box$

# 2-1 • Guided Problem Solving

**GPS** **Student Page 64, Exercise 23:**

Shelby made a list of her test scores: 88, 100, 92, 80, 85, 94, and 90. What is the lowest score she can get on her next test to have a mean score of 90?

## Understand

1. What are you being asked to do?

   _____

   _____

2. If you already know the mean and all her test scores but one, how can you find the missing test score?

   _____

   _____

## Plan and Carry Out

3. What is her mean score right now?

   _____

4. Does her next test score need to be higher or lower than 90?

   _____

5. How many tests will there be, including the next test? Multiply that number by 90.

   _____

6. Subtract the first seven scores from your answer to Step 5.

   _____

## Check

7. Take all her test scores, including the one that you found, and find the mean. Is it 90?

   _____

## Solve Another Problem

8. The mean of five numbers is 55. If four of the numbers are 86, 77, 14, and 12, what is the other number?

   _____

# Practice 2-2

*Mode = the # you see the most*

Median and Mode

**Find the median and the mode(s) of each data set.**

**1.** 6, 10, 12, 5, 7, 12, 9

**2.** 19.32, 19.44, 19.54, 19.44, 19.33, 19.27, 19.31

_____

**3.** 24, 24, 28, 32, 40, 42

**4.** 2, 4, 5, 4, 3, 4, 2, 3, 3

_____

**Use the table for Exercises 5–7.**

| Last Year's Monthly Rainfall | |
|---|---|
| **Month** | **Rainfall (inches)** |
| January | 5 |
| February | 4.5 |
| March | 6 |
| April | 15 |
| May | 5 |
| June | 3 |
| July | 2 |
| August | 2 |
| September | 1 |
| October | 2 |
| November | 3 |
| December | 4.5 |

**5.** What was the mean monthly rainfall last year? _____

**6.** What is the mode of all the months listed? _____

**7.** Does the mean, median, or mode best describe last year's

rainfall? _____

**Each student in a class has taken five tests. The teacher allows the students to pick the mean, median, or mode of each set of scores to be their final score. Which measure should each of these students pick in order to have the highest final score?**

**8.** 100, 87, 81, 23, 19

**9.** 79, 78, 77, 76, 85

_____

**10.** 80, 80, 70, 67, 68

**11.** 75, 78, 77, 70, 70

_____

# 2-2 • Guided Problem Solving

**GPS** Student Page 69, Exercise 21:

**Number Sense** The median of four numbers is 48. Three of the numbers are 42, 51, and 52. What is the other number?

## Understand

1. What are you being asked to do?

   _____

2. What is the median?

   _____

3. How do you find the median when there is an even number of data items?

   _____

## Plan and Carry Out

4. Order the three numbers. _____

5. Between which two numbers does the missing number belong?

   _____

6. 48 is the number between the missing number and which other

   number? _____

7. What is the difference between the answer to Step 6 and 48?

   _____

8. What is the difference between the missing number and 48? Why?

   _____

9. What is the missing number? _____

## Check

10. Explain how to check your answer.

    _____

    _____

## Solve Another Problem

11. The median of six numbers is 37. If five of the numbers are 29, 38, 34, 38, and 40, what is the other number?

    _____

Guided Problem Solving

# Practice 2-3

1.  **a.** Choose a page from a book you are reading. Choose 50 words on
        that page. Using these 50 words, complete the frequency table.

| Letter | Tally | Frequency |
|--------|-------|-----------|
| t      |       |           |
| s      |       |           |
| r      |       |           |
| n      |       |           |

   **b.** Make a line plot for your frequency table.

   **c.** Which letter occurred most frequently in your sample? least frequently?

   _____

**Use the line plot at the right for Exercises 2–4.**

2.  What information is displayed in the line plot?

    _____

3.  How many students spent at least half an hour
    on homework?

    _____

4.  What is the range of time spent on homework last night?

    _____

**Time Spent Doing
Homework Last Night
(min)**

```
                    X
            X       X
    X       X       X               X
    X       X       X               X       X
    X       X       X       X       X       X
    X       X       X       X       X       X
    <+-------+-------+-------+-------+-------+->
    15      20      25      30      35      40
```

5.  A kennel is boarding dogs that weigh the following amounts
    (in pounds).

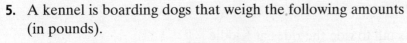

| 5 | 62 | 43 | 48 | 12 | 17 | 29 | 74 |
|---|----|----|----|----|----|----|----|
| 8 | 15 | 4  | 11 | 15 | 26 | 63 |    |

   What is the range of the dogs' weights?

   _____

# 2-3 • Guided Problem Solving

**GPS** Student Page 73, Exercise 13:

**Speed Limits** On a highway, the minimum speed allowed is 40 miles per hour. The maximum speed is 65 miles per hour. What is the range of speeds allowed on the highway?

## Understand

1. Underline the words that indicate which numbers you are to use to answer this question.

2. What is the range?

   _____

   _____

## Plan and Carry Out

3. What is the least possible highway speed allowed?

   _____

4. What is the greatest possible highway speed allowed?

   _____

5. Write a subtraction expression to answer the question.

   _____

6. What is the range?

   _____

## Check

7. How can you check your answer? Does your answer check?

   _____

   _____

## Solve Another Problem

8. You have to be at least 36 inches tall to ride the rides at Kiddie Land, but you cannot be any taller than 48 inches. What is the range of heights for these rides?

   _____

# Practice 2-4

**Use the table below for Exercises 1–3.**

| All-Time Favorite Sports Figures | |
|---|---|
| **Sports Figure** | **Number of Votes** |
| Babe Ruth | 29 |
| Babe Didrikson Zaharias | 22 |
| Jackie Robinson | 18 |
| Billie Jean Moffitt King | 17 |
| Muhammad Ali | 14 |
| Jim Thorpe | 13 |

1. What would you label the horizontal axis for a bar graph of the data?

   _____

2. What interval would you use for the vertical axis of the bar graph?

   _____

3. Construct a bar graph displaying the number of votes for all-time favorite sports figures.

**Use the table below for Exercises 4 and 5.**

| Daily Use of Petroleum in the U.S. (millions of barrels) | | | | | | | | | |
|---|---|---|---|---|---|---|---|---|---|
| **Year** | 1950 | 1955 | 1960 | 1965 | 1970 | 1975 | 1980 | 1985 | 1990 |
| **Number** | 6.5 | 8.5 | 9.8 | 11.5 | 14.7 | 16.3 | 17.1 | 15.7 | 16.9 |

4. Make a line graph for the amount of petroleum used daily in the U.S.

5. What does the line graph show?

   _____

   _____

# 2-4 • Guided Problem Solving

**GPS** Student Page 77, Exercise 11:

**Prime Ministers** Make a bar graph to show how many years each prime minister was in office.

## Understand

1. What is a bar graph?

   _____

   _____

Gro Harlem Brundtland
Norway 10 years

## Plan and Carry Out

2. If the bars are to be vertical, what should go along the horizontal axis?

   _____

3. What should go along the vertical axis? _____

4. What is the maximum number of years?

   What scale should you use? _____

5. Draw the bar graph.

Indira Gandhi
India  18 years

Golda Meir
Israel  5 years

## Check

6. What should you title your graph?

   _____

## Solve Another Problem

7. Draw a bar graph to show how many of each pet the students at Moore Middle School have. 52 students have dogs, 68 students have cats, 22 students have birds, 15 students have lizards, and 4 students have rabbits.

Margaret Thatcher
UK  11 years

# Practice 2-5

Gervase works after school and on weekends at a pet store, where he is paid $5 per hour. He uses the following spreadsheet to keep track of the time he works and the money he earns.

| | A | B | C | D | E |
|---|---|---|---|---|---|
| 1 | Day | Time In (P.M.) | Time Out (P.M.) | Hours Worked | Amount Earned |
| 2 | Monday | 4 | 7 | | |
| 3 | Tuesday | 4 | 7 | | |
| 4 | Thursday | 4 | 8 | | |
| 5 | Saturday | 1 | 9 | | |
| 6 | | | Total | | |

**Write the value for the given cell.**

**1.** A2

_____

**2.** B2

_____

**3.** C4

_____

**4.** A4

_____

**Write a formula to find the value of each cell. Then calculate the value.**

**5.** D5

_____

**6.** E5

_____

**7.** D6

_____

**8.** E6

_____

**9.** Rosario worked for $14.50 an hour on the weekdays and $15.25 an hour on the weekends. On Monday and Sunday she worked 8 hours each day.

   **a.** Make a spreadsheet similar to the one above. Use column B for hourly wage, column C for hours worked, and column D for amount earned.

   **b.** How much money did Rosario make each day and at the end of one week?

_____

_____

_____

# 2-5 • Guided Problem Solving

**GPS** **Student Page 82, Exercise 16:**

| | A | B | C | D | E |
|---|---|---|---|---|---|
| 1 | Day | Time In (P.M.) | Time Out (P.M.) | Hours Worked | Amount Earned |
| 2 | 9/15 | 3 | 8 | ? | ? |
| 3 | 9/17 | 4 | 8 | ? | ? |
| 4 | 9/19 | 3 | 6 | ? | ? |
| 5 | | | Total: | ? | ? |

**Wages** Suppose your cousin works part-time and earns $7 per hour. The spreadsheet shows a typical schedule for a week.

Write a formula for cell D2. Then calculate the value in cell D2.

## Understand

1. What are you being asked to do?

   _____

   _____

2. What does column D represent? _____

3. What does row 2 represent?

   _____

   _____

## Plan and Carry Out

4. What operation do you use to figure the number of hours worked? _____

5. What cells do you need for the formula? _____

6. Write the formula for D2. _____

7. Calculate the value of D2. _____

## Check

8. Explain how you can check your answer.

   _____

   _____

## Solve Another Problem

9. Your cousin's friend worked from 12 noon to 9 P.M. on 9/15. Create a row like your cousin's row 2 for his friend.

# Practice 2-6

**Use the stem-and-leaf plot for Exercises 1–5.**

1. What is the age of the youngest grandparent? _____

2. How many grandparents are 79 years old? _____

3. What is the range of the data? _____

4. What is the median? _____

5. What is the mode? _____

**Ages of Grandparents**

| stem | leaf |
|------|------|
| 6 | 7 8 8 |
| 7 | 0 1 2 3 4 9 9 |
| 8 | 1 3 3 3 4 7 |
| 9 | 0 2 5 |

**Key:** 6 | 7 means 67.

**Make a stem-and-leaf plot for each set of data.**

6. scores on a history test

   84, 93, 72, 87, 86, 97, 68, 74, 86, 91, 64, 83

   | stem | leaf |
   |------|------|
   |  |  |

   **Key:** 6 | 4 means 64.

7. number of badges earned by local scouts

   7, 12, 9, 2, 17, 24, 0, 3, 10, 20

   | stem | leaf |
   |------|------|
   |  |  |

   **Key:** 1 | 0 means 10.

8. minutes to travel to a friend's house

   12, 31, 5, 10, 23, 17, 21, 12, 8, 33

   | stem | leaf |
   |------|------|
   |  |  |

   **Key:** 3 | 1 means 31.

# 2-6 • Guided Problem Solving

**GPS Student Page 90, Exercise 14:**

The heights of nine people are below. Use a stem-and-leaf plot to find the median, the mode, and any outliers.

Heights in inches:

| | | |
|---|---|---|
| 70 | 59 | 64 |
| 66 | 79 | 67 |
| 82 | 68 | 61 |

## Understand

1. Looking at the data, which numbers should be the stems? Explain.

_____

## Plan and Carry Out

2. Order the heights from least to greatest.

_____

_____

3. Write the stems in order. Draw a vertical line next to the stems.

4. Write the leaves in order for each stem.

5. Include a key to explain what the stems and leaves represent. _____

## Check

6. How can you check to make sure you used all the data values?

_____

_____

## Solve Another Problem

7. Eight friends were in a race. Their times in seconds are given below.

108  114  140  118  182  165  150  123

Make a stem-and-leaf plot for the data.

# Practice 2-7

**Use the information below for Exercises 1–2.**

There are only two used car dealers in Auto City. Monthly auto sales for January, February, and March are shown for one dealer.

| Monthly Auto Sales | |
|---|---|
| January | 15 |
| February | 14 |
| March | 13 |

1. A competitor created the graph below.

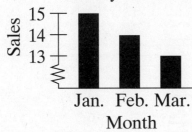

What impression is given by the graph?

_____

2. Why is the graph misleading?

_____

_____

_____

**Use the line graph for Exercises 3–4.**

3. What is misleading about the way the graph is drawn?

_____

_____

_____

4. What impression does the graph try to create?

_____

_____

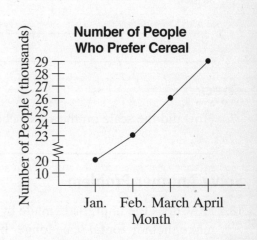

# 2-7 • Guided Problem Solving

**Student Page 96, Exercise 10:**

**Reasoning** How does the impression made by a line graph change when you make the horizontal scale shorter but keep the vertical scale the same?

## Understand

1. What does a line graph look like?

   _____

2. What does it mean to "make the horizontal scale shorter"?

   _____

   _____

## Plan and Carry Out

3. Graph the points $(1, 1)$ and $(2, 3)$ on the top graph to the right.

4. Graph the points $(1, 1)$ and $(2, 3)$ on the bottom graph to the right.

5. Compare the two lines from Steps 3 and 4.

   _____

6. How does the impression made by a line graph change when you make the horizontal scale shorter but keep the vertical scale the same?

   _____

   _____

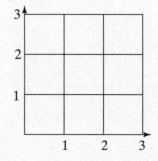

## Check

7. How did the scale on the *x*-axis change in Step 4?

   _____

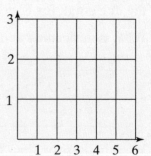

## Solve Another Problem

8. How does the impression made by a line graph change when you make the horizontal scale longer but keep the vertical scale the same?

   _____

   _____

# 2A: Graphic Organizer

**For use before Lesson 2-1**

**Study Skill** Take notes when your teacher presents new material in class. Organize those notes as a way to study, reviewing them as you go.

**Write your answers.**

1.  What is the chapter title? _____

2.  How many lessons are there in this chapter? _____

3.  What is the topic of the Test-Taking Strategies page? _____

4.  Complete the graphic organizer below as you work through the chapter.

    •   In the center, write the title of the chapter.

    •   When you begin a lesson, write the lesson name in a rectangle.

    •   When you complete a lesson, write a skill or key concept in a circle linked to that lesson block.

    •   When you complete the chapter, use this graphic organizer to help you review.

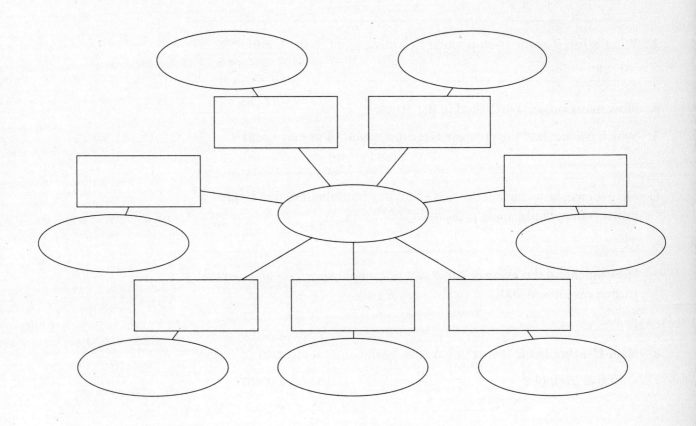

# 2B: Reading Comprehension

**Study Skill** Read direction lines carefully before beginning an exercise set.

**Read the paragraph and answer the questions.**

According to the National Gardening Association, Americans spent $37.7 billion in 2001 decorating and maintaining their lawns and gardens. The most popular flowering plants used in landscaping are impatiens, petunias, and pansies. Eighteen percent of all flowering plants sold in the United States are impatiens, 13% are petunias, and 8% are pansies. Twenty-three percent of all garden vegetables sold are tomatoes.

The average amount of money spent per household on lawn and garden projects in 2001 is shown.

| | | | |
|---|---|---|---|
| Flower bulbs | $40 | Flower gardening | $58 |
| Indoor houseplants | $40 | Insect control | $60 |
| Landscaping | $174 | Lawn care | $220 |
| Tree care | $97 | Vegetable gardening | $58 |

1. What is the paragraph about? _____

2. What was the total amount of money that Americans spent on their lawns and gardens in 2001?

   _____

3. What is listed as the most popular flowering plant in the United States?

   _____

4. How many projects are listed in the article? _____

5. Which project had the greatest average amount of money spent?

   _____

6. On average, how much more was spent per household on lawn care projects than landscaping projects in 2001?

   _____

7. How much did the average American household spend on *all* lawn and garden projects in 2001?

   _____

8. **High-Use Academic Words** In Exercise 7, what does it mean to *determine*?

   a. to give examples             b. to find a result

# 2C: Reading/Writing Math Symbols

**For use after Lesson 2-2**

**Study Skill** Learning is when you figure out how to get past an obstacle.

**Match each number with its word form.**

1. 6.8

    **A.** two and sixteen hundredths

2. 2.16

    **B.** eight tenths

3. 860

    **C.** eight hundred sixty

4. 0.218

    **D.** six and eight tenths

5. 0.8

    **E.** two hundred eighteen thousandths

**Write a mathematical expression for each word description.**

6. seven plus three hundredths

    _____

7. Two tenths is greater than six hundredths.

    _____

8. Ten divided by four equals two and five tenths.

    _____

9. three and one tenth multiplied by ten and one half

    _____

10. seven minus eleven and four thousandths

    _____

**Write out the following numbers in a word form.**

11. 3.9 _____

12. 4.01 _____

13. 0.039 _____

14. 0.5 _____

15. 60.908 _____

Name ______________________ Class ______________ Date ______________

# 2D: Visual Vocabulary Practice

For use after Lesson 2-6

**Study Skill** Mathematics builds on itself, so build a strong foundation.

**Concept List**

| | | |
|---|---|---|
| mean | median | mode |
| range | outlier | line graph |
| line plot | frequency table | stem-and-leaf plot |

**Write the concept that best describes each exercise. Choose from the concept list above.**

**1.**

**Number of Pets**

| Pets | Tally | Frequency |
|---|---|---|
| 0 | 卌 | 5 |
| 1 | 卌 \| | 6 |
| 2 | \|\| | 2 |

______________

**2.**

**Bowling League Scores**

| | |
|---|---|
| 15 | 0 1 1 2 7 7 9 |
| 16 | 1 2 2 3 3 |
| 17 | 0 9 |
| 18 | 1 5 |

**Key:** 15 | 0 means 150.

______________

**3.**

The prices of the same item at five stores are \$1.15, \$2.05, \$1.35, \$2.25, and \$1.65.

What does the amount \$2.25 − \$1.15 = \$1.10 represent for this set of prices?

______________

**4.**

**Books Purchased**

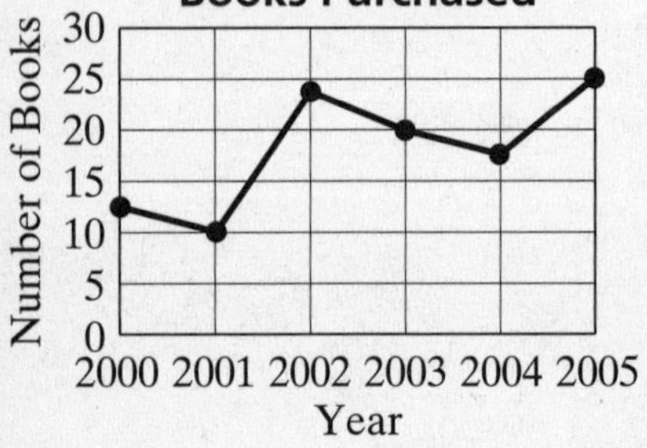


______________

**5.**

The high temperatures in a city over five days included 64°F, 61°F, 67°F, 82°F, and 64°F.

What does the temperature of 82°F represent for this set of temperatures?

______________

**6.**

The ages of five employees at a company are 32, 25, 28, 37, and 28.

What does the number $\frac{32 + 25 + 28 + 37 + 28}{5} = 30$ represent for this set of ages?

______________

**7.**

Sandra's grades in math class are 80, 82, 100, 96, 90, and 82.

What does the number $\frac{82 + 90}{2} = 86$ represent for this set of grades?

______________

**8.**

The number 3 represents this in the data set {1, 3, 4, 1, 3, 8, 2, 3}.

______________

**9.**

**Runs Batted In**

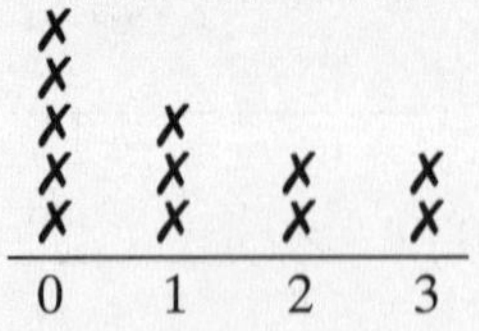


______________

# 2E: Vocabulary Check

**Study Skill** Strengthen your vocabulary. Use these pages and add cues and summaries by applying the Cornell Notetaking style.

**Write the definition for each word or term at the right. To check your work, fold the paper back along the dotted line to see the correct answers.**

_____

_____ mean

_____

_____

_____ median

_____

_____

_____ mode

_____

_____

_____ outlier

_____

_____

_____ range

_____

# 2E: Vocabulary Check (continued)

**Write the vocabulary word or term for each definition. To check your work, fold the paper forward along the dotted line to see the correct answers.**

the sum of the data divided by the
number of data items

_____

the middle value of a data set
that is arranged in numerical order

_____

the item in a data set that occurs
with the greatest frequency

_____

a data item that is much higher or
lower than the other item in the set

_____

the difference between the greatest
and least values in a data set

_____

# 2F: Vocabulary Review

**Study Skill** Pay attention in class. Some concepts are very difficult to grasp unless you devote your full attention to learning them.

**Circle the word that best completes the sentence.**

1. The (*median*, *mean*) is the sum of the data values divided by the number of items.

2. A (*line*, *bar*) graph is used to show a change in data over time.

3. You can use the (*commutative*, *associative*) property to change the order in an addition or multiplication expression.

4. (*Standard form*, *Expanded form*) is a different way to write a number to show the place and value of each digit.

5. The (*Associative*, *Commutative*) Property of Addition states that changing the grouping of the addends does not change the sum.

6. To find the (*mode*, *range*) of a data set, you must subtract the least value from the greatest value.

7. If a data set has an outlier that is very far apart from the rest of the data, the (*mean*, *mode*) may not be the best way to describe that data.

8. The (*median*, *mode*) is the middle number in a set of ordered data.

9. A (*spreadsheet*, *cell*) is a table made up of rows and columns used to organize data.

10. The (*mean*, *mode*) of a data set is the data item that appears most often.

11. A (*frequency table*, *line plot*) is a graph that shows the shape of the data set by stacking X's above each data value on a number line.

Name _____ Class _____ Date _____

# Practice 3-1

**Describing a Pattern**

**Sketch the next two designs in each pattern.**

**1.**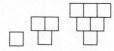

**2.**

**Write the next three terms in each pattern.**

**3.** 3, 5, 7, 9, _____

**4.** 34, 31, 28, 25, _____

**5.** 2, 6, 18, 54, _____

**6.** 7, 8, 10, 13, _____

**Write a rule for each number pattern, and then write the next three terms.**

**7.** 4, 7, 10, 13, _?_, _?_, _?_

_____

_____

**8.** 2, 4, 8, 16, _?_, _?_, _?_

_____

_____

**9.** 135, 125, 115, 105, _?_, _?_, _?_

_____

_____

_____

**10.** 5, 10, 20, 40, _?_, _?_, _?_

_____

_____

_____

**11.** Make a number pattern that starts with the number 6. Write the rule for your pattern, and then write the first five terms.

_____

_____

_____

**Find the missing term.**

**12.** 7, 21, 63, _?_, 567

_____

**13.** _?_, 20, 80, 320, 1280

_____

# 3-1 • Guided Problem Solving

**GPS Student Page 111, Exercise 18:**

**Business** A dry cleaner charges $5.00 to clean one item. She offers to clean a second item for $4.50 and a third item for $4.00.

**a.** If she continues to subtract $.50 for each additional item, how much will it cost to clean six items?

**b.** If the pattern continues, which item will be cleaned for free?

## Understand

**1.** What are you being asked to do in part (a)?

_____

**2.** What are you being asked to do in part (b)?

_____

**3.** What problem solving strategy will best solve this problem?

_____

## Plan and Carry Out

**4.** What is the price of cleaning the 4th item? _____

**5.** What is the price for the 5th item? _____

**6.** What is the price for the 6th item? _____

**7.** Write and evaluate an expression for the total cost of cleaning six items.

_____

**8.** What are the prices for the 7th, 8th, 9th, and 10th items?

_____

**9.** Which item will be cleaned for free? _____

## Check

**10.** Can you think of another way to solve the problem? Explain.

_____

## Solve Another Problem

**11.** Susie is trying to increase the distance she runs. The first week she runs $\frac{1}{2}$ mile. The second week she runs $\frac{3}{4}$ mile. The third week she runs 1 mile. If the pattern continues, how far will she run during the sixth week? _____

# Practice 3-2

Write a variable expression for each model. Squares represent ones.
Shaded rectangles represent variables.

1.

    _____

2.

    _____

3.

    _____

**Evaluate each expression.**

4. $56 \div b$ for $b = 7$

   _____

5. $3m$ for $m = 9$

   _____

6. $v + 16$ for $v = 9$

   _____

7. $2t - 8$ for $t = 21$

   _____

8. $2(4e)$ for $e = 5$

   _____

9. $12 - 2g$ for $g = 3$

   _____

10. $3pq$ for $p = 3$ and $q = 5$

    _____

11. $9r + 16$ for $r = 8$

    _____

**Copy and complete each table.**

12.

| x | x + 7 |
|---|---|
| 2 | 9 |
| 5 | 12 |
| 8 | |
| 11 | |
| | 21 |

13.

| x | 5x |
|---|---|
| 3 | |
| 6 | |
| 9 | |
| 12 | |
| | 75 |

14.

| x | 125 − x |
|---|---|
| 15 | |
| 30 | |
| 45 | |
| 60 | |
| | 50 |

15. A cellular phone company charges a $49.99 monthly fee for 600
    free minutes. Each additional minute costs $0.35. This month you
    used 750 minutes. How much do you owe?

    _____

# 3-2 • Guided Problem Solving

**GPS** **Student Page 116, Exercise 28:**

**Dogs** A dog walker charges $10 to walk a large dog and $6 to walk a small dog. She uses $10d + 6s$ to calculate her earnings, where $d$ is the number of large dogs and $s$ is the number of small dogs. How much does she earn for walking each group?

  **a.** 4 large and 2 small dogs

  **b.** 6 small dogs

## Understand

1. What are you being asked to do?

    _____

    _____

## Plan and Carry Out

2. What is the expression for calculating the dog walker's earnings?

    _____

3. What do you replace $d$ and $s$ with in part (a)? _____

4. Replace $d$ and $s$ with the values and simplify the expression.

    _____

5. How much does she earn to walk 4 large dogs and 2 small dogs?

    _____

6. Repeat Steps 3–5 to determine the dog walker's earnings for

    walking 6 small dogs. _____

## Check

7. How can you check your answer? Use your method to see if your answer is correct.

    _____

    _____

## Solve Another Problem

8. The sum of the interior angles of a polygon can be found using the formula $S = (N - 2) \times 180°$, where $N$ is the number of sides of the polygon. What is the sum of the interior angles of a polygon with 8 sides?

    _____

# Practice 3-3

**Write two word phrases for each variable expression.**

**1.** $5m$

**2.** $8 + b$

**3.** $q \div 15$

**4.** $c - 10$

**5.** $18 \div a$

**6.** $27 - m$

**7.** You buy 5 bags of peanuts to share with your friends. Each bag contains $p$ ounces of peanuts. How many ounces of peanuts did you buy? Draw a model for this situation. Then write an expression to describe the relationship.

**8.** Write an expression to describe the relationship of the data in the table.

| n | |
|---|---|
| 15 | 19 |
| 20 | 24 |
| 25 | 29 |

**Write a variable expression for each word phrase.**

**9.** nine less than $t$

**10.** eleven more than a number

**11.** the quotient of 700 and a number

**12.** two times the number of windows

**13.** $b$ divided by seven

**14.** 81 increased by $n$

# 3-3 • Guided Problem Solving

**GPS** Student Page 122, Exercise 28

**Painting** Customers in a paint store use the table at the right to decide how much paint they need.

a. Write an expression for the number of gallons of paint needed for an area of $A$ square feet.

b. Paint costs $17.95 per gallon. Write an expression to find the cost of the paint needed for an area of $A$ square feet.

| Area sq. ft. | Gallons |
|---|---|
| 400 | 1 |
| 800 | 2 |
| 2,000 | 5 |
| 3,200 | 8 |

## Understand

1. What are you being asked to do?

_____

_____

_____

2. Circle the information you will need to solve the problem.

## Plan and Carry Out

3. How much does paint cost per gallon?

_____

4. Write an expression for the number of gallons of paint needed for an area of $A$ square feet.

_____

5. Write an expression to find the cost of the paint needed for an area of $A$ square feet.

_____

## Check

6. Use your expression to find out how much it would cost a customer to paint an area of 2,000 square feet. Does your answer make sense?

_____

## Solve Another Problem

7. Anna and Tom are window washers. They are working on a house that has $r$ rooms, with 4 windows in each room. They have 2 windows left to wash before the job is complete. Write an expression for the number of windows they have already washed.

_____

# Practice 3-4

**Using Number Sense to Solve One-Step Equations**

**Find the missing number that makes the equation true.**

**1.** $7 + \boxed{\phantom{x}} = 12$   **2.** $\boxed{\phantom{x}} \times 5 = 30$   **3.** $13 - \boxed{\phantom{x}} = 4$

_____   _____   _____

**Tell whether each equation is true or false.**

**4.** $12 + 10 = 10 + 12$   **5.** $31 + 4 = 41 + 3$   **6.** $3.5 \times 1 = 1$

_____   _____   _____

**7.** $(3 \times 5) \times 4 = 3 \times (5 \times 4)$   **8.** $(7 \times 2) + 6 = 7 \times (2 + 6)$   **9.** $0 \times a = a$

_____   _____   _____

**Solve each equation. Use either mental math or the strategy *Guess,* *Check,* and *Revise.***

**10.** $8b = 72$   **11.** $n + 14 = 45$

_____   _____

**12.** $h - 3.6 = 8$   **13.** $w \div 12 = 3$

_____   _____

**14.** $53 = z - 19$   **15.** $86 = 29 + y$

_____   _____

**16.** The winners of a slam dunk basketball competition receive T-shirts. The coach spends $50.40 on shirts for the entire team. Each T-shirt costs $4.20. Solve the equation $(4.20)n = 50.40$ to find the number of team members.

_____

_____

# 3-4 • Guided Problem Solving

**GPS** **Student Page 127, Exercise 29**

You have $c$ pounds of cashews and 2.7 pounds of peanuts. You have 6 pounds of nuts altogether. Solve the equation $c + 2.7 = 6$ to find out how many pounds of cashews you have.

### Understand

1. What are you being asked to do?

   _____

   _____

2. How can mental math help you to solve this problem?

   _____

   _____

### Plan and Carry Out

3. What does the equation $c + 2.7 = 6$ mean?

   _____

   _____

4. What is $6 - 2.7$? _____

5. How many pounds of cashews do you have?

   _____

### Check

6. Explain how you can check your answer. Then check your answer.

   _____

   _____

## Solve Another Problem

7. At a school, there are 60 teachers for 1,500 students. Each teacher has the same number of students. Use the equation $60n = 1,500$ to find how many students each teacher has.

   _____

# Practice 3-5

right**Solving Addition Equations**

**Solve each equation. Then check the solution. Remember, you can draw a diagram to help you solve an equation.**

**1.** $38 + b = 42$

**2.** $n + 14 = 73$

**3.** $12.4 = 9 + t$

**4.** $m + 7.3 = 9.1$

**Write and solve an equation. Then check each solution.**

**5.** The height of the male giraffe in one zoo is 17.3 feet. The male is 3.2 feet taller than the female giraffe. How tall is the female giraffe?

**6.** Three of the top best-selling record albums of all time are Michael Jackson's *Thriller* (24 million copies), Fleetwood Mac's *Rumours* (17 million copies), and Boston's *Boston* ($b$ million copies). The three albums sold a combined total of 56 million copies. How many copies of *Boston* were sold?

**Solve each equation. Then check the solution.**

**7.** $a + 22 = 120$

**8.** $10 = e + 2.7$

**9.** $3.89 + x = 5.2$

# 3-5 • Guided Problem Solving

GPS **Student Page 133, Exercise 21**

**Music** You add a 4-minute song to your digital music player.
The player now has 2 hours of music. Use an equation to find out
how much music was on the player before you added the song.

## Understand

1. What are you being asked to do? _____

   _____

2. What will the variable represent in the equation?

   _____

3. Circle the information you will need to solve.

## Plan and Carry Out

4. How long was the song that you added? _____

5. Write an expression for the length of the song you added plus
   the amount of music that was on the player before you added the
   new song. Choose any variable for the amount of music that was
   on the player. _____

6. How much music (in minutes)
   was on the player after you

   added the song? _____

7. Write an equation comparing
   the amounts in Steps 5 and 6.

   _____

8. What do you do to both sides of
   the equation to isolate the variable?

   _____

9. Solve the equation.

   _____

10. How much music was on the player before you added the song?

    _____

## Check

11. Explain how you can check your answer. Then check your answer.

    _____

## Solve Another Problem

12. The book *A Tree Grows in Brooklyn* has 420 pages. It is 206
    pages longer than *The Catcher in the Rye*. Use an equation to
    find the number of pages in *The Catcher in the Rye*.

    _____

# Practice 3-6

**Solving Subtraction Equations**

Solve each equation. Then check the solution. Remember, you can draw a diagram to help you solve an equation.

**1.** $x - 10 = 89$

_____

**2.** $14 = y - 15$

_____

**3.** $12.3 = b - 7$

_____

**4.** $n - 2.7 = 8.3$

_____

**Write and solve an equation. Then check each solution.**

**5.** The owner of a used music store bought a compact disc for $4.70. When she sold it, her profit was $4.75. What was the selling price?

_____

_____

**6.** Yesterday, Stephanie spent $38.72 on new shoes and $23.19 on computer software. When she was finished, she had $31.18. How much money did she have before she went shopping?

_____

_____

**Solve each equation. Then check the solution.**

**7.** $x - 7 = 77$

_____

**8.** $3.1 = r - 7.5$

_____

**9.** $k - 5.13 = 2.9$

_____

# 3-6 • Guided Problem Solving

**GPS** Student Page 136, Exercise 20:

You buy several posters. The total cost is $18.95. You have $7.05 left after you pay. Write and solve an equation to find how much money you had before this purchase.

## Understand

1. What are you being asked to do?

   _____

2. What will the variable represent in the equation?

   _____

3. Circle the information you will need to solve.

## Plan and Carry Out

4. How much did you pay for the posters? _____

5. Write an expression for the amount of money you had before the purchase minus the amount you paid for the posters. Choose any variable for the amount of money you had.

   _____

6. How much money did you have left after the purchase?

   _____

7. Write an equation comparing the amounts in Steps 5 and 6.

   _____

8. What do you do to both sides of the equation to isolate the variable?

   _____

9. Solve the equation.

   _____

10. How much money did you have before the purchase?

    _____

## Check

11. Check your answer by substituting the result in step 10 into the equation you wrote in step 7. Does it check?

    _____

## Solve Another Problem

12. Jim has saved $78. This is $23 less than his sister has saved. Write and solve an equation to find how much his sister has saved.

# Practice 3-7

**State whether the number given is a solution to the equation.**

1. $8c = 80$; $c = 10$

2. $b \div 7 = 8$; $b = 56$

3. $9m = 108$; $m = 12$

4. $y \div 9 = 17$; $y = 163$

5. $9r = 72$; $r = 7$

6. $14b = 56$; $b = 4$

7. $48 = y \div 4$; $y = 12$

8. $32 = y \div 8$; $y = 256$

9. $17a = 41$; $a = 3$

**Solve each equation. Then check each solution.**

10. $905 = 5a$

11. $6v = 792$

12. $12 = y \div 12$

13. $80 = 16b$

14. $19m = 266$

15. $d \div 1{,}000 = 10$

16. $672 = 21f$

17. $z \div 27 = 63$

18. $43h = 817$

**Write and solve an equation for each situation.**
**Then check the solution.**

19. Lea drove 420 miles and used 20 gallons of gas. How many miles per gallon did her car get?

20. Ty spent $15 on folders that cost $3 each. How many folders did he buy?

21. Julia wants to buy copies of a book to give as presents. How many books can she buy if they are on sale for $12 each, and she has $100 to spend?

# 3-7 • Guided Problem Solving

**GPS** Student Page 141, Exercise 29

**Biology** An elephant's height is about 5.5 times the length of her hind footprint. Use an equation to find the approximate height of an elephant whose hind footprint is 1.5 feet long.

## Understand

1. What are you being asked to do?

   _____

   _____

   _____

2. Circle the information you will need to solve.

3. The phrase "*5.5 times*" tells you to perform what operation?

   _____

## Plan and Carry Out

4. What is the length of the hind footprint
   of this particular adult female elephant? _____

5. Write an expression to represent the phrase
   "*5.5 times the length of the hind footprint.*"

   _____

6. Write an equation for the height of the elephant. _____

7. What is the height of the elephant? _____

## Check

8. Explain how you can check your answer. Does your answer check?

   _____

   _____

## Solve Another Problem

9. Angela makes 1.75 times the amount of money that Janet makes.
   If Janet makes $38,200, how much does Angela make? Write and
   solve an equation.

   _____

Name _____ Class _____ Date _____

# Practice 3-8

The Distributive Property

**Write an expression to represent the total area of each figure. Then use your expression to find the total area. Show all your work.**

1. 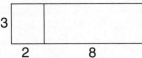   2. 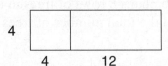   3.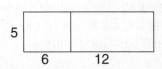

_____    _____    _____

_____    _____    _____

**Use the Distributive Property to find the missing numbers in the equations.**

4. $8 \times (9 + 4) = (\boxed{\phantom{x}} \times 9) + (8 \times \boxed{\phantom{x}})$

5. $(4 \times 7) + (4 \times 5) = 4 \times (\boxed{\phantom{x}} + 5)$

6. $3 \times (7 + 9) = (\boxed{\phantom{x}} \times 7) + (3 \times \boxed{\phantom{x}})$

7. $8 \times (9 - 6) = (8 \times \boxed{\phantom{x}}) - (\boxed{\phantom{x}} \times 6)$

**Use the Distributive Property to multiply mentally.**

8. $7 \times 53$

9. $8 \times 97$

**Use the Distributive Property to simplify each expression.**

10. $9 \times (5 + 3) \times 4 - 6$

11. $(8 + 7) \times 3 \times 2$

12. The auditorium at the School for the Arts has 7 rows of seats, and each row has 102 seats in it. Use the Distributive Property to find the number of seats in the auditorium.

13. The largest television screen ever made was featured at the Tsukuba International Exposition near Tokyo, Japan, in 1985. The screen was called the Sony JUMBOtron and measured 40 meters by 25 meters. Use the Distributive Property to find the area of the screen.

All rights reserved.

© Pearson Education, Inc., publishing as Pearson Prentice Hall.

L1 Practice

Course 1 Lesson 3-8

253

# 3-8 • Guided Problem Solving

**GPS** Student Page 147, Exercise 22:

**Gardening** Your school's ecology club plants 8 rows of trees in a vacant lot. Each row has 27 trees. Find the total number of trees that the ecology club plants.

## Understand

1. What are you being asked to do?

   _____

2. Circle the information you will need to solve.

## Plan and Carry Out

3. How many rows of trees are there?

   _____

4. How many trees are there in each row?

   _____

5. Write an expression for the total number of trees.

   _____

6. Use the Distributive Property to simplify the expression.

   _____

7. How many trees are there total?

   _____

## Check

8. Explain how you can check your answer. Does your answer check?

   _____

   _____

## Solve Another Problem

9. Alyce is tiling her living room. There are 29 rows of tiles, with 9 tiles in each row. How many tiles are there total?

   _____

# 3A: Graphic Organizer

**For use before Lesson 3-1**

**Study Skill** Read over the lesson before you come to class. Reading ahead of time will help you to grasp new concepts quicker.

**Write your answers.**

1. What is the chapter title? _____

2. How many lessons are there in this chapter? _____

3. What is the topic of the Test-Taking Strategies page? _____

4. Complete the graphic organizer below as you work through the chapter.

   • In the center, write the title of the chapter.

   • When you begin a lesson, write the lesson name in a rectangle.

   • When you complete a lesson, write a skill or key concept in a circle linked to that lesson block.

   • When you complete the chapter, use this graphic organizer to help you review.

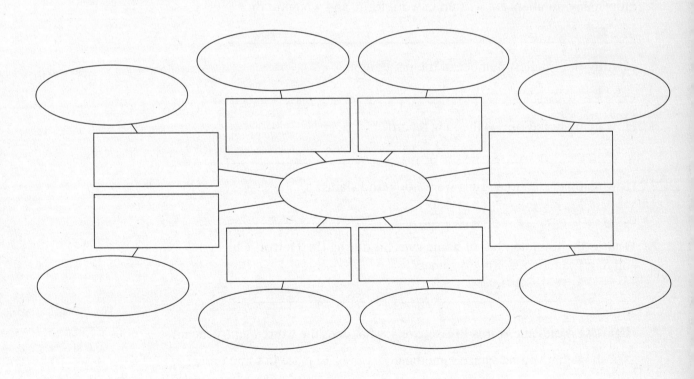

# 3B: Reading Comprehension

**Study Skill** Practice storing and recalling information while it is still fresh in your mind.

**Read the paragraph and answer the questions.**

> On July 3, 2002, the major league record for the most home runs hit in one day was set topping by 5 the previous record of 57 set on April 7, 2000. Fifty-three different players contributed to this milestone. A game between Detroit and Chicago added twelve home runs. San Francisco and Colorado added 10 more. Around the league, an amazing four grand slams were also hit. But this was not the only record broken on that day. Nine different players hit more than one home run in a game.

1. What is the paragraph about?

   _____

2. On what date did the new record occur?

   _____

3. How many numbers are written in word form, and what are they?

   _____

4. Identify the smallest number in the paragraph.

   _____

5. How many home runs is the new record?

   _____

6. How many of the home runs were not grand slams?

   _____

7. What is the total number of home runs hit during the Detroit-Chicago and San Francisco-Colorado games?

   _____

8. **High-Use Academic Words** In Exercise 4, what does the word *identify* mean?

   a. to show that you recognize something          b. to place in some order

# 3C: Reading/Writing Math Symbols

**For use after Lesson 3-3**

**Vocabulary and Study Skills**

**Study Skill** Bring all necessary tools with you to class. Never go to class unprepared.

**Match the phrase in Column A with its expression in Column B.**

| Column A | Column B |
|---|---|
| 1. 4 increased by a number | A. $4 - n$ |
| 2. a number divided by 4 | B. $4 + n$ |
| 3. a number subtracted from 4 | C. $n \div 4$ |
| 4. 4 multiplied by a number | D. $n - 4$ |
| 5. 4 less than a number | E. $4n$ |

| Column A | Column B |
|---|---|
| 6. the difference of 6 and a number | A. $n \div 6$ |
| | B. $6n$ |
| 7. the product of 6 and a number | C. $6 - n$ |
| 8. the sum of a number and 6 | D. $n - 6$ |
| 9. 6 divided into a number | E. $6 + n$ |
| 10. 6 less than a number | |

| Column A | Column B |
|---|---|
| 11. the quotient of 12 and a number | A. $12 \div n$ |
| | B. $n - 12$ |
| 12. a number times 12 | C. $n + 12$ |
| 13. 12 decreased by a number | D. $12 - n$ |
| 14. the total of 12 and a number | E. $12n$ |
| 15. 12 subtracted from a number | |

# 3D: Visual Vocabulary Practice

For use after Lesson 3-4

*High-Use Academic Words*

**Study Skill** If a word is not in the glossary, use a dictionary to find its meaning.

**Concept List**

solve                  compare                define
order                  organize               sum
table                  estimate               evaluate

**Write the concept that best describes each exercise. Choose from the concept list above.**

| 1. | 2. | 3. |
|---|---|---|
| $x - 1 = 9$ <br> $x - 1 + 1 = 9 + 1$ <br> $x = 10$ | $4 + 6 + 11 + 2 = 23$ | **2004 Olympic Medal Totals** <br><br> Country / Number <br> Russia / 38 <br> U.S.A. / 29 <br> China / 14 |
| 4. | 5. | 6. |
| An equation is a mathematical sentence that has an equal sign. | 2, 1.85, 3.2, 1.6, 3.27 <br> becomes <br> 1.6, 1.85, 2, 3.2, 3.27 | $3.05 < 3.5$ |
| 7. | 8. | 9. |
| $59 \div 3.1 \approx 60 \div 3$ | 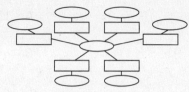 | $2z - 4$ for $z = 13$ |

Table 3:

| Country | Number |
|---|---|
| Russia | 38 |
| U.S.A. | 29 |
| China | 14 |

# 3E: Vocabulary Check

**Study Skill** Strengthen your vocabulary. Use these pages and add cues and summaries by applying the Cornell Notetaking style.

**Write the definition for each word or term at the right. To check your work, fold the paper back along the dotted line to see the correct answers.**

_____ equation

_____

_____

_____ inverse operations

_____

_____ variable

_____

_____

_____ numerical expression

_____

_____

_____ open sentence

_____

# 3E: Vocabulary Check (continued)

**For use after Lesson 3-5**

Write the vocabulary word or term for each definition. To check your work, fold the paper forward along the dotted line to see the correct answers.

a mathematical sentence with an equal sign

_____

operations that undo each other

_____

a letter that stands for a number

_____

an expression with only numbers and operation symbols

_____

an equation with one or more variables

_____

# 3F: Vocabulary Review Puzzle

**For use with the Chapter Review**

**Study Skill** Follow directions carefully.

**Complete the crossword puzzle. For help, use the glossary in your textbook.**

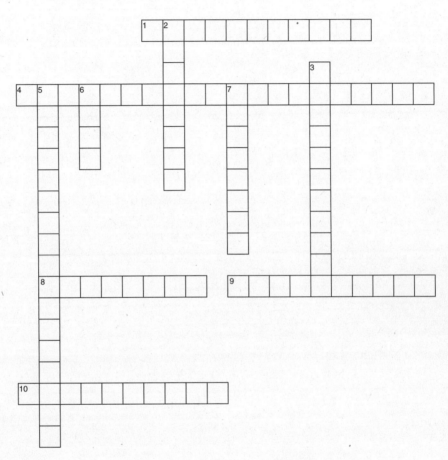

**ACROSS**

1.  $12 + (3 + 9) = (12 + 3) + 9$ is an example of this property

4.  $7(4 + 3) = 7(4) + 7(3)$ is an example of this property.

8.  mathematical sentence that contains an equal sign

9.  mathematical phrase containing numbers and operations

10. predicts how a pattern may continue

**DOWN**

2.  number that makes an equation true

3.  $100 + 32 = 32 + 100$ is an example of this property

5.  operations that undo one another

6.  each number in a number pattern

7.  a symbol that stands for an unknown number

# Practice 4-1

**Is the first number divisible by the second? Use mental math.**

1. 475 by 5 _____

2. 5,296 by 3 _____

3. 843 by 2 _____

4. 456,790 by 5 _____

5. 3,460 by 2 _____

6. 4,197 by 3 _____

**Test each number for divisibility by 2, 3, 5, 9, or 10.**

7. 126

8. 257

9. 430

_____

_____

_____

10. 535

11. 745

12. 896

_____

_____

_____

13. 729

14. 945

15. 4,580

_____

_____

_____

16. 6,331

17. 7,952

18. 8,000

_____

_____

_____

**Find the digit that makes each number divisible by 9.**

19. 54,78☐

20. 42,☐97

21. 83,2☐4

22. Name the numbers that are divisible by the numbers given: numbers between 10 and 20, divisible by 2, 3, and 9

_____

_____

23. There are 159 students to be grouped into relay teams. Each team is to have the same number of students. Can each team have 3, 5, or 6 students?

_____

Name _____ Class _____ Date _____

# 4-1 • Guided Problem Solving

**Money** Elissa and eight friends have lunch at a restaurant. The bill is $56.61. Can the friends split the bill into nine equal shares? Use the divisibility rule for 9 to explain your answer.

## Understand

1. What are you being asked to do?

   _____

   _____

2. What do you have to use to explain your answer?

   _____

3. What is the divisibility rule for 9?

   _____

   _____

## Plan and Carry Out

4. How much is the bill? _____

5. What are the digits? _____

6. What is the sum of the digits? _____

7. Does 9 divide evenly into the sum? _____

8. Can the friends split the bill into nine equal shares?_____

## Check

9. How can you check that your answer is correct?

   _____

   _____

## Solve Another Problem

10. Melissa, Dyanna, and Cristina are counselors at a summer camp. They want to divide the campers evenly among them. If there are 137 campers, use the rule for divisibility by 3 to detemine if this is possible.

   _____

# Practice 4-2

**Exponents**

**Write each expression using an exponent. Name the base and the exponent.**

**1.** $3 \times 3 \times 3 \times 3$

_____

_____

**2.** $7 \times 7 \times 7 \times 7 \times 7 \times 7$

_____

_____

**3.** $9 \times 9 \times 9$

_____

_____

**Write each number in expanded form using powers of 10.**

**4.** 98,364

_____

_____

_____

**5.** 20,351,401

_____

_____

_____

**6.** 875,020

_____

_____

_____

**Simplify each expression.**

**7.** $9^2$

_____

**8.** $6^4$

_____

**9.** $5^3$

_____

**10.** $156 + (256 \div 8^2)$

_____

**11.** $32 + 64 + 2^3$

_____

**12.** $53 + 64 \div 2^3$

_____

**13.** $(3 \times 4)^2$

_____

**14.** $60 \div (8 + 7) + 11$

_____

**15.** $2^2 \times 5^2 + 106$

_____

**16.** $4 + 7 \times 2^3$

_____

**17.** $60 + (5 \times 4^3) + 2^2 \times 55$

_____

**18.** $7^2 + 4$

_____

**19.** $7^2 - 7 \times 2$

_____

**20.** $48 \div 4 \times 5 - 2 \times 5$

_____

**21.** $(4^2 - 4) \times 10$

_____

**22.** $(4 + 3) \times (2 + 1)$

_____

# 4-2 • Guided Problem Solving

**GPS** **Student Page 165, Exercise 33:**

**Biology** A single-celled animal splits in two after one hour. Each new cell also splits in two after one hour. How many cells will there be after eight hours? Write your answer using an exponent.

## Understand

1. What are you being asked to do?

   _____

   _____

2. Explain what it means to write a number with an exponent.

   _____

   _____

## Plan and Carry Out

3. How many cells are there after 3 hours?
   Write the number using an exponent.

   _____

4. How many cells are there after 4 hours?
   Write the number using an exponent.

   _____

5. How many cells are there after 6 hours?
   Write the number using an exponent.

   _____

6. How many cells are there after 8 hours?
   Write the number using an exponent.

   _____

## Check

7. Why is the exponent 8?

   _____

## Solve Another Problem

8. An organism divides into 3 different organisms after the first hour. Each of those 3 organisms divide into 3 different organisms after the second hour. If this pattern continues, how many organisms are there after 4 hours? Write the number using an exponent.

   _____

# Practice 4-3

**Tell whether each number is prime or composite.**

**1.** 53

**2.** 86

**3.** 95

_____

_____

_____

**4.** 24

**5.** 27

**6.** 31

_____

_____

_____

**7.** 103

**8.** 47

**9.** 93

_____

_____

_____

**Complete each factor tree.**

**10.**

**11.**   75
          /  \
         _    15
              /  \
             _    _

**12.**   84
          /  \
         _    21
        /|   /  \
       _ _  _    _

**Find the prime factorization of each number.**

**13.** 58

**14.** 72

_____

_____

**15.** 40

**16.** 30

_____

_____

**Find the number with the given prime factorization.**

**17.** $2 \times 2 \times 5 \times 7 \times 11$

**18.** $2 \times 3 \times 5 \times 7 \times 11$

_____

_____

**19.** $2 \times 2 \times 13 \times 17$

**20.** $7 \times 11 \times 13 \times 17$

_____

_____

**21.** There are 32 students in a class. How many ways can the class be
divided into groups with equal numbers of students? What are they?

_____

_____

# 4-3 • Guided Problem Solving

**GPS** Student Page 169, Exercise 30:

**Parades** A group has 36 ceremonial guards. When they march, they form rows of equal numbers of guards. What numbers of rows can they make? How many guards will be in each row?

## Understand

1. What are you being asked to do?

   _____

   _____

2. What do you have to know to do this problem?

   _____

3. How many answers are there to this question?

   _____

## Plan and Carry Out

4. List the factors of 36.

   _____

5. What are the possible numbers of rows?

   _____

6. For each number of rows, how many guards are in each row?

   _____

   _____

## Check

7. How can you check your answer?

   _____

   _____

## Solve Another Problem

8. Louise is planting 30 bunches of pansies in her garden. She wants to put them in rows of equal numbers of bunches. What numbers of rows can they make? How many bunches will be in each row?

   _____

# Practice 4-4

**List the factors to find the GCF of each set of numbers.**

**1.** 8, 12                  **2.** 18, 27                **3.** 15, 23

_____          _____       _____

**4.** 24, 12                 **5.** 18, 24                **6.** 5, 25

_____          _____       _____

**Use a division ladder to find the GCF of each set of numbers.**

**7.** 10, 15                 **8.** 25, 75                **9.** 14, 21

_____          _____       _____

**10.** 32, 24, 40           **11.** 25, 60, 75           **12.** 12, 35, 15

_____          _____       _____

**Use factor trees to find the GCF of each set of numbers.**

**13.** 28, 24                           **14.** 27, 36

_____                    _____

**15.** 15, 305                          **16.** 57, 27

_____                    _____

**17.** 24, 48                           **18.** 56, 35

_____                    _____

**Solve.**

**19.** The GCF of two numbers is 850. Neither number is divisible by the other. What is the smallest that these two numbers could be?

_____

**20.** The GCF of two numbers is 479. One number is even and the other number is odd. Neither number is divisible by the other. What is the smallest that these two numbers could be?

_____

# 4-4 • Guided Problem Solving

**GPS** **Student Page 174, Exercise 30:**

Three friends pool their money to buy baseball cards. Brand A has 8 cards in each pack, Brand B has 12 cards, and Brand C has 15 cards. If they want to split each pack of cards equally, which two brands should they buy? Explain.

## Understand

1. What does *split each pack of cards equally* mean?

   _____

## Plan and Carry Out

2. How many cards will they have if they buy Brand A and Brand B?

   _____

3. Is the number you found in Step 2 divisible by 3? Why or why not?

   _____

4. How many cards will they have if they buy Brand A and Brand C?

   _____

5. How many cards will they have if they buy Brand B and Brand C?

   _____

6. Which of the answers to Steps 4 and 5 is divisible by 3? _____

7. Which two brands should they buy?

   _____

## Check

8. Explain your decision.

   _____

## Solve Another Problem

9. Carrie is lining up 45 students in the drill team and 25 students in the color guard. She wants each row to have the same number of students in both groups. How many rows are there, and how many students are in each row?

   _____

   _____

# Practice 4-5

**Equivalent Fractions**

**Name the fractions modeled and determine if they are equivalent.**

1.

2.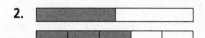

3.

_____    _____    _____

**By what number can you multiply the numerator and denominator of the first fraction to get the second fraction?**

4. $\frac{2}{3}, \frac{4}{6}$

5. $\frac{3}{8}, \frac{15}{40}$

6. $\frac{7}{10}, \frac{42}{60}$

_____    _____    _____

**By what number can you divide the numerator and denominator of the first fraction to get the second fraction?**

7. $\frac{6}{8}, \frac{3}{4}$

8. $\frac{70}{80}, \frac{7}{8}$

9. $\frac{15}{60}, \frac{1}{4}$

_____    _____    _____

**Write two equivalent fractions for each fraction.**

10. $\frac{3}{10}$ _____

11. $\frac{7}{8}$ _____

12. $\frac{5}{6}$ _____

13. $\frac{15}{20}$ _____

14. $\frac{8}{12}$ _____

15. $\frac{15}{45}$ _____

**State whether each fraction is in simplest form. If it is not, write it in simplest form.**

16. $\frac{15}{35}$ _____

17. $\frac{22}{55}$ _____

18. $\frac{34}{36}$ _____

19. $\frac{19}{57}$ _____

20. $\frac{27}{54}$ _____

21. $\frac{30}{41}$ _____

**Solve.**

22. A library has 10 camping guide books, 4 fishing guide books, and 6 hiking guide books. In simplest form, what fraction of the guide books are camping or hiking guide books?

_____

# 4-5 • Guided Problem Solving

**GPS** **Student Page 179, Exercise 28:**

**Traffic Planning** Two traffic engineers are writing about the average driving time between two towns. One engineer writes the time as 45, but the other writes it as $\frac{3}{4}$. What could explain the difference?

## Understand

1. What are you being asked to do?

   _____

   _____

2. What is the relationship between the two measurements?

   _____

## Plan and Carry Out

3. Name some units in which time can be measured.

   _____

   _____

4. What is a reasonable unit for the engineer who wrote 45?

   _____

5. What is a reasonable unit for the engineer who wrote $\frac{3}{4}$?

   _____

6. What explains the difference?

   _____

   _____

## Check

7. Why did you choose those units?

   _____

   _____

## Solve Another Problem

8. A scientist measured the time it took for a reaction to take place as $\frac{1}{4}$ hour. To use the results, he needs to write the numbers as minutes. How many minutes did it take for the reaction to take place?

   _____

# Practice 4-6

**What mixed number represents the amount shaded?**

1.

_____

2.

_____

3.

_____

**Write each mixed number as an improper fraction.**

4. $1\frac{7}{8}$ _____   5. $2\frac{3}{4}$ _____   6. $7\frac{1}{3}$ _____

7. $3\frac{3}{4}$ _____   8. $4\frac{1}{4}$ _____   9. $5\frac{5}{6}$ _____

10. $2\frac{3}{8}$ _____   11. $4\frac{7}{8}$ _____   12. $2\frac{3}{5}$ _____

**Write each improper fraction as a mixed number in simplest form.**

13. $\frac{15}{2}$ _____   14. $\frac{8}{3}$ _____   15. $\frac{5}{2}$ _____

16. $\frac{11}{10}$ _____   17. $\frac{7}{6}$ _____   18. $\frac{9}{8}$ _____

19. $\frac{27}{12}$ _____   20. $\frac{26}{18}$ _____   21. $\frac{35}{21}$ _____

22. Find the improper fraction with a denominator of 6 that is equivalent to $5\frac{1}{2}$.

_____

# 4-6 • Guided Problem Solving

**GPS** **Student Page 185, Exercise 30:**

**Catering** A caterer plans to serve two slices of melon to each of 50 guests. She estimates getting 12 slices from each melon. Write the number of melons she will use as a mixed number. How many whole melons does she need?

## Understand

1. Circle the information you will need to solve.

2. What are you being asked to do?

   _____

   _____

## Plan and Carry Out

3. How many slices does she need to feed 50 guests?

   _____

4. How many slices does she get from each melon?

   _____

5. What operation do you use to find the number of melons she needs?

   _____

6. Write the number of melons she will use as a mixed number.

   _____

7. How many *whole* melons does she need?

   _____

## Check

8. Why does she need to know how many whole melons are needed?

   _____

## Solve Another Problem

9. Three hundred twenty-one students are going on a field trip. One bus can seat 48 students. Write the number of buses needed as a mixed number. How many whole buses are needed?

   _____

**Guided Problem Solving**

Name _____ Class _____ Date _____

# Practice 4-7

**List multiples to find the LCM of each set of numbers.**

**1.** 5, 10

**2.** 2, 3

**3.** 6, 8

_____          _____          _____

**4.** 8, 10

**5.** 5, 6

**6.** 12, 15

_____          _____          _____

**7.** 9, 15

**8.** 6, 15

**9.** 6, 9

_____          _____          _____

**10.** 3, 5

**11.** 4, 5

**12.** 9, 21

_____          _____          _____

**Use prime factorizations to find the LCM of each set of numbers.**

**13.** 18, 21

**14.** 15, 21

**15.** 18, 24

_____          _____          _____

**16.** 15, 30

**17.** 24, 30

**18.** 24, 72

_____          _____          _____

**19.** 8, 42

**20.** 16, 42

**21.** 8, 56

_____          _____          _____

**22.** At a store, hot dogs come in packages of eight and hot dog buns come in packages of twelve. What is the least number of packages of each type that you can buy and have no hot dogs or buns left over?

_____

[L1] Practice

*Course 1 Lesson 4-7*

# 4-7 • Guided Problem Solving

**GPS** **Student Page 190, Exercise 29:**

**Business** During a promotion, a music store gives a free CD to every fifteenth customer and a free DVD to every fortieth customer. Which customer will be the first to get both gifts?

## Understand

1. Circle the information you will need to solve.

2. What are you being asked to do?

   _____

   _____

## Plan and Carry Out

3. Which customers will receive a free CD?

   _____

   _____

4. Which customers will receive a free DVD?

   _____

   _____

5. Which customer will be the first to get both gifts?

   _____

## Check

6. Explain how you can check your answer.

   _____

   _____

## Solve Another Problem

7. Emanuel, Michelle, and Kim volunteer at the swimming pool. Emanuel works every 5 days. Michelle works every 6 days. Kim works every 15 days. They are working together today. How many days will it be until the next time they work together?

   _____

   _____

   _____

   _____

# Practice 4-8

**Comparing and Ordering Fractions**

**Compare each pair of numbers using <, =, or >.**

1. $2\frac{14}{17}$ ☐ $1\frac{16}{17}$

2. $\frac{15}{21}$ ☐ $\frac{5}{7}$

3. $2\frac{7}{8}$ ☐ $2\frac{5}{6}$

4. $3\frac{15}{16}$ ☐ $3\frac{21}{32}$

5. $4\frac{7}{8}$ ☐ $3\frac{9}{10}$

6. $5\frac{9}{10}$ ☐ $5\frac{18}{20}$

**Order each set of numbers from least to greatest.**

7. $\frac{9}{10}, \frac{5}{6}, \frac{14}{15}$

8. $1\frac{7}{8}, 1\frac{7}{12}, 1\frac{5}{6}$

_____

_____

9. $\frac{14}{15}, \frac{9}{10}, \frac{11}{12}$

10. $2\frac{1}{4}, 3\frac{7}{8}, 3\frac{5}{6}$

_____

_____

11. $\frac{2}{3}, \frac{4}{5}, \frac{7}{30}, \frac{11}{15}$

12. $2\frac{1}{6}, 1\frac{3}{4}, 3\frac{7}{8}, 2\frac{1}{10}$

_____

_____

**Use mental math to compare each pair of fractions using <, =, or >.**

13. $\frac{1}{6}$ ☐ $\frac{1}{8}$

14. $\frac{8}{9}$ ☐ $\frac{8}{12}$

15. $\frac{1}{4}$ ☐ $\frac{1}{5}$

16. $\frac{3}{9}$ ☐ $\frac{3}{7}$

17. $\frac{5}{50}$ ☐ $\frac{1}{60}$

18. $\frac{9}{10}$ ☐ $\frac{10}{12}$

19. $\frac{1}{12}$ ☐ $\frac{1}{15}$

20. $\frac{5}{6}$ ☐ $\frac{3}{4}$

21. $\frac{1}{65}$ ☐ $\frac{3}{60}$

22. Four puppies measured $5\frac{1}{4}$ in., $5\frac{3}{8}$ in., $5\frac{5}{8}$ in., and $5\frac{5}{16}$ in. long at birth. Put the lengths in order from least to greatest.

_____

# 4-8 • Guided Problem Solving

**GPS** **Student Page 195, Exercise 34:**

Two sports drinks have the same price. The cherry-flavored drink contains $12\frac{9}{20}$ ounces. The blueberry-flavored drink contains $12\frac{7}{16}$ ounces. Which drink is the better buy?

## Understand

1. Circle the information you will need to solve.

2. What are you being asked to do?

   _____

3. Since both drinks are priced the same, what do you have to determine?

   _____

## Plan and Carry Out

4. What is the common denominator for $12\frac{9}{20}$ and $12\frac{7}{16}$? _____

5. Rewrite the fractional part of each mixed number with the common denominator. _____

6. Which fraction is bigger? _____

7. Which drink is the better buy? _____

## Check

8. What is another way you could answer this question?

   _____

   _____

## Solve Another Problem

9. Mary, Ana, and Tim shared the driving on a trip. Mary drove $\frac{1}{8}$ of the distance. Ana drove $\frac{1}{4}$ of the distance. Did Mary or Ana drive more miles? Explain how you know.

   _____

# Practice 4-9

**Write the decimal represented by each model as a fraction in simplest form.**

**1.**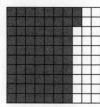

**2.**

**3.**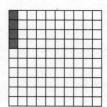

_____  _____  _____

**Write each decimal as a fraction or mixed number in simplest form.**

**4.** 0.6 _____     **5.** 1.25 _____

**6.** 0.74 _____     **7.** 0.635 _____

**8.** 0.8 _____     **9.** 6.16 _____

**Write each fraction or mixed number as a decimal.**

**10.** $\frac{5}{4}$ _____     **11.** $\frac{7}{8}$ _____

**12.** $\frac{9}{16}$ _____     **13.** $\frac{1}{8}$ _____

**14.** $1\frac{4}{5}$ _____     **15.** $\frac{9}{100}$ _____

**16.** You buy $2\frac{3}{4}$ pounds of apples. What number should appear on the digital scale when the apples are weighed?

_____

**Rewrite each set of numbers in order from least to greatest.**

**17.** $\frac{2}{5}$, 1.4, $\frac{1}{3}$, 0.5     **18.** $2\frac{1}{5}$, 2.25, $\frac{8}{20}$, 2.8     **19.** $\frac{1}{3}$, 0.4, $\frac{4}{9}$, 2.5

_____     _____     _____

**Determine whether each statement of equality is true or false.**

**20.** $\frac{2}{5} = 0.4$     **21.** $0.4 = \frac{6}{15}$     **22.** $0.5 = \frac{8}{15}$

_____     _____     _____

# 4-9 • Guided Problem Solving

**GPS** Student Page 201, Exercise 34:

**Shopping** You order $1\frac{1}{4}$ pounds of cheese at a delicatessen. What decimal number appears on the digital scale?

## Understand

1. What are you being asked to do?

   _____

2. How do you read $\frac{1}{4}$ as a division problem?

   _____

## Plan and Carry Out

3. How do you write 1 as a decimal?

   _____

4. Divide 1 by 4.

   _____

5. Write $1\frac{1}{4}$ as a decimal.

   _____

6. What decimal number appears on the digital scale?

   _____

## Check

7. How can you check your answer?

   _____

   _____

## Solve Another Problem

8. A recipe calls for $3\frac{3}{4}$ pounds of flour. Your scale only measures in decimals. What will the scale read?

   _____

# 4A: Graphic Organizer

**For use before Lesson 4-1**

**Study Skill** As you read over the material in the chapter, keep a paper and pencil handy to write down notes and questions that you have.

**Write your answers.**

1. What is the chapter title? _____

2. How many lessons are there in this chapter? _____

3. What is the topic of the Test-Taking Strategy page? _____

4. Complete the graphic organizer below as you work through the chapter.
   - In the center, write the title of the chapter.
   - When you begin a lesson, write the lesson name in a rectangle.
   - When you complete a lesson, write a skill or key concept in a circle linked to that lesson block.
   - When you complete the chapter, use this graphic organizer to help you review.

Vocabulary and Study Skills

# 4B: Reading Comprehension

**Study Skill** Read aloud or recite when you are learning. Reciting a rule or a formula may help you remember and recall it.

**Read the following and answer the questions.**

The following is the ingredient list for peanut butter cookies. This recipe makes 36 cookies.

| Peanut Butter Cookies | |
| --- | --- |
| $1\frac{1}{4}$ cup brown sugar | $\frac{3}{4}$ cup peanut butter |
| $\frac{1}{2}$ cup shortening | 3 tablespoons milk |
| 2 teaspoons vanilla | 2 eggs |
| $1\frac{3}{4}$ cup flour | $\frac{3}{4}$ teaspoon salt |
| $\frac{3}{4}$ teaspoon baking soda | 1 cup roasted peanuts |

1. What does the list of ingredients make? _____

2. What is the greatest measured quantity in the ingredient list? _____

3. What is the smallest measured quantity in the ingredient list? _____

4. What fraction of a cup of milk does the recipe call for? (There are 16 tablespoons in a cup.) _____

5. How many cups of peanuts and peanut butter does the recipe use all together? _____

6. If you double the recipe, how many cups of shortening would you need? _____

7. How many dozen cookies does the recipe make? (There are 12 cookies in a dozen.)

   _____

8. Suppose you wanted to make 24 cookies. What fraction of the recipe should you make?

   _____

9. **High-Use Academic Words** In the study skill given at the top of the page, what does it mean to *recall*?

   a. to bring back to mind          b. to change something

# 4C: Reading/Writing Math Symbols

**For use after Lesson 4-2**

**Study Skill** After completing homework, take a break. Then spend some time checking each exercise.

**Write the following statements using mathematical symbols.**

1. the quantity of a number plus 4

    _____

2. the quantity of a number plus three, increased by 2

    _____

3. three more than the quantity *n* plus five

    _____

4. the quantity *n* plus 10, decreased by three squared

    _____

5. six decreased by the quantity of a number increased by 2

    _____

6. four to the third power plus the quantity *n* decreased by 3

    _____

7. eight squared decreased by the quantity of the sum of a number and 4

    _____

8. six cubed decreased by the quantity of the difference of a number and 1

    _____

**Write the meaning in words of each mathematical expression.**

9. $(n - 5)$

    _____

10. $(n + 3) + 1$

    _____

11. $2 + (n + 10)$

    _____

12. $5^2 + (n - 6)$

    _____

13. $(n + 7) - 6$

    _____

14. $(n + 3) + 4^3$

    _____

15. $10^2 - (n + 2)$

    _____

Name _____ Class _____ Date _____

# 4D: Visual Vocabulary Practice

For use after Lesson 4-9

**Study Skill** When a math exercise is difficult, try to determine what makes it difficult. Is it a word that you don't understand? Are the numbers difficult to use?

**Concept List**

| | | |
|---|---|---|
| mixed number | improper fraction | base |
| prime factorization | greatest common factor | least common denominator |
| least common multiple | equivalent fractions | exponent |

**Write the concept that best describes each exercise. Choose from the concept list above.**

| | | |
|---|---|---|
| **1.**<br><br>$8$ in $8^4$<br><br>_____ | **2.**<br>The number 4 represents this for the numbers 28 and 48.<br><br>_____ | **3.**<br><br>$120\frac{5}{6}$<br><br>_____ |
| **4.**<br>The number 120 represents this for the numbers 24 and 30.<br><br>_____ | **5.**<br><br>$90 = 2 \times 3^2 \times 5$<br><br>_____ | **6.**<br><br>$\frac{4}{10}$ and $\frac{24}{60}$<br><br>_____ |
| **7.**<br><br>$4$ in $(2 + 1 \times 3)^4$<br><br>_____ | **8.**<br><br>$\frac{34}{15}$<br><br>_____ | **9.**<br>The number 60 represents this for the fractions $\frac{5}{12}$ and $\frac{23}{30}$.<br><br>_____ |

© Pearson Education, Inc., publishing as Pearson Prentice Hall.

**284** *Course 1* Chapter 4 — Vocabulary and Study Skills

# 4E: Vocabulary Check

**Study Skill** Strengthen your vocabulary. Use these pages and add cues and summaries by applying the Cornell Notetaking style.

**Write the definition for each word or term at the right. To check your work, fold the paper back along the dotted line to see the correct answers.**

_____ equivalent fractions

_____

_____

_____ mixed number

_____

_____

_____ prime number

_____

_____

_____ composite number

_____

_____

_____ proper fraction

_____

_____

# 4E: Vocabulary Check (continued)     For use after Lesson 4-6

**Write the vocabulary word or term for each definition. To check your work, fold the paper forward along the dotted line to see the correct answers.**

fractions that name the same
amount

_____

the sum of a whole number
and a fraction

_____

a whole number whose only factors
are 1 and the number itself

_____

a whole number greater than 1 with
more than 2 factors

_____

a fraction that has a numerator that
is less than the denominator

_____

Name _____ Class _____ Date _____

# 4F: Vocabulary Review Puzzle

**For use with the Chapter Review**

**Study Skill** Combine clue words and pictures to prompt your memory.

Use the word list below to find hidden words in the puzzle. Once you have found a word, draw a circle around it and cross the word off in the word list. Words can be displayed forwards, backwards, up, down, or diagonally but they are always in a straight line.

| | | | |
|---|---|---|---|
| divisible | prime factor | improper fraction | factor tree |
| multiple | composite number | equivalent fractions | simplest form |
| mixed number | base | least common multiple | |
| fraction | power | common factor | |

```
A Z E L P I T L U M N O M M O C T S A E L
C E B A S E W X T Y N U Z N A O G P H O E
O J V G R O T C A F N O M M O C S Q A P Q
M W A G H M L L I F H P F D O P O W E R U
P H P O W E R H E M N O B Q E R Y F Z I I
O I B P E L B I S I V I D C M X A R B M V
S K K G L L C R M E N D B I W C D A P E A
I X J K T S F J L U Q R X V T I V C D F L
T I Y W T D X P K R M E A O P U Y T O A E
E J Z U A E I F G Q D L R F A J E I G C N
N I V M E T R F L N Z T Q B C C T O Z T T
U B L X L K W M U I R D K X E Y Z N C O F
M W K U F E C M J E P A H S V B S T U R R
B N M V V O B U E X T J H M R W W N X A A
E U O I N E S D Z Y M U L T I P L E Q G C
R Y L Q R T P M R O F T S E L P M I S Y T
I M P R O P E R F R A C T I O N R S F Z I
K S I R B M T B Q A H O F M D G F H N I O
D A U C E W E N D O Z P V L Q L X A J C N
J T G U H S V G E P I C W R X M Z Y B K S
```

# Practice 5-1

**Write the fraction shown by each model. Then choose a benchmark for each measurement. Use $0, \frac{1}{2}$, or 1.**

**1.** _____

**2.** _____

**Estimate each sum or difference. Use the benchmarks $0, \frac{1}{2}$, and 1.**

**3.** $\frac{5}{16} + \frac{5}{8}$

**4.** $\frac{10}{12} + \frac{4}{5}$

**5.** $\frac{8}{10} - \frac{1}{2}$

_____  _____  _____

**6.** $\frac{3}{4} + \frac{3}{8}$

**7.** $\frac{7}{10} - \frac{1}{6}$

**8.** $\frac{13}{15} - \frac{1}{12}$

_____  _____  _____

**Estimate each sum or difference.**

**9.** $4\frac{1}{4} - 1\frac{7}{9}$

**10.** $8\frac{6}{8} - 2\frac{1}{3}$

**11.** $5\frac{7}{8} + 3\frac{3}{4}$

_____  _____  _____

**12.** Name three fractions whose benchmark is $\frac{1}{2}$.

_____

**13.** Name three fractions whose benchmark is 1.

_____

**14.** One bag of oranges costs $2.99 and weighs about $3\frac{7}{8}$ pounds. Individual oranges are sold at $.89 per pound. Which is the better buy? Explain.

_____

_____

_____

# 5-1 • Guided Problem Solving

**GPS** Student Page 215, Exercise 27:

**Coins** Use the table at the right to estimate the total width of the coins.

| U.S. Coins | |
| --- | --- |
| Coin | Diameter (inches) |
| Dime | $\frac{11}{16}$ |
| Penny | $\frac{3}{4}$ |
| Nickel | $\frac{13}{16}$ |
| Quarter | $\frac{15}{16}$ |

## Understand

1. What are you being asked to do?

   _____

2. How are you supposed to use the table?

   _____

## Plan and Carry Out

3. What is the actual width of the dime? _____

4. Is this fraction closer to $0, \frac{1}{2}$, or 1? _____

5. What are the actual widths of the dime, nickel, penny, and quarter?

   _____

6. Is the nickel's width closer to $0, \frac{1}{2}$, or 1? _____

7. Is the penny's width closer to $0, \frac{1}{2}$, or 1? _____

8. Is the quarter's width closer to $0, \frac{1}{2}$, or 1? _____

9. Estimate the total width of the coins. _____

## Check

10. Do you expect that your estimate is more or less than the actual length? Explain.

   _____

## Solve Another Problem

11. The table shows the average precipitation for four months. Estimate the total amount of precipitation.

| January | February | March | April |
| --- | --- | --- | --- |
| $3\frac{2}{3}$ in. | $1\frac{4}{7}$ in. | $2\frac{7}{8}$ in. | $4\frac{1}{2}$ in. |

# Practice 5-2

**Fractions With Like Denominators**

**Write each sum or difference in simplest form.**

1. $\frac{1}{4} + \frac{2}{4}$

2. $\frac{7}{10} - \frac{4}{10}$

3. $\frac{5}{8} - \frac{3}{8}$

_____

4. $\frac{1}{8} + \frac{5}{8}$

5. $\frac{5}{8} + \frac{2}{8}$

6. $\frac{3}{10} + \frac{6}{10}$

_____

7. What is the total amount of sugar in the recipe at the right?

_____

| **Martha's Cookie Recipe** |
| --- |
| 1 cup shortening |
| 2 eggs |
| $\frac{1}{4}$ cup white sugar |
| $\frac{1}{4}$ cup brown sugar |
| $1\frac{1}{2}$ cup flour |
| 1 teaspoon vanilla |

8. Martha decides to double the recipe. How much brown sugar will she use?

_____

**Estimate each sum or difference.**

9. $\frac{3}{8} + \frac{2}{8} - \frac{4}{8}$

10. $\frac{1}{10} + \frac{2}{10} + \frac{4}{10}$

_____

11. $\frac{9}{20} - \left(\frac{2}{20} - \frac{4}{20}\right)$

12. $\frac{6}{9} + \frac{2}{9} - \frac{1}{9}$

_____

**Solve.**

13. At the tea shop, $\frac{5}{15}$ of the customers purchased green tea, $\frac{2}{15}$ of the customers purchased jasmine tea, and $\frac{5}{15}$ of the customers purchased herbal tea. What portion of the customers purchased another type of tea?

_____

14. A piece of fabric is $\frac{7}{9}$ yard long. A piece of ribbon is $\frac{2}{9}$ yard long. How many more yards of ribbon do you need to have equal lengths of fabric and ribbon?

_____

# 5-2 • Guided Problem Solving

**GPS** **Student Page 220, Exercise 28:**

**Biology** Plasma makes up $\frac{11}{20}$ of your blood. Blood cells make up the other $\frac{9}{20}$. How much more of your blood is plasma than blood cells?

## Understand

1. What are you being asked to do?

   _____

2. What operation do you have to use to answer this question?

   _____

## Plan and Carry Out

3. How much of your blood is plasma?

   _____

4. How much of your blood is blood cells?

   _____

5. Write an expression you can use to answer the question.

   _____

6. How much more of your blood is plasma than blood cells?

   _____

## Check

7. How can you check your answer?

   _____

   _____

## Solve Another Problem

8. Maddie has a window that is $15\frac{3}{8}$ inches long. She bought blinds that are $16\frac{5}{8}$ inches. How much longer are the blinds than the window?

   _____

# Practice 5-3

**Write each sum or difference in simplest form.**

1. $\frac{1}{4} + \frac{2}{3}$

2. $\frac{2}{5} - \frac{1}{10}$

3. $\frac{1}{6} + \frac{1}{4}$

4. $\frac{5}{8} - \frac{1}{4}$

5. $\frac{7}{8} - \frac{1}{2}$

6. $\frac{3}{10} + \frac{4}{5}$

7. $\frac{5}{6} - \frac{2}{5}$

8. $\frac{5}{12} - \frac{1}{4}$

9. $\frac{7}{16} + \frac{1}{8}$

10. $\frac{11}{16} + \frac{5}{8}$

11. Jeanie has a $\frac{3}{4}$-yard piece of ribbon. She needs one $\frac{3}{8}$-yard piece and one $\frac{1}{2}$-yard piece. Can she cut the piece of ribbon into the two smaller pieces? Explain.

**Simplify by using mental math.**

12. $\frac{7}{10} + \frac{2}{5} - \frac{1}{10}$

13. $\frac{5}{100} + \frac{20}{100} + \frac{30}{100}$

14. $\frac{2}{8} - \frac{2}{4} + \frac{5}{8}$

15. $\frac{6}{10} - \frac{2}{10} + \frac{1}{2}$

# 5-3 • Guided Problem Solving

GPS **Student Page 225, Exercise 27:**

**Weather** A meteorologist records the rainfall as $\frac{3}{10}$ inch from 9:00 to 10:00. You measure $\frac{7}{8}$ inch of rain from 10:00 to 11:00.

a. **Estimation** Estimate the rainfall from 9:00 to 11:00.

b. Find the total rainfall from 9:00 to 11:00.

## Understand

1. What is the difference between part (a) and part (b)?

_____

_____

## Plan and Carry Out

2. Estimate $\frac{3}{10}$ and $\frac{7}{8}$ separately. _____

3. Use the answers to Step 2 to estimate
   the total rainfall between 9:00 and 11:00. _____

4. What do you need to find the sum of the two measurements?

_____

5. What is the least common denominator for $\frac{3}{10}$ and $\frac{7}{8}$? _____

6. Rewrite each fraction using the answer to Step 5. _____

7. What is the total rainfall from 9:00 to 11:00?

_____

## Check

8. Does your answer match your estimate? Explain.

_____

## Solve Another Problem

9. A recipe for party mix calls for $\frac{3}{4}$ cup of cereal, $\frac{1}{4}$ cup of walnuts, $\frac{5}{8}$ cup of crackers, and $\frac{1}{2}$ cup of raisins. Estimate the number of cups in the mix. Determine the actual number of cups in the mix.

_____

# Practice 5-4

**Adding Mixed Numbers**

**Complete to rename each mixed number.**

**1.** $3\frac{9}{8} = 4\frac{?}{8}$ _____

**2.** $5\frac{7}{4} = 6\frac{?}{4}$ _____

**3.** $2\frac{17}{12} = 3\frac{?}{12}$ _____

**Write each sum in simplest form.**

**4.** $4\frac{3}{10} + 5\frac{2}{5}$

**5.** $3\frac{7}{8} + 2\frac{1}{2}$

**6.** $5\frac{2}{3} + 3\frac{1}{4}$

**7.** $6\frac{3}{4} + 2\frac{1}{2}$

**8.** $1\frac{1}{12} + 3\frac{1}{6}$

**9.** $9\frac{2}{5} + 10\frac{3}{10}$

**10.** $7\frac{1}{3} + 5\frac{11}{12}$

**11.** $11\frac{7}{10} + 4$

**12.** $2\frac{2}{3} + 4\frac{3}{4}$

**13.** $7\frac{3}{4} + 2\frac{7}{8}$

**14.** $4\frac{1}{2} + 3\frac{5}{6}$

**15.** $7\frac{2}{3} + 1\frac{5}{6}$

**16.** Estimate the length of rope needed to go around a triangle with sides $6\frac{1}{2}$ feet, $7\frac{3}{4}$ feet, and $10\frac{1}{4}$ feet.

**17.** Sam grew three pumpkins for the pumpkin growing contest. The pumpkins weighed $24\frac{1}{8}$ pounds, $18\frac{2}{4}$ pounds, and $32\frac{5}{16}$ pounds. Find the combined total weight of Sam's pumpkins.

**Compare using <, =, or >. Use benchmarks to help.**

**18.** $50\frac{7}{10} + 49\frac{1}{5}$ ☐ $101$

**19.** $5\frac{3}{4} + 5\frac{1}{8}$ ☐ $11\frac{1}{2}$

**20.** $20\frac{1}{5} + 4\frac{9}{10}$ ☐ $25$

# 5-4 • Guided Problem Solving

**GPS** Student Page 231, Exercise 23a:

**Tides** At low tide, the depth of the water is $4\frac{11}{12}$ feet. At high tide, the water depth increases by $2\frac{3}{4}$ feet. How deep is the water at high tide?

## Understand

1. Circle the information you will need to solve.

2. What operation do you need to answer the question?

_____

## Plan and Carry Out

3. What is the least common denominator for $4\frac{11}{12}$ feet and $2\frac{3}{4}$ feet?

_____

4. Rewrite both fractions using the least common denominator.

_____

5. Write an expression you can use to answer the question.

_____

6. How deep is the water at high tide?

_____

## Check

7. How can you check your answer?

_____

_____

## Solve Another Problem

8. Suppose Don will need to leave his fishing spot when the river reaches 30 feet. The river is predicted to rise $5\frac{7}{12}$ feet from its present level of $21\frac{7}{10}$ feet. Will he need to leave?

_____

# Practice 5-5

**Write each difference in simplest form.**

**1.** $10\frac{11}{16} - 3\frac{7}{8}$

**2.** $8\frac{1}{3} - 2\frac{3}{8}$

**3.** $9 - 3\frac{2}{5}$

_____

_____

_____

**4.** $5\frac{3}{16} - 2\frac{3}{8}$

**5.** $8\frac{1}{6} - 3\frac{2}{5}$

**6.** $7\frac{1}{2} - 3$

_____

_____

_____

**7.** $2\frac{3}{4} - 1\frac{1}{8}$

**8.** $4\frac{1}{8} - 2\frac{1}{16}$

**9.** $9\frac{2}{3} - 3\frac{5}{6}$

_____

_____

_____

**10.** $2\frac{1}{10} - 1\frac{2}{5}$

**11.** $15\frac{7}{12} - 8\frac{1}{2}$

**12.** $6\frac{7}{16} - 2\frac{7}{8}$

_____

_____

_____

**Solve.**

**13.** Robbie needs to buy fencing for his square vegetable garden, which measures $16\frac{3}{4}$ feet on a side. One side borders the back of the garage. The fencing costs $4 per feet. Estimate how much the fencing will cost.

_____

**14.** Use a ruler or measuring tape to find the perimeter of your desk. Measure to the nearest half inch.

width:_____     length:_____     perimeter:_____

Now find the perimeter of your teacher's desk.

width:_____     length:_____     perimeter:_____

# 5-5 • Guided Problem Solving

**GPS** Student Page 235, Exercise 23:

**Weather** On Monday, the snowfall in the mountains was $15\frac{3}{4}$ inches. On Tuesday, the snowfall was $18\frac{1}{2}$ inches. How much more snow fell on Tuesday?

## Understand

1. Circle the information you will need to solve.

2. What are you being asked to do?

   _____

   _____

## Plan and Carry Out

3. How many inches fell on Monday?

   _____

4. How many inches fell on Tuesday?

   _____

5. What common denominator do you need to use?

   _____

6. Rewrite each fraction using the least common denominator.

   _____

7. What was the difference in snowfall?

   _____

## Check

8. How can you check your answer?

   _____

## Solve Another Problem

9. The perimeter of the lid to a rectangular box is $\frac{14}{6}$ yards. If the longer sides are $\frac{5}{6}$ yard, how long are the shorter sides? Explain.

   _____

# Practice 5-6

**Solve each equation using mental math. Write your solution in simplest form.**

**1.** $\frac{5}{17} + x = \frac{8}{17}$

_____

**2.** $\frac{2}{7} + x = \frac{5}{7}$

_____

**3.** $x - \frac{1}{2} = 10\frac{1}{10}$

_____

**4.** $5\frac{7}{8} - x = \frac{13}{16}$

_____

**Solve each equatiion. Remember you can use a model.**

**5.** $\frac{4}{7} - x = \frac{6}{35}$

_____

**6.** $x - \frac{1}{5} = \frac{3}{10}$

_____

**7.** $x + \frac{7}{22} = \frac{13}{22}$

_____

**8.** $\frac{7}{9} - x = \frac{1}{36}$

_____

**9.** $x - \frac{1}{6} = \frac{1}{6}$

_____

**10.** $x + 9\frac{1}{4} = 12\frac{7}{16}$

_____

**Write and solve an equation for each situation.**

**11.** Lori and Fraz ate $\frac{7}{12}$ of a vegetable pizza. If Lori ate $\frac{1}{3}$ of the pizza, how much of it did Fraz eat?

_____

_____

**12.** Irene's gas tank was $\frac{9}{10}$ full when she left her house, and it was $\frac{7}{15}$ full when she arrived for her vacation. What fraction of a tank of gas did she use driving there?

_____

_____

# 5-6 • Guided Problem Solving

**GPS** **Student Page 243, Exercise 27:**

**Landscaping** The Service Club buys a 10-yard roll of edging to put around two trees in front of the school. The club uses $5\frac{2}{3}$ yards of edging for one tree and $3\frac{1}{2}$ yards for the other tree. How much edging is left?

## Understand

1. Circle the information you will need to solve.

2. How do you plan to solve this problem?

   _____

   _____

## Plan and Carry Out

3. How much of the edging has been used?

   _____

4. Add these amounts together using a common denominator.

   _____

5. How much edging did the club purchase?

   _____

6. How much edging is left over?

   _____

## Check

7. Explain how you can check your answer.

   _____

## Solve Another Problem

8. Linda bought a 15-yard roll of fabric to make a suit. She used $8\frac{1}{3}$ yards of fabric for the blouse and $5\frac{1}{4}$ yards for the pants. How much fabric is left?

   _____

# Practice 5-7

**Clark is trying to plan his Saturday. He estimates each activity will take the following times.**

Make a schedule for Clark's day if he wakes up at 7:00 A.M. Assume all his activities are done in the given order.

| | Activity | Amount of Time | Time of Day |
|---|---|---|---|
| 1. | Get up, eat breakfast | 30 min | _____ |
| 2. | Mow lawn | 1 h | _____ |
| 3. | Rake yard | 2 h | _____ |
| 4. | Wash, wax car | 45 min | _____ |
| 5. | Walk dog | 15 min | _____ |
| 6. | Clean room | 45 min | _____ |
| 7. | Eat lunch | 30 min | _____ |
| 8. | Shop for school clothes | 1 h 30 min | _____ |
| 9. | Read book | 45 min | _____ |
| 10. | Do homework | 1 h 15 min | _____ |
| 11. | Baby-sit brother | 2 h | _____ |
| 12. | Eat supper | 45 min | _____ |
| 13. | Get ready for party | 30 min | _____ |
| 14. | Ride to party | 20 min | _____ |
| 15. | Party | 2 h | _____ |
| 16. | Ride home | 20 min | _____ |

**Find the elapsed time.**

**17.** from 2:12 P.M. to 10:18 P.M.

_____

**18.** from 9:35 A.M. to 8:48 P.M.

_____

**19.** The movie begins at 7:45 P.M. and lets out at 10:20 P.M. How long is the movie?

_____

**20.** A plane left at 10:45 A.M. and landed at 4:37 P.M. How long was the flight?

_____

# 5-7 • Guided Problem Solving

**GPS** **Student Page 250, Exercise 27:**

**Clowns** A clown wants to perform a 45-minute show at three birthday parties. The first party begins at 10:00 A.M. He needs to leave the third party by 2:15 P.M. He wants to allow one hour between each party. Make a schedule for the clown.

## Understand

1. Circle the information you will need to solve.

2. What are you being asked to do?

    _____

3. What problem-solving method can you use to help create the schedule?

    _____

## Plan and Carry Out

4. If the clown starts the first show at 10:00 A.M. when will he finish?

    _____

5. If he allows an hour between each show, when will the next show begin?

    _____

6. When will he finish the second show? _____

7. If he allows an hour between each show, when will the next show begin?

    _____

8. When will he finish the third show? _____

## Check

9. Did the clown finish when he was supposed to? _____

## Solve Another Problem

10. If the clown's schedule changed and he doesn't have to leave until 6:00 P.M., how many more shows with breaks can the clown have?

    _____

# 5A: Graphic Organizer

**For use before Lesson 5-1**

**Study Skill** Spend time previewing the chapter. Highlight new vocabulary words and their definitions.

**Write your answers.**

1. What is the chapter title? _____

2. How many lessons are there in this chapter? _____

3. What is the topic of the Test-Taking Strategies page? _____

4. Complete the graphic organizer below as you work through the chapter.
   • In the center, write the title of the chapter.
   • When you begin a lesson, write the lesson name in a rectangle.
   • When you complete a lesson, write a skill or key concept in a circle linked to that lesson block. Use this graphic organizer to help you review the chapter.

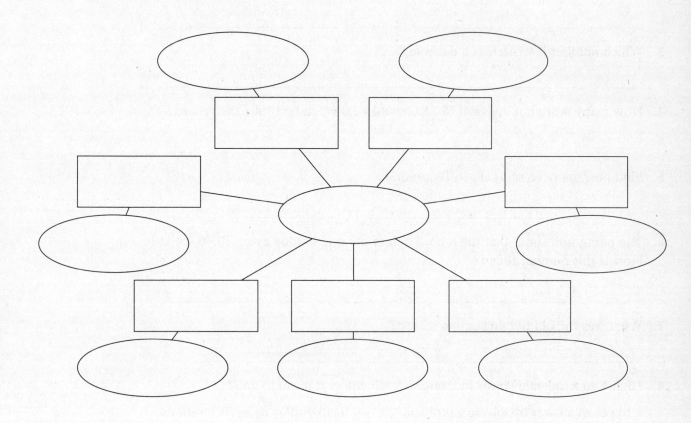

# 5B: Reading Comprehension

**Study Skill** Make a realistic study schedule which takes into account your after-school activities, homework assignments, and chores at home.

**Read the paragraph and answer the questions.**

---

Takeru Kobayashi of Japan holds the world record for hotdog eating. His old world record was $50\frac{1}{2}$ hot dogs in 12 minutes, but he recently broke that record by eating $53\frac{1}{2}$ hot dogs in 12 minutes. Mr. Kobayashi ate one hot dog every 13.46 seconds to hold on to his world record title. Mr. Kobayashi, who is 5 ft 7 in., weighed in at 131 pounds before the contest but weighed 144 pounds after the contest.

---

1. What is the greatest number in the paragraph?

   _____

2. Which numbers are written as mixed numbers?

   _____

3. Which number is written as a decimal?

   _____

4. How many *more* hot dogs did Mr. Kobayashi eat when he broke the record?

   _____

5. Find how many seconds are in 12 minutes.

   _____

6. The paragraph states that the record holder ate one hotdog every 13.46 seconds. How is this number found?

   _____

   _____

7. What was the old hot dog eating record?

   _____

8. **High-Use Academic Words** In Exercise 5, what does it mean to *find*?

   a. to get an answer by solving a problem         b. to display using illustrations

# 5C: Reading/Writing Math Symbols

**For use after Lesson 5-5**

**Study Skill** Mathematics builds on itself so build a strong foundation.

**Match each number with its word form.**

1. $9^3$

2. .030

3. 910

4. $2^5$

5. $\dfrac{12}{5}$

**A.** thirty thousandths

**B.** two raised to the fifth power

**C.** nine cubed

**D.** twelve fifths

**E.** nine hundred ten

**Write a mathematical expression for each word description**

6. seven raised to the seventh power

   _____

7. one third less than two fifths equals one fifteenth

   _____

8. twenty is equal to two squared multiplied by five

   _____

9. three less than a number to the fourth power

   _____

**Write out the following numbers in a word form.**

10. $10^3 = 10 \times 10 \times 10$ _____

11. $2^3 < 3^2$ _____

12. $45 = 3^2 \times 5$ _____

Name _____ Class _____ Date _____

# 5D: Visual Vocabulary Practice

**For use after Lesson 5-7**

**Study Skill** When you come across something you don't understand, view it as an opportunity to increase your brain power.

## Concept List

| | | |
|---|---|---|
| benchmark | elapsed time | front-end estimation |
| scatter plot | spreadsheet | Addition Property of Equality |
| Distributive Property | common factor | common multiple |

**Write the concept that best describes each exercise. Choose from the concept list above.**

| 1. 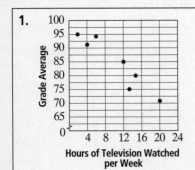 Hours of Television Watched per Week | 2. $\frac{1}{2} + 1$ can be used to estimate $\frac{9}{19} + \frac{47}{46}$. | 3. An interview started at 11:15 A.M. and ended at 1:00 P.M. One hour and 45 minutes represents this. |
|---|---|---|
| **4.** The number 54 is an example of this for the numbers 18 and 54. | **5.** <br> |   | A | B | <br>| 1 | \$1.25 | −\$8.25 | <br>| 2 | \$4.50 | −\$1.75 | <br>| 3 | \$2.75 | −\$2.50 | <br>| 4 | \$7.00 | −\$3.25 | | **6.** $2.91 + 7.94 \approx 3 + 8 = 11$ |
| **7.** If $3(x-1) - 2 = -1$, then $3(x-1) = 1$. | **8.** The number 6 is an example of this for the numbers 60 and 48. | **9.** $-12 \times (1-3) = (-12) \times 1 - (-12) \times 3$ |

# 5E: Vocabulary Check

**Study Skill** Strengthen your vocabulary. Use these pages and add cues and summaries by applying the Cornell Notetaking style.

**Write the definition for each word or term at the right. To check your work, fold the paper back along the dotted line to see the correct answers.**

_____  benchmark

_____

_____

_____  elapsed time

_____

_____

_____  term

_____

_____

_____  conjecture

_____

_____

_____  cell

_____

_____

# 5E: Vocabulary Check (continued)

**Write the vocabulary word or term for each definition. To check your work, fold the paper forward along the dotted line to see the correct answers.**

a convenient number used to
replace fractions that are less than 1

_____

the time between two events

_____

a number in a pattern

_____

a prediction that suggests what
can be expected to happen

_____

a box in a spreadsheet where a
row and a column meet

_____

Vocabulary and Study Skills

# 5F: Vocabulary Review Puzzle

**For use with the Chapter Review**

**Study Skill** Pay attention in class and when reading your text so information does not slip out of your "short-term" memory.

**Use the clues to fill in the puzzle.**

**ACROSS**

1. a mathematical sentence with an equal sign

2. can be divided by

3. an equation that is true for every value

4. the time between two events

5. the top number in a fraction

6. a value that makes an equation true

**DOWN**

1. having the same value as

2. a letter that stands for a number

3. a convenient number used to replace fractions that are less than 1

4. a mathematical phrase containing numbers and operation symbols

5. a quotient of two quantities shown as a numerator over a denominator

6. the bottom number in a fraction

# Practice 6-1

**Multiplying Fractions**

**Draw a model to find each product.**

1. $\frac{1}{6} \times \frac{3}{4}$

2. $\frac{2}{5} \times \frac{1}{2}$

**Find each product.**

3. $\frac{3}{5}$ of 10

_____

4. $\frac{1}{4}$ of 12

_____

5. $\frac{2}{3}$ of 6

_____

6. $\frac{5}{6}$ of $\frac{3}{8}$

_____

7. $\frac{3}{5}$ of $\frac{1}{2}$

_____

8. $\frac{3}{4}$ of 12

_____

9. $\frac{3}{16}$ of 8

_____

10. $\frac{1}{2} \times \frac{5}{6}$

_____

11. $\frac{3}{4} \times \frac{7}{8}$

_____

12. $\frac{3}{5}$ of $\frac{3}{4}$

_____

13. $\frac{1}{2} \cdot \frac{1}{3}$

_____

14. $\frac{1}{8} \times \frac{3}{4}$

_____

15. $\frac{2}{3}$ of $\frac{1}{4}$

_____

16. $\frac{2}{5} \cdot \frac{1}{2}$

_____

17. $\frac{1}{4}$ of $\frac{4}{5}$

_____

18. What product does the model represent?

_____

**Solve.**

19. A kitten eats $\frac{1}{4}$ cup of cat food. Another cat in the same household eats 6 times as much. How much food does the cat eat?

_____

20. You brought home $\frac{1}{2}$ of a can of paint. You then used $\frac{2}{3}$ of the paint to cover a table top. What fraction of a full can of paint did you use?

_____

# 6-1 • Guided Problem Solving

**GPS** Student Page 264, Exercise 30:

**Monuments** The width of the base of the Washington Monument is about $\frac{1}{10}$ of its height. The height of the monument is about 555 feet tall. Find the width of the base.

## Understand

1. What are you being asked to do?

   _____

2. Which word group tells you what operation to perform?

   _____

## Plan and Carry Out

3. When multiplying a fraction by a whole number how do you rewrite the whole number?

   _____

4. Write an expression to solve the problem. _____

5. Simplify the expression. _____

6. Multiply the numerators, multiply the denominators, and simplify. _____

7. What is the width of the base of the monument? _____

## Check

8. To estimate $\frac{1}{10}$ of 555, use compatible numbers. Find $\frac{1}{10}$ of 600. Is your answer reasonable?

   _____

## Solve Another Problem

9. A concert hall has 12,360 seats. For the last concert, only $\frac{2}{3}$ of the hall was full. How many seats were unused?

   _____

# Practice 6-2

**Estimate each product.**

1. $2\frac{5}{6} \times 1\frac{3}{4}$ _____

2. $3\frac{3}{8} \times 7\frac{1}{4}$ _____

3. $5\frac{3}{8} \times 2\frac{7}{8}$ _____

4. $2\frac{3}{8} \times 4\frac{4}{5}$ _____

5. $6\frac{7}{12} \times 5\frac{9}{10}$ _____

6. $7\frac{1}{3} \times 10\frac{11}{12}$ _____

**Find each product.**

7. $2\frac{5}{6} \cdot 1\frac{3}{4}$

8. $3\frac{3}{8} \cdot 7\frac{1}{4}$

9. $5\frac{3}{8} \cdot 2\frac{7}{8}$

_____

_____

_____

10. $2\frac{3}{8} \cdot 4\frac{4}{5}$

11. $12\frac{1}{4} \times 3\frac{3}{4}$

12. $8\frac{1}{6} \cdot 2\frac{1}{4}$

_____

_____

_____

13. $\frac{1}{4} \times 5\frac{2}{5}$

14. $2\frac{3}{8} \cdot \frac{4}{5}$

15. $1\frac{1}{2} \cdot 5\frac{1}{3}$

_____

_____

_____

16. $3\frac{3}{8} \times 6$

17. $\frac{3}{4} \times 1\frac{3}{5}$

18. $9\frac{3}{5} \cdot \frac{1}{3}$

_____

_____

_____

19. $1\frac{1}{4} \times 2\frac{2}{3}$

20. $1\frac{3}{5} \cdot \frac{1}{4}$

21. $6\frac{1}{4} \times 1\frac{2}{5}$

_____

_____

_____

**Solve.**

22. Deanna's cake recipe needs to be doubled for a party. How much of each ingredient should Deanna use?

| Cake Recipe | | |
|---|---|---|
| *ingredient* | *amount* | *doubled amount* |
| flour | $2\frac{1}{4}$ cups | _____ |
| sugar | $1\frac{3}{4}$ cups | _____ |
| butter | $1\frac{1}{2}$ cups | _____ |
| milk | $\frac{3}{4}$ cup | _____ |

# 6-2 • Guided Problem Solving

**GPS** Student Page 270, Exercise 28a:

A mother is $1\frac{3}{8}$ times as tall as her daughter. The girl is $1\frac{1}{3}$ times as tall as her brother. The mother is how many times as tall as her son?

## Understand

1. What are you being asked to do?

   _____

2. What do you do first when you multiply mixed numbers?

   _____

## Plan and Carry Out

3. Write an equation for the sentence "A mother is $1\frac{3}{8}$ times as tall as her daughter," where $m$ represents the height of the mother and $d$ represents the height of the daughter.

   _____

4. Write an equation for the sentence "The girl is $1\frac{1}{3}$ times as tall as her brother," where $d$ represents the height of the girl and $b$ represents the height of the brother.

   _____

5. Substitute the expression for $d$ from Step 4 for $d$ in the equation you wrote in Step 3. _____

6. Simplify by multiplying the two mixed numbers. _____

7. The mother is how many times as tall as her son? _____

## Check

8. Divide $1\frac{5}{6}$ by either $1\frac{3}{8}$ or $1\frac{1}{3}$.

   _____

## Solve Another Problem

9. Nora is building a birdhouse. The height of the birdhouse is $2\frac{1}{2}$ times the length of the birdhouse. If the length is $8\frac{2}{3}$ in., how tall is the birdhouse?

   _____

# Practice 6-3

**Dividing Fractions**

**Write the reciprocal of each number.**

**1.** $\frac{7}{10}$ _____

**2.** 4 _____

**3.** $\frac{1}{3}$ _____

**4.** Draw a diagram to show how many $\frac{3}{4}$-ft pieces of string can be cut from a piece of string $4\frac{1}{2}$ ft long.

**Find each quotient.**

**5.** $\frac{3}{10} \div \frac{4}{5}$

_____

**6.** $\frac{3}{8} \div 3$

_____

**7.** $\frac{1}{3} \div \frac{2}{7}$

_____

**8.** $\frac{1}{4} \div \frac{1}{4}$

_____

**9.** $\frac{7}{8} \div \frac{2}{7}$

_____

**10.** $\frac{1}{4} \div \frac{1}{8}$

_____

**11.** $\frac{1}{2} \div \frac{2}{5}$

_____

**12.** $\frac{8}{9} \div \frac{1}{2}$

_____

**13.** $3 \div \frac{3}{8}$

_____

**Solve.**

**14.** How many $\frac{3}{4}$-cup servings are there in a 6-cup package of rice?

_____

**15.** George cut 5 oranges into quarters. How many pieces of orange did he have?

_____

**16.** Maureen, Frank, Tashia, Zane, Eric, and Wesley are addressing envelopes for volunteer work at a local charity. They were given $\frac{3}{4}$ of an entire mailing to address to be evenly divided among six of them. What fraction of the entire mailing does each person address?

_____

# 6-3 • Guided Problem Solving

**GPS** Student Page 275, Exercise 30:

**Baking**  A recipe for a loaf of banana bread requires $\frac{2}{3}$ cup of vegetable oil. You have 3 cups of oil. How many loaves of banana bread can you make with the oil?

## Understand

1. What are you being asked to do?

   _____

   _____

2. Explain how to divide fractions.

   _____

   _____

## Plan and Carry Out

3. What number are you dividing by? Why?

   _____

4. How many cups of oil are available
   to make the banana bread? _____

5. What number are you dividing? Why?

   _____

6. Write a division expression to solve the problem. _____

7. Re-write the expression using multiplication. _____

8. Evaluate the expression. _____

9. How many loaves of banana bread can
   you make with the oil? _____

## Check

10. Multiply $\frac{2}{3} \times 4\frac{1}{2}$. Does your answer check? _____

## Solve Another Problem

11. Greg bought 24 bags of mulch for the planters in his front yard. If each
    planter uses $\frac{3}{4}$ bag, how many planters can he fill with mulch?

    _____

# Practice 6-4

**Estimate each quotient.**

1. $\frac{4}{5} \div \frac{7}{8}$

2. $2\frac{3}{7} \div \frac{5}{6}$

3. $12\frac{3}{8} \div 3\frac{3}{4}$

4. $\frac{1}{8} \div \frac{11}{12}$

5. $17\frac{11}{13} \div 2\frac{7}{9}$

6. $51\frac{1}{5} \div 4\frac{9}{10}$

**Find each quotient.**

7. $1\frac{4}{5} \div \frac{1}{3}$

8. $1\frac{2}{3} \div \frac{1}{8}$

9. $3\frac{4}{7} \div 3\frac{1}{2}$

10. $\frac{2}{5} \div 4\frac{3}{5}$

11. $4\frac{1}{8} \div \frac{3}{7}$

12. $2\frac{4}{5} \div 4\frac{3}{4}$

13. $1\frac{5}{7} \div 1\frac{2}{3}$

14. $\frac{1}{3} \div 2\frac{1}{6}$

15. $1\frac{4}{9} \div \frac{6}{7}$

16. $\frac{1}{2} \div 3\frac{1}{4}$

17. $\frac{1}{4} \div 1\frac{5}{9}$

18. $1\frac{1}{2} \div 1\frac{2}{3}$

**Anna bought a strip of fabric 10 yd long. She needs a $1\frac{1}{3}$-yd piece to make a pillow.**

19. How many pillows can Anna make?

_____

20. Anna decides to make smaller pillows using $\frac{2}{3}$-yd pieces.
    How many small pillows can she make?

_____

# 6-4 • Guided Problem Solving

**GPS** **Student Page 279, Exercise 22:**

**Construction** An attic ceiling 24 feet wide needs insulation. Each strip of insulation is $1\frac{1}{3}$ feet wide. Estimate the number of insulation strips that are needed.

## Understand

1. What are you being asked to do?

   _____

   _____

2. Which number(s) will you round to estimate?

   _____

   _____

## Plan and Carry Out

3. To what number do you round $1\frac{1}{3}$?

   _____

4. Divide 24 by the rounded number. What is the result?

   _____

5. Approximately how many strips do you need?

   _____

## Check

6. How do you check your answer?

   _____

   _____

## Solve Another Problem

7. A closet bar is $8\frac{3}{4}$ in. long. If a standard shirt is $1\frac{1}{2}$ in. wide, estimate how many shirts can you hang on the bar?

   _____

# Practice 6-5

**Solve each equation. Check the solution.**

**1.** $\frac{n}{4} = \frac{1}{2}$  

**2.** $\frac{x}{7} = 6$  

**3.** $\frac{y}{19} = 3$

$n =$ _____  

$x =$ _____  

$y =$ _____

**4.** $\frac{m}{18} = 2$  

**5.** $\frac{n}{8} = 1$  

**6.** $\frac{n}{30} = \frac{3}{5}$

$m =$ _____  

$n =$ _____  

$n =$ _____

**7.** $\frac{3}{7}q = \frac{3}{8}$  

**8.** $\frac{5}{14}c = \frac{1}{2}$  

**9.** $\frac{3}{2}b = \frac{6}{7}$

$q =$ _____  

$c =$ _____  

$b =$ _____

**10.** $\frac{1}{4}n = 2$  

**11.** $\frac{7}{8}t = 3$  

**12.** $\frac{5}{12}h = \frac{3}{5}$

$n =$ _____  

$t =$ _____  

$h =$ _____

**13.** $\frac{4}{9}v = \frac{1}{4}$  

**14.** $\frac{8}{25}h = 2$  

**15.** $\frac{10}{7}h = \frac{1}{2}$

$v =$ _____  

$h =$ _____  

$h =$ _____

**Solve.**

**16.** The largest U.S. standard postage stamp ever issued has a width of about 1 inch, which was $\frac{3}{4}$ of the height of the stamp. Write and solve an equation to find the height of the stamp.

_____

_____

**17.** Candace said, "I'm thinking of a fraction. If I divide it by $\frac{1}{2}$, I get $\frac{3}{11}$." What fraction was Candace thinking of?

_____

_____

# 6-5 • Guided Problem Solving

**GPS** Student Page 285, Exercise 26:

**Shopping** The price of a shirt is $\frac{5}{6}$ the price of a pair of pants. The shirt costs $12.50. How much do the pants cost?

## Understand

1. What are you being asked to do?

   _____

2. Define a variable to represent the unknown.

   _____

3. Fill in the boxes with the correct information.

## Plan and Carry Out

4. Write an expression for the phrase "$\frac{5}{6}$ the price of the pants" if the pants cost $p$ dollars. _____

5. How much does the shirt cost? _____

6. Write an equation to solve the problem. _____

7. What do you do to both sides of the equation to solve for $p$? _____

8. Solve the equation. _____

9. How much did the pants cost? _____

## Check

10. Determine if 12.50 is $\frac{5}{6}$ of 15.

    _____

## Solve Another Problem

11. Lupe and Carlos are $\frac{1}{4}$ of the way done painting their new house. So far they have used $6\frac{2}{3}$ cans of paint. How many cans of paint will they use to paint the entire house?

    _____

Name _____ Class _____ Date _____

# Practice 6-6

The Customary System

Use the table to choose an appropriate unit of measurement for each item. Explain.

## Customary Units of Measure

| | Name | Approximate Comparison |
|---|---|---|
| Length | inch | Length of a soda bottle cap |
| | foot | Length of an adult male's foot |
| | mile | Length of 14 football fields |
| Weight | ounce | Weight of a slice of bread |
| | pound | Weight of a loaf of bread |
| | ton | Weight of two grand pianos |
| Capacity | cup | Amount of water in a drinking glass |
| | quart | Amount in a bottle of fruit punch |
| | gallon | Amount in a large can of paint |

**1.** height of a stop sign

_____

_____

**2.** length of a leaf

_____

_____

**3.** width of a door

_____

_____

**4.** depth of the ocean

_____

_____

**5.** weight of a small notebook

_____

_____

**6.** weight of a couch

_____

_____

**7.** water in a swimming pool

_____

_____

**8.** water in a bathtub

_____

_____

**Compare using <, =, or >.**

**9.** water you use to wash dishes ☐ 1 cup

**10.** the depth of the Grand Canyon ☐ 30 miles

**11.** the weight of a cereal bowl ☐ 6 ounces

# 6-6 • Guided Problem Solving

**Prehistoric Creatures** Scientists discovered the fossil of a huge African crocodile that was more than 40 feet long. About how many door widths are equal to the length of the crocodile?

## Understand

1. What are you being asked to do?

   _____

   _____

2. What information do you need to answer the question?

   _____

   _____

## Plan and Carry Out

3. What is a reasonable estimate for the width of a door? _____

4. What units should you use when estimating a door's width in this problem? Explain. _____

   _____

   _____

5. Divide the length of the crocodile by the width of the door.

   _____

## Check

6. Use a yardstick to measure the width of your classroom's door. Was your estimate close?

   _____

## Solve Another Problem

7. Marie is 68 in. tall and her boyfriend Mario is 6 ft 2 in. tall. Who is taller? Explain.

   _____

   _____

# Practice 6-7

**Complete each statement.**

1. $7\frac{1}{2}$ ft = _____ yd

2. 45 in. = _____ ft

3. 28 fl oz = _____ c

4. $2\frac{3}{4}$ T = _____ lb

5. 3 lb = _____ oz

6. 10 pt = _____ qt

**Add or subtract.**

7.     8 ft 3 in.
  − 3 ft 5 in.
  _____

8.     12 qt 1 pt
  + 11 qt 1 pt
  _____

9.     9 yd 15 in.
  + 7 yd 28 in.
  _____

10.     105 lb  8 oz
  − 98 lb 12 oz
  _____

11.     3 c 7 fl oz
  + 4 c 6 fl oz
  _____

12.     13 yd 2 ft
  − 6 yd 1 ft
  _____

**Solve.**

13. The odometer of an automobile shows tenths of a mile. How many feet are in $\frac{1}{10}$ mi?

_____

14. How many inches are in one mile?

_____

15. Jarel bought 3 containers of cottage cheese, each weighing 24 oz. How many pounds did she buy?

_____

**Use <, =, or > to complete each statement.**

16. $4\frac{1}{3}$ ft ☐ 50 in.

17. 136 oz ☐ $8\frac{1}{2}$ lb

18. 26 fl oz ☐ 3 c

# 6-7 • Guided Problem Solving

**GPS** **Student Page 295, Exercise 32:**

**Costume Design**  A costume designer makes a figure skater's costume. The designer needs two 34-inch strips of fabric. How many yards of fabric does the designer need?

## Understand

1. Circle the information you will need to solve.

2. What are you being asked to do?

_____

_____

3. How many inches are in a yard?

_____

## Plan and Carry Out

4. How many strips of fabric does she need? _____

5. How long does each strip need to be? _____

6. How many inches of fabric do you need total? _____

7. How do you convert this into yards? _____

8. How many yards is it exactly?

_____

9. How many whole yards of fabric does she need? _____

## Check

10. Approximately how many yards is each strip? Is your answer reasonable? Explain.

_____

_____

## Solve Another Problem

11. Jessica is making fruit juice and it calls for 6 pints of water. Jessica only has a 2-quart pitcher. Will her fruit juice fit in the pitcher? Explain.

_____

_____

# 6A: Graphic Organizer

**Study Skill** As you read over the material in the chapter, keep a paper and pencil handy to write down notes and questions that you have.

**Write your answers.**

1. What is the chapter title? _____

2. How many lessons are there in this chapter? _____

3. What is the topic of the Test-Taking Strategies page?

   _____

4. Complete the graphic organizer below as you work through the chapter.
   • In the center, write the title of the chapter.
   • When you begin a lesson, write the lesson name in a rectangle.
   • When you complete a lesson, write a skill or key concept in a circle linked to that lesson block.
   • When you complete the chapter, use this graphic organizer to help you review.

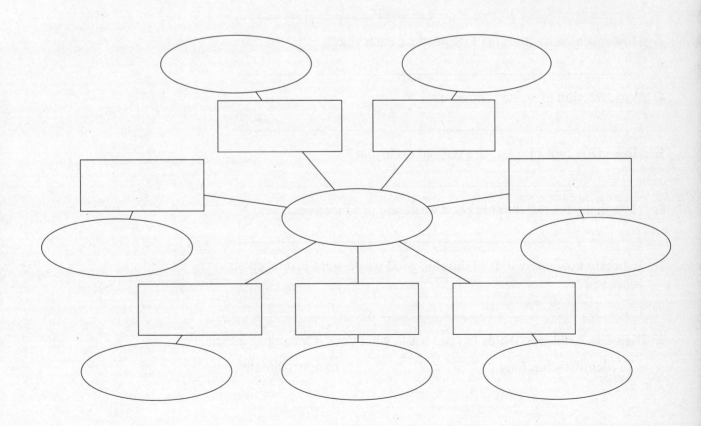

# 6B: Reading Comprehension

For use after Lesson 6-2

**Study Skill** Attitude is everything.

**Read the paragraph below and answer the questions that follow.**

> The amount of solid waste produced by the United States has doubled in the last 30 years. Solid waste is the trash you create every day. One tenth of this trash is food and yard waste, $\frac{7}{25}$ is containers and packaging, $\frac{8}{25}$ is durable goods, and $\frac{3}{10}$ is nondurable goods. Durable goods are things like washing machines that are made to last a long time. Nondurable goods are not made to last long, like newspapers and napkins. In recent years, Americans have produced more than 232 million tons of trash a year. Most of our waste is disposed of in landfills, about $\frac{3}{20}$ is burned, and another $\frac{3}{10}$ is recycled.

1. How is most of the waste produced in the U.S. disposed of?

   _____

2. What fraction of solid waste is disposed of in this way?

   _____

3. How much waste does the U.S. produce each year?

   _____

4. What fraction of waste is burned?

   _____

5. How many tons of waste are burned each year?

   _____

6. How many tons of durable good waste are produced each year?

   _____

7. Estimate how many tons of durable good waste were produced 30 years ago.

   _____

8. **High-Use Academic Words** In Exercise 7, what does it mean to *estimate*?

   a. to identify something                    b. to approximate

# 6C: Reading/Writing Math Symbols

For use after Lesson 6-5

**Study Skill** Write assignments down; do not try to rely only on your memory.

**Match the customary units in Column A with the appropriate abbreviation in Column B.**

| Column A | | Column B | |
|---|---|---|---|
| **1.** ounces | | **A.** c | |
| **2.** feet | | **B.** yd | |
| **3.** pounds | | **C.** qt | |
| **4.** cup | | **D.** ft | |
| **5.** inches | | **E.** in. | |
| **6.** quart | | **F.** oz | |
| **7.** yards | | **G.** T | |
| **8.** tons | | **H.** lb | |

**Write out the measurements without using abbreviations.**

**9.** 14 ft 3 in. _____

**10.** 6 lb 3 oz _____

**11.** 2 gal 9 qt _____

**12.** 3 pt 1 c _____

**13.** 1 mi 1000 yd _____

**14.** 4 T 300 lb _____

**15.** 4 qt 10 oz _____

**16.** 7 yd 2 ft _____

# 6D: Visual Vocabulary Practice

**For use after Lesson 6-6**

*High-Use Academic Words*

**Study Skill** When making a sketch, make it simple but make it complete.

## Concept List

| | | |
|---|---|---|
| equivalent | model | convert |
| graph | locate | notation |
| calculate | pattern | verify |

**Write the concept that best describes each exercise. Choose from the concept list above.**

---

**1.**

$$1 \text{ mi} = 5{,}280 \text{ ft}$$

_____

**2.**

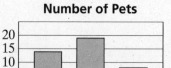

**Number of Pets**

_____

**3.**

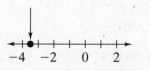

_____

**4.**

$$\left(\tfrac{1}{2} - 3\right) \div \tfrac{1}{2} = \left(\tfrac{-5}{2}\right) \div \tfrac{1}{2}$$
$$= \left(\tfrac{-5}{2}\right) \times 2 = -5$$

_____

**5.**

$$\tfrac{9}{27} \text{ and } \tfrac{1}{3}$$

_____

**6.**

If $6n - 2 = -\tfrac{1}{2}$,
then $n = \tfrac{1}{4}$.

$$\left(6 \times \tfrac{1}{4}\right) - 2 = 1\tfrac{1}{2} - 2 = -\tfrac{1}{2}$$

_____

**7.**

$$3.589 \times 10^5$$

_____

**8.**

$$1, \quad 2, \quad 4, \quad 7, \quad 11$$
$$+1 \quad +2 \quad +3 \quad +4$$

_____

**9.**

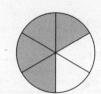

_____

# 6E: Vocabulary Check

**Study Skill** Strengthen your vocabulary. Use these pages and add cues and summaries by applying the Cornell Notetaking style.

**Write the definition for each word or term at the right. To check your work, fold the paper back along the dotted line to see the correct answers.**

_____ reciprocals

_____

_____

_____ frequency table

_____

_____

_____ Customary System

_____

_____

_____ convert

_____

_____

_____ spreadsheet

_____

_____

Vocabulary and Study Skills

# 6E: Vocabulary Check (continued)

**Write the vocabulary word or term for each definition. To check your work, fold the paper back along the dotted line to see the correct answers.**

two numbers whose product is 1

_____

a table that lists each item in a data set with the number of times the item occurs

_____

a system of measurement used in the United States

_____

to change from one unit of measure to another

_____

a tool used for organizing data, arranged in numbered rows and lettered columns

_____

# 6F: Vocabulary Review Puzzle

For use with the Chapter Review

**Study Skill** Take notes while you study. They will provide you with a helpful outline when you study for a quiz or test.

**Complete the crossword puzzle. For help, use the glossary in your textbook.**

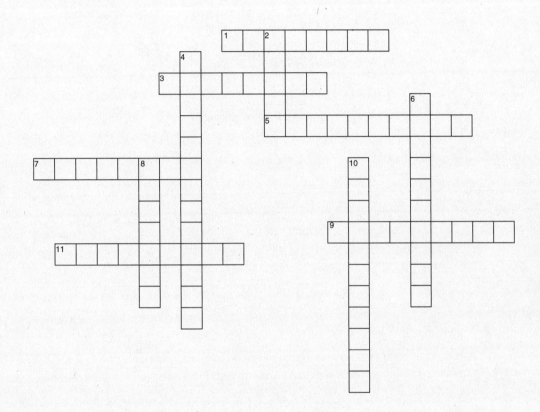

## ACROSS

1. a fraction whose numerator is greater than or equal to its denominator

3. a number that makes an equation true

5. fractions or decimals that name the same amount

7. a number that can be used to indicate part of a whole

9. a whole number greater than one with more than two factors

11. the top number in a fraction

## DOWN

2. a whole number with only two factors—one and itself

4. factors that are the same for two or more numbers

6. one of two numbers whose product is 1

8. operations that undo one another

10. the bottom number in a fraction

# Practice 7-1

**Write each ratio in three ways.**

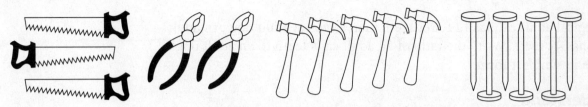

**1.** saws to pliers

_____

**2.** hammers to nails

_____

**3.** saws to nails

_____

**4.** nails to saws

_____

**5.** hammers to pliers

_____

**6.** pliers to saws

_____

**Write each ratio as a fraction in simplest form.**

**7.** pencils : squares

_____

**8.** flowers : pencils

_____

**9.** pencils : flowers

_____

**10.** squares : flowers

_____

**Find the value that makes the ratios equal.**

**11.** 4 to 10, 2 to __?__

_____

**12.** 8 : 3, __?__ : 9

_____

**13.** 51 to 18, __?__ to 6

_____

**14.** $\frac{12}{12}$, $\frac{?}{20}$

_____

**15.** 98 : 46, 49 : __?__

_____

**16.** $\frac{15}{7}$, $\frac{?}{21}$

_____

# 7-1 • Guided Problem Solving

**GPS** **Student Page 309, Exercise 29:**

A typical adult cat has 12 fewer teeth than a typical adult dog. An adult dog has 42 teeth. Write the ratio of an adult cat's teeth to an adult dog's teeth in simplest form.

## Understand

1. What are you being asked to do?

   _____

   _____

2. What does "in simplest form" mean?

   _____

   _____

## Plan and Carry Out

3. Which number goes in the numerator, cat's teeth or dog's teeth? _____

4. How many teeth does a typical adult cat have? _____

5. Write the ratio of cat's teeth to dog's teeth. _____

6. What is the greatest common factor of the numerator and denominator? _____

7. Rewrite the ratio using the greatest common factor. _____

8. Simplify the ratio. _____

## Check

9. Which have fewer teeth, cats or dogs? Does this agree with your ratio? Explain.

   _____

   _____

## Solve Another Problem

10. The faculty softball league has 56 female players and 84 male players. Write the ratio of female players to male players in simplest form.

    _____

# Practice 7-2

**Find the unit rate for each situation.**

1. 44 breaths in 2 minutes

     _____

2. 72 players on 9 teams

     _____

3. 60 miles in 2 hours

     _____

4. 15 pages in 30 minutes

     _____

**Write the unit rate as a ratio. Then find an equal ratio.**

5. There are 12 inches in a foot. Find the number of inches in 6 feet.

6. The cost is $8.50 for 1 shirt. Find the cost of 4 shirts.

7. There are 365 days in a year. Find the number of days in 3 years.

8. There are 6 cans per box. Find the number of cans in 11 boxes.

9. There are 5 students in a group. Find the number of students in 5 groups.

**Find each unit price.**

10. $5 for 10 pounds

     _____

11. 40 ounces for $12

     _____

12. $6 for 10 pens

     _____

13. $60 for 5 books

     _____

# 7-2 • Guided Problem Solving

**GPS** **Student Page 315, Exercise 22:**

**Jump Rope** Crystal jumps 255 times in 3 minutes. The United States record for 11-year-olds is 882 jumps in 3 minutes.

a. Find Crystal's unit rate for jumps per minute.

b. Find the record holder's unit rate for jumps per minute.

c. How many more times per minute did the record holder jump than Crystal?

## Understand

1. What are you being asked to do in part (a) and part (b)?

   _____

   _____

2. What is a unit rate?

   _____

   _____

## Plan and Carry Out

3. What is Crystal's rate? _____

4. What is Crystal's unit rate? _____

5. What is the record holder's rate? _____

6. What is the record holder's unit rate? _____

7. How many more times did the record holder jump per minute?

   _____

## Check

8. How can you check your answer for parts (a) and (b)?

   _____

   _____

## Solve Another Problem

9. Mike can make 60 egg sandwiches in 1.25 hours. What is his unit rate?

   _____

Guided Problem Solving

Name _____ Class _____ Date _____

# Practice 7-3

**Do the ratios in each pair form a proportion?**

1. $\frac{8}{9}$, $\frac{4}{3}$

   _____

2. $\frac{20}{16}$, $\frac{18}{15}$

   _____

3. $\frac{18}{12}$, $\frac{21}{14}$

   _____

4. $\frac{21}{27}$, $\frac{35}{45}$

   _____

5. $\frac{18}{22}$, $\frac{45}{55}$

   _____

6. $\frac{38}{52}$, $\frac{57}{80}$

   _____

**Find the value that completes each proportion.**

7. $\frac{4}{5} = \frac{?}{15}$

   _____

8. $\frac{8}{?} = \frac{4}{15}$

   _____

9. $\frac{3}{2} = \frac{21}{?}$

   _____

10. $\frac{?}{5} = \frac{32}{20}$

   _____

11. $\frac{7}{8} = \frac{?}{32}$

   _____

12. $\frac{5}{4} = \frac{15}{?}$

   _____

**Solve.**

13. In 1910, there were about 220 families for every 1,000 people in the United States. If a certain town had a population of 56,000, about how many families would you expect to find in the town?

    _____

    _____

14. For every 100 families with TV sets, about 12 families like watching sports. In a town of 23,400 families who all have TV sets, how many families would you expect to like watching sports?

    _____

    _____

# 7-3 • Guided Problem Solving

GPS **Student Page 318, Exercise 21:**

**Cooking** A recipe calls for 2 cups of flour to make 3 dozen cookies. Is 3 cups of flour enough to make 60 cookies? Explain.

## Understand

1. Circle the relevant information in the problem.

2. What are you being asked to do?

   _____

## Plan and Carry Out

3. How many cookies are in 3 dozen? _____

4. Write a ratio comparing 2 cups of flour and the number of cookies in 3 dozen.

   _____

5. Write a ratio comparing 3 cups of flour and an unknown number of cookies.

   _____

6. Write a proportion using the ratios from Steps 4 and 5.

   _____

7. Find the value that completes the proportion. _____

8. How many cookies will 3 cups of flour make? _____

9. Are 3 cups of flour enough to make 60 cookies? Explain.

   _____

## Check

10. Write a proportion between the ratio in Step 4 and a ratio comparing an unknown amount of flour to 60 cookies. Solve this proportion. How many cups of flour are needed to make 60 cookies? Is this number greater than 3?

   _____

## Solve Another Problem

11. Twelve cans of chicken soup contain 48 servings. How many servings do 8 cans of soup contain?

   _____

# Practice 7-4

**Does each pair of ratios form a proportion?**

1. $\frac{14}{21}, \frac{8}{12}$ _____

2. $\frac{12}{18}, \frac{16}{24}$ _____

3. $\frac{24}{25}, \frac{12}{15}$ _____

4. $\frac{28}{42}, \frac{26}{39}$ _____

**Solve each proportion.**

5. $\frac{9}{7} = \frac{27}{x}$

6. $\frac{17}{12} = \frac{34}{y}$

_____

_____

7. $\frac{6}{a} = \frac{36}{54}$

8. $\frac{m}{25} = \frac{9}{75}$

_____

_____

9. $\frac{31}{c} = \frac{93}{15}$

10. $\frac{14}{35} = \frac{m}{5}$

_____

_____

**Write and solve a proportion for each problem.**

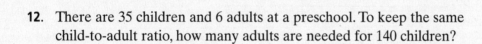

11. It costs $15 to buy 5 packs of baseball cards. How much will it cost to buy 25 packs of baseball cards?

_____

_____

12. There are 35 children and 6 adults at a preschool. To keep the same child-to-adult ratio, how many adults are needed for 140 children?

_____

_____

13. Sam is making dinner for four people. The recipe calls for 15 ounces of steak for 4 people. How much steak will he need if he makes dinner for 10 people?

_____

_____

14. Brenda is selling magazine subscriptions. Two subscriptions sell for $15.99. How much will 8 subscriptions cost?

_____

_____

# 7-4 • Guided Problem Solving

**GPS** Student Page 323, Exercise 25:

**Printing** Your friend has a poster printed from a photograph that is 4 inches wide by 6 inches long. The poster is 22 inches wide and is proportional to the photograph. What is the length of the poster?

## Understand

1. Circle the information you will need to solve.

2. What does it mean to be *proportional* to the photograph?

   _____

   _____

## Plan and Carry Out

3. Write a ratio comparing 4 inches and 6 inches. _____

4. Write a ratio comparing 22 inches and an unknown length. _____

5. Write a proportion using the two ratios from Steps 3 and 4. _____

6. Use cross products to find the value that completes the proportion. _____

7. How long will the poster be? _____

## Check

8. How can you check your answer? Does your answer check?

   _____

   _____

## Solve Another Problem

9. You need to have a picture enlarged for a birthday party. The original picture is 3 inches long by 5 inches wide. You need the enlarged picture to be 15 inches wide. How long should the picture be if it is going to be proportional to the original picture?

   _____

   _____

# Practice 7-5

· · · · · · · · · · · · · · · · · · · · · · · · · · · · · · · · · · · · · · · · · · · · · · · · · · · · · ·

**Use a ruler to measure the scale drawing. Then find the dimensions of the actual object with the given scale.**

1.

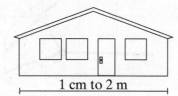

1 cm to 2 m

_____

2.

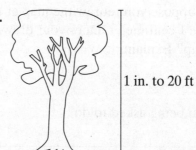

1 in. to 20 ft

_____

3.

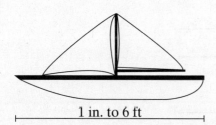

1 in. to 6 ft

_____

4.

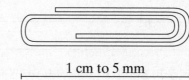

1 cm to 5 mm

_____

5.

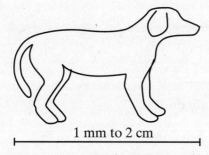

1 mm to 2 cm

_____

6.

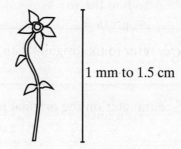

1 mm to 1.5 cm

_____

**Solve.**

7. The length of a wall in a floor plan is $6\frac{1}{2}$ inches. The actual wall is 78 feet long. Find the scale of the floor plan.

_____

8. The height of a building is $3\frac{3}{8}$ inches on a scale drawing. Find the actual height of the building if the scale used is 1 inch : 4 feet.

_____

# 7-5 • Guided Problem Solving

**Student Page 329, Exercise 21a:**

**Number Sense** Suppose you redraw the map at the right using a scale of 0.5 centimeter : 1 centimeter. Does your drawing enlarge or reduce the size of the map? Explain.

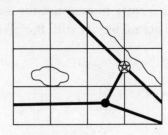

## Understand

1. What are you being asked to do?

   _____

   _____

2. What is a scale?

   _____

   _____

3. What scale are you going to use to redraw the map?

   _____

## Plan and Carry Out

4. Does *0.5 centimeter* refer to the original map or the new map?

   _____

5. Does *1 centimeter* refer to the original map or the new map?

   _____

6. A length of 0.5 centimeter on the original map will be how long on your map?

   _____

7. Does your drawing enlarge or reduce the size of the map?

   _____

## Check

8. Suppose a road is 3 cm long on the original map. How long would it be on your map? Does that agree with your answer?

   _____

## Solve Another Problem

9. You are going to redraw a painting exactly as it is in the original. What is the scale?

   _____

# Practice 7-6

**Percents, Fractions, and Decimals**

**Write each percent as a decimal and as a fraction in simplest form.**

**1.** 46% _____  **2.** 17% _____  **3.** 90% _____

**Write each decimal as a percent and as a fraction in simplest form.**

**4.** 0.02 _____  **5.** 0.45 _____  **6.** 0.4 _____

**Write each fraction as a decimal and as a percent.**

**7.** $\frac{3}{5}$ _____  **8.** $\frac{7}{10}$ _____  **9.** $\frac{13}{25}$ _____

**The table shows the fraction of students who participated in extracurricular activities from 1965 to 2000. Complete the table by writing each fraction as a percent.**

### Students' Extracurricular Choices

| Year | 1965 | 1970 | 1975 | 1980 | 1985 | 1990 | 1995 | 2000 |
|------|------|------|------|------|------|------|------|------|
| Student participation (fraction) | $\frac{3}{4}$ | $\frac{8}{10}$ | $\frac{17}{20}$ | $\frac{39}{50}$ | $\frac{21}{25}$ | $\frac{19}{25}$ | $\frac{87}{100}$ | $\frac{9}{10}$ |
| Student participation (percent) | | | | | | | | |

**Write each fraction or decimal as a percent. Write the percent (without the percent sign) in the puzzle.**

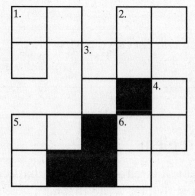

**ACROSS**

**1.** $\frac{3}{5}$

**2.** $\frac{1}{5}$

**3.** 0.55

**4.** $\frac{1}{100}$

**5.** 0.23

**6.** $\frac{7}{20}$

**DOWN**

**1.** $\frac{13}{20}$

**2.** 0.25

**3.** $\frac{1}{2}$

**4.** $\frac{3}{20}$

**5.** 0.24

**6.** $\frac{3}{10}$

# 7-6 • Guided Problem Solving

**Biology** At least ninety-nine percent of all the kinds of plants and animals that have ever lived are now extinct. Write ninety-nine percent as a fraction and as a decimal.

## Understand

1. What percent of plants and animals are extinct?

   _____

2. A percent is a ratio of a number to what other number?

   _____

## Plan and Carry Out

3. Ninety-nine percent means 99 out of what number?

   _____

4. Write this number as a fraction.

   _____

5. Which decimal place is the hundredths place?

   _____

6. Write ninety-nine percent as a decimal.

   _____

## Check

7. Explain how you can check your answer.

   _____

   _____

## Solve Another Problem

8. Sixty-one percent of a school's students participate in extra-curricular activities. Write this number as a fraction and as a decimal.

   _____

# Practice 7-7

**Find each answer.**

**1.** 15% of 20

**2.** 40% of 80

**3.** 20% of 45

_____

_____

_____

**4.** 90% of 120

**5.** 65% of 700

**6.** 25% of 84

_____

_____

_____

**7.** 60% of 50

**8.** 45% of 90

**9.** 12% of 94

_____

_____

_____

**10.** 37% of 80

**11.** 25% of 16

**12.** 63% of 800

_____

_____

_____

**Solve each problem.**

**13.** Teri used 60% of 20 gallons of paint. How much did she use?

_____

**14.** The Badgers won 75% of their 32 games this year. How many games did they win?

_____

**15.** A survey of the students at Lakeside School yielded the results shown below. There are 1,400 students enrolled at Lakeside School. Complete the table for the number of students in each activity.

### How Lakeside Students Spend Their Time on Saturday

| Activity | Percent of Students | Number of Students |
|---|---|---|
| Baby-sitting | 22% | $0.22 \times 1,400 = 308$ |
| Sports | 26% | |
| Job | 15% | |
| At home | 10% | |
| Tutoring | 10% | |
| Other | 17% | |

# 7-7 • Guided Problem Solving

**GPS** **Student Page 339, Exercise 34a:**

**Vision** In the United States, about 46% of the population wear glasses or contact lenses. A sample of 85 people is taken.

   **a.** About how many people would you expect to wear glasses or contact lenses?

## Understand

1. Circle the information you will need to solve.

2. What are you being asked to do?

   _____

   _____

3. What method can you use to solve this problem?

   _____

## Plan and Carry Out

4. Write 46% as a ratio. _____

5. Write a ratio comparing the
   unknown out of 85 people. _____

6. Write a proportion using the
   two ratios from Steps 4 and 5. _____

7. Solve the proportion for the unknown. _____

8. About how many people would you expect
   to wear glasses or contact lenses? _____

## Check

9. How can you check your answer? Does your answer check?

   _____

   _____

## Solve Another Problem

10. About 77% of all band members received either an A or a B on
    the last test. If this trend continues throughout the entire school of
    1,260 students, about how many students do you expect to receive
    A's or B's?

    _____

© Pearson Education, Inc., publishing as Pearson Prentice Hall.

Name _____ Class _____ Date _____

# Practice 7-8

**Sketch a circle graph for the given percents.**

**1.** Favorite Foods

| Pizza | Spaghetti | Hamburger |
|-------|-----------|-----------|
| 60%   | 30%       | 10%       |

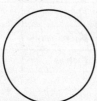

**2.** Favorite Type of Book

| Animal | Sports | Adventure | Mystery |
|--------|--------|-----------|---------|
| 20%    | 25%    | 10%       | 45%     |

**3.** Favorite Color

| Blue | Purple | Red |
|------|--------|-----|
| 40%  | 35%    | 25% |

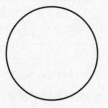

**4.** Favorite Sport

| Swimming | Softball | Soccer | Hockey |
|----------|----------|--------|--------|
| 20%      | 30%      | 5%     | 45%    |

**Use the circle graph for Exercises 5–6.**

**5.** Which element is found in the greatest quantity in the body?

_____

_____

**6.** List the three elements, from least to greatest quantity.

_____

_____

**Major Elements Found in the Body**

Oxygen

Other

Hydrogen

Carbon

# 7-8 • Guided Problem Solving

**GPS** **Student Page 343, Exercise 16:**

**Science** The human body is made up of 21 chemical elements. Use the table at the right to make a circle graph.

**Human Body Composition**

| Element | Percent |
|---------|---------|
| Oxygen | 65 |
| Carbon | 18 |
| Hydrogen | 10 |
| Nitrogen | 3 |
| Other | 4 |

## Understand

1. How do you determine how much of the circle each element gets?

_____

## Plan and Carry Out

2. Approximately how much of the circle should oxygen represent?

_____

3. Approximately how much of the circle should carbon represent?

_____

4. Approximately how much of the circle should hydrogen represent?

_____

5. Draw the circle graph.

## Check

6. Why should oxygen take up most of the graph?

_____

## Solve Another Problem

7. The bake sale profits came from the sale of cookies (52%), brownies (24%), pies (12%), and cupcakes (12%). Make a circle graph to show the components of the bake sale's profits.

Guided Problem Solving

# Practice 7-9

**Estimate each amount.**

1. 81% of 60

   _____

2. 20% of 490

   _____

3. 48% of 97

   _____

4. 72% of 80

   _____

5. 18% of 90

   _____

6. 21% of 80

   _____

7. 39% of 200

   _____

8. 81% of 150

   _____

**Solve each problem.**

9. Mr. Andropolis wants to leave the waitress a 12% tip. Estimate the tip he should leave if the family's bill is $32.46.

   _____

   _____

10. Michael receives a 9.8% raise. He currently earns $1,789.46 per month. Estimate the amount by which his monthly earnings will increase.

    _____

    _____

11. Estimate the sales tax and final cost of a book that costs $12.95 with a sales tax of 6%.

    _____

    _____

12. A jacket costs $94.95. It is on sale for 30% off. Estimate the sale price.

    _____

    _____

# 7-9 • Guided Problem Solving

**GPS** **Student Page 350, Exercise 20:**

**Jobs** You get the following tips. Estimate the value of each tip.

a. 20% of $14.20        b. 10% of $24.75

c. 15% of $19.70        d. Which tip has the greatest value?

## Understand

1. What is the easiest way to find 10% of an amount?

   _____

## Plan and Carry Out

2. Estimate 10% of $24.75. _____

3. What is the relationship
   between 10% and 20%? _____

4. How do you use 10% in order to find 20%?

   _____

5. Estimate 20% of $14.20. _____

6. What is the relationship between 10%, 20%, and 15%?

   _____

7. How can you use 10% and 20% of an amount to find 15% of an
   amount?

   _____

   _____

8. Estimate 15% of $19.70.

   _____

   _____

## Check

9. Which tip had the greatest value? Explain.

   _____

## Solve Another Problem

10. Estimate 15% of $24.80 and determine if it is more or less than
    20% of $22.40.

    _____

# 7A: Graphic Organizer

**For use before Lesson 7-1**

**Study Skill** Preview the chapter material. Make a list of new formulas, properties, and vocabulary. Add to this list as your teacher covers each new concept.

**Write your answers.**

1. What is the chapter title? _____

2. How many lessons are there in this chapter? _____

3. What is the topic of the Test-Taking Strategies page? _____

4. Complete the graphic organizer below as you work through the chapter.
   • In the center, write the title of the chapter.
   • When you begin a lesson, write the lesson name in a rectangle.
   • When you complete a lesson, write a skill or key concept in a circle linked to that lesson block. When you complete the chapter, use this graphic organizer to help you review.

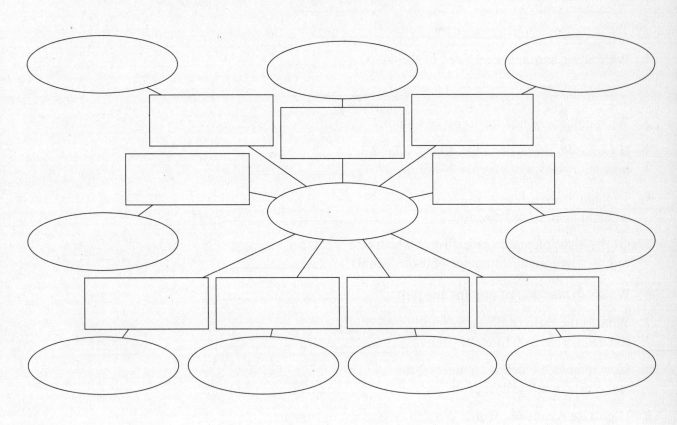

# 7B: Reading Comprehension

**Study Skill** Use tables and charts when you need to organize complex information.

Food coloring comes in red, blue, green, and yellow colors. By mixing these standard colors, you can make many different colors.

**Use the chart below to answer the questions.**

### Number of Drops Required

| Blended Shades | RED | YELLOW | BLUE | GREEN |
|---|---|---|---|---|
| Turquoise | 0 | 0 | 4 | 1 |
| Brown | 7 | 4 | 0 | 2 |
| Grape | 5 | 0 | 1 | 0 |
| Lime | 0 | 3 | 0 | 1 |
| Pistachio | 0 | 1 | 0 | 4 |
| Orange | 2 | 3 | 0 | 0 |
| Peach | 1 | 2 | 0 | 0 |
| Salmon | 3 | 2 | 0 | 0 |

1. What information is contained in the chart?

   _____

2. What colors are needed to make salmon? _____

3. If you use 6 drops of yellow to make lime,
   how many drops of green will you need? _____

4. To make brown, how many colors
   will you need to mix together? _____

5. Of the eight blended shades listed, which one
   requires the greatest number of drops (total)? _____

6. Which shades do not require any red? _____

7. What is the ratio of blue drops to
   red drops required to make grape? _____

8. How many total drops are needed to
   make brown if 8 yellow drops are used? _____

9. **High-Use Academic Words** What does it mean to *organize*
   information, as mentioned in the study skill?

   a. to arrange information so that      b. to store information on
      it is more easily understood            a computer

# 7C: Reading/Writing Math Symbols

**For use after Lesson 7-5**

**Study Skill** Use word clues such as rhyming words and pictures of familiar places and things to prompt your memory.

**Write the meaning of each mathematical expressions in word form.**

1. 4 qt : 1 gal _____

2. 1 yd : 3 ft _____

3. 16 oz : 1 lb _____

4. $\dfrac{1{,}760 \text{ yd}}{1 \text{ mile}}$ _____

5. $\dfrac{1\text{T}}{2{,}000 \text{ lb}}$ _____

6. $\dfrac{2 \text{ c}}{1 \text{ pt}}$ _____

7. 1 m : 100 cm _____

**Write each of the following as a ratio or rate. Use appropriate abbreviations.**

8. 1 mile to 5,280 feet

_____

9. 72 hours to 3 days

_____

10. 2,000 milligrams to 2 grams

_____

11. 9 square feet to 1 square yard

_____

12. 4 quarts to 8 pints

_____

13. 62 miles per hour

_____

14. 203 calories per serving

_____

15. $1.25 per pound

_____

*Course 1* Chapter 7

# 7D: Visual Vocabulary Practice

For use after Lesson 7-6

**Study Skill** Mathematics is like learning a foreign language. You have to know the vocabulary before you can speak the language correctly.

## Concept List

cross products          equivalent ratios          percent
proportion              rate                       ratio
scale                   unit price                 unit rate

**Write the concept that best describes each exercise. Choose from the concept list above.**

| | | |
|---|---|---|
| **1.**  A pie was sliced into 5 equal pieces and 3 slices remain. This is represented by the variable $x$ in the equation $\frac{3}{5} = \frac{x}{100}$. <br><br> _____ | **2.** Jared can run 6 miles in 50 minutes. This can also be represented as $\frac{6 \text{ miles}}{50 \text{ minutes}}$. <br><br> _____ | **3.** $\$6 : \$4$ and $\frac{\$15}{\$10}$ <br><br> _____ |
| **4.** 9 to 11 <br><br> _____ | **5.** $\frac{6}{15} = \frac{14}{z}$ <br><br> _____ | **6.** Jesse purchased 2.5 lb of bananas for $2.00. The amount $0.80/lb represents this. <br><br> _____ |
| **7.** Xavier biked 36 miles in 3 hours. $\frac{12 \text{ miles}}{1 \text{ hour}}$ or 12 mi/h represents this. <br><br> _____ | **8.** For the equation $\frac{a}{6} = \frac{6}{9}$, these are represented by $a \times 9$ and $6 \times 6$. <br><br> _____ | **9.** The width of a room in a house is 16 feet. The width of the same room in a blueprint drawing is 2 inches. The equation 2 inches = 16 feet represents this in the blueprint. <br><br> _____ |

Name _____ Class _____ Date _____

# 7E: Vocabulary Check

For use after Lesson 7-7

**Study Skill** Strengthen your vocabulary. Use these pages and add cues and summaries by applying the Cornell Notetaking style.

**Write the definition for each word or term at the right. To check your work, fold the paper back along the dotted line to see the correct answers.**

unit rate

ratio

proportion

percent

rate

# 7E: Vocabulary Check (continued)

**For use after Lesson 7-7**

Write the vocabulary word or term for each definition. To check your work, fold the paper forward along the dotted line to see the correct answers.

the rate for one unit of
a given quantity

_____

a comparison of two
quantities by division

_____

an equation stating that
two ratios are equal

_____

a ratio that compares a
number to 100

_____

a ratio that compares two
quantities that are measured
in different units

_____

# 7F: Vocabulary Review Puzzle

**For use with the Chapter Review**

**Study Skill** Turn off the television and the radio while studying or doing homework.

**Read the definition, determine the word, and then find the hidden words in the puzzle. Once you have found a word, draw a circle around it and cross out the word definition. Words can be displayed forwards, backwards, up, down, or diagonally.**

```
K F L R A T I O K G N A Q H E J Z V O G
P O L K O C X E M A H Z U R S D N F J E
D N L C R R F Q I R S H U U E E E F S Z
P O S E E F A D G V E T H V S N P I O L
I I N D C J M S N N C K I B C O R V L V
E T D G I J R U S E R T T S A M O F U A
I A J Q P K A E J O U X D I L I P Q T D
K U O V R N F N W B C I T N E N O N I N
E Q H J O I O B I Y T I V X G A R C O R
E E H U C C H R I M N L A I B T T J N E
V K O O A I T V G N E N W T M O I N P B
I E S G L S K V S O C U H W I R O O U M
T S K K I X V P H B R M R I I V N I N U
A R C D S O L O O B E E S S D G E T Q N
T E C O A Q S E Y L P R O E Z S Z C X D
U V N K Z T I E B P Y A G X E H C A W E
M N L D W W S V X P A T V L H N N R U X
M I N H I J G F F B E O Q B S P W F W I
O Y K A U X Z J M U R R X D A E J U C M
C U V X X E T A R K A X K O W N F P R V
```

- comparison of two numbers by division
- $4(8 + 6) = 4(8) + 4(6)$ is an example of this property.
- ratio that compares a number to 100
- predicts how a pattern may continue
- The variable $b$ in the fraction $\frac{a}{b}$ is known as this.
- ratio that compares two quantities measured in different units
- one of two numbers whose product is 1
- an equation that states that two ratios are equal
- a number that describes a part of a set of a part of a whole that is divided into equal parts
- $12 + (3 + 6) = (12 + 3) + 6$ is an example of this property.
- The number 4 in the fraction $\frac{4}{7}$ is referred to as this.
- the number of square units a figure encloses
- $7 + 8 = 8 + 7$ is an example of this property.
- a number that makes an equation true
- mathematical statement that contains an equal sign
- operations that undo one another
- ratio that compares a length on a model to the actual length of a real object
- shows the sum of a whole number and a fraction

# Practice 8-1

Points, Lines, Segments, and Rays

**Use the diagram at the right. Name each of the following.**

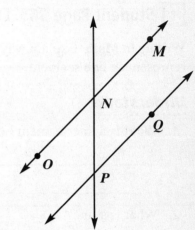

1. three segments

   _____

2. three rays

   _____

3. two pairs of intersecting lines

   _____

4. Draw a line segment.

5. Draw a ray.

6. Use *sometimes, always,* or *never* to complete the sentence:

   A ray _____ has one endpoint.

**Name the segments that appear to be parallel.**

7.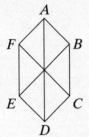

   _____

   _____

8.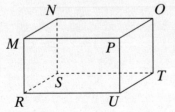

   _____

   _____

# 8-1 • Guided Problem Solving

GPS **Student Page 365, Exercise 19:**

**Writing in Math** Explain why $\overleftrightarrow{AB}$ represents a line and $\overline{AB}$ represents a line segment.

## Understand

1. What is a line segment?

   _____

   _____

2. What is a line?

   _____

   _____

## Plan and Carry Out

3. What must you include on a line when drawing a line in a plane?

   _____

4. Why does $\overleftrightarrow{AB}$ represent a line?

   _____

5. How is a line segment drawn differently?

   _____

6. Why does $\overline{AB}$ represent a line segment?

   _____

## Check

7. What facts should you use in explaining your answer?

   _____

## Solve Another Problem

8. Explain why a ray is represented as $\overrightarrow{AB}$.

   _____

   _____

# Practice 8-2

**Use the diagram at the right.**

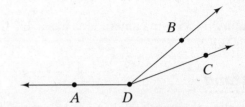

1. Name three rays.

   _____

2. Name three angles. Classify each angle as acute, right, obtuse, or straight.

   _____

**Measure each angle with a protractor.**

3. _____

4. _____ 

**Use a protractor to draw angles with the following measures.**

5. 88°

6. 66°

**Use the diagram at the right.**

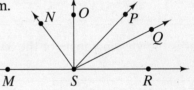

7. Use a protractor to measure ∠MSN, ∠NSO, ∠OSP, ∠PSQ, and ∠QSR. Mark the measurements on the diagram.

8. List all the obtuse angles shown.

   _____

9. List all the right angles shown.

   _____

10. What are the angle measures in the figure shown at the right?

    _____

    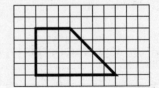

# 8-2 • Guided Problem Solving

**GPS** **Student Page 371, Exercise 25:**

**Photography** A 35-mm camera lens has a 45° field of view. What kind of angle is this?

## Understand

1. Underline the number(s) to use to answer this question.

2. List some different types of angles.

   _____

## Plan and Carry Out

3. What is an acute angle?

   _____

4. What is a right angle?

   _____

5. What is an obtuse angle?

   _____

   _____

6. What is a straight angle?

   _____

7. What is the viewing angle of the 35-mm camera lens?

   _____

8. What kind of angle is this?

   _____

## Check

9. Why did you choose this type of angle?

   _____

## Solve Another Problem

10. Chrissy is using brick pavers to line one corner of her front yard. The corner has a 120° angle. What type of angle is this? Explain.

    _____

    _____

# Practice 8-3

**Complete each sentence with *sometimes*, *always*, or *never*.**

1. Two right angles are _____ complementary.

2. Two acute angles are _____ supplementary.

**Find the value of *x* in each figure.**

3.

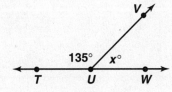

_____

4.

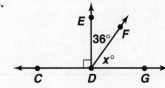

_____

5.

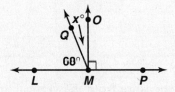

_____

6.

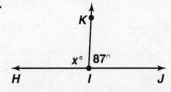

_____

**Use the diagram at the right to identify each of the following.**

7. two pairs of supplementary angles

_____

8. a pair of acute vertical angles

_____

9. a pair of obtuse vertical angles

_____

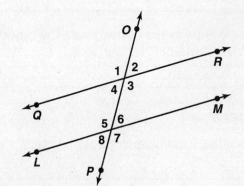

# 8-3 • Guided Problem Solving

**GPS** Student Page 377, Exercise 24:

**Architecture** Before renovations, the Leaning Tower of Pisa stood at an angle of about 5° from vertical. What was the measure of the acute angle that the tower made with the ground? What was the measure of the obtuse angle?

## Understand

1. What is the first thing you are being asked to do?

   _____

   _____

2. What is the second thing you are being asked to do?

   _____

   _____

## Plan and Carry Out

3. If the tower did not lean, what angle would the tower form with the ground?

   _____

4. By what angle measure from the vertical line was the tower leaning before the renovations?

   _____

5. Write a subtraction expression that you can use to find the acute angle.

   _____

6. What was the acute angle the tower made with the ground?

   _____

7. What was the obtuse angle the other side of the tower made with the ground?

   _____

## Check

8. How can you check your answer?

   _____

   _____

## Solve Another Problem

9. A stop sign stands at an angle of 90° with the ground. During a snowstorm, a car slid off the road and hit the sign so that it now forms a 62° angle with the ground. What is the obtuse angle formed on the other side of the sign?

   _____

# Practice 8-4

**Measure the sides and angles of each triangle. Then name each triangle by its angles and its sides.**

1.

2.

3.

_____      _____      _____

_____      _____      _____

**Classify each triangle with the following side lengths.**

4. 8, 9, 8 _____      5. 3, 4, 5 _____

**Classify each triangle with the following angles.**

6. 60°, 60°, 60°      7. 90°, 63°, 27°

_____      _____

**Sketch each triangle. If you cannot sketch a triangle, explain why.**

8. a right obtuse triangle      9. an acute equilateral triangle      10. an isosceles scalene triangle

_____      _____      _____

_____      _____      _____

_____      _____      _____

_____      _____      _____

# 8-4 • Guided Problem Solving

**GPS** **Student Page 383, Exercise 24:**

A designer for a boat company describes the sail shown in the photo at the right. Describe the triangle, classifying it by its angles.

## Understand

1. Name the three ways you can classify a triangle by its angle measures.

   _____

2. Name the three ways you can classify a triangle by the number of congruent segments or sides.

   _____

## Plan and Carry Out

3. Can a triangle be classified in more than one way? _____

4. Look at the picture of the sailboat. What appears to be true about the angle measures of the sail?

   _____

5. What appears to be true about the measures of the side lengths of the sail?

   _____

6. Classify the sail by the measures of its angles. _____

7. Classify the sail by the number of congruent sides.

   _____

8. Give all possible names for the triangular sail.

   _____

## Check

9. Did you classify the triangular sail correctly?

   _____

## Solve Another Problem

10. A sailboat has a sail shaped as shown. Judging by *its appearance*, give all names possible for the triangle in the diagram.

    _____

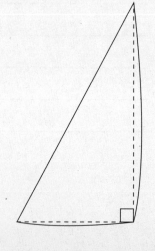

Name _____ Class _____ Date _____

# Practice 8-5

**Exploring and Classifying Polygons**

**Identify each polygon according to the number of sides.**

1. _____

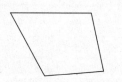

2. _____

3. _____

4. _____

**Use the dot paper below to draw an example of each polygon.**

5. a quadrilateral with one right angle

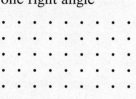

6. a hexagon with two right angles

**Use the diagram to identify all the polygons for each name.**

7. parallelogram

_____

8. rhombus

_____

9. rectangle

_____

10. trapezoid

_____

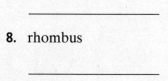
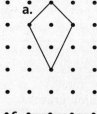
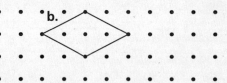
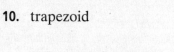
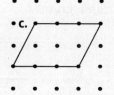
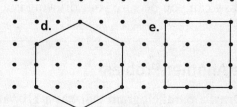

# 8-5 • Guided Problem Solving

**GPS** Student Page 390, Exercise 23:

Draw a parallelogram that has a 30° angle.

## Understand

1. What type of tool do you need to use to draw a 30° angle?

   _____

2. What do you know about the measures of opposite angles in a parallelogram?

   _____

## Plan and Carry Out

3. What is the sum of the angles in a parallelogram? _____

4. How many 30° angles are there in the parallelogram? _____

5. What is the sum of the other two angle measures?

   _____

6. What is the measure of the two other angles?

   _____

7. Use a protractor to draw the parallelogram.

## Check

8. How can you be sure your drawing is a parallelogram?

   _____

## Solve Another Problem

9. Draw a parallelogram that has a 110° angle.

# Practice 8-6                          Congruent and Similar Figures

For each figure tell whether it is congruent to
the parallelogram at the right.

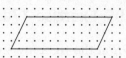

**1.**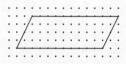

_____

**2.**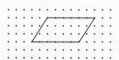

_____

**3.**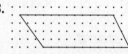

_____

Which trapezoids appear to be similar to the trapezoid
at the right?

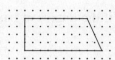

**4.**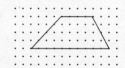

_____

**5.**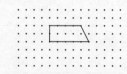

_____

**6.**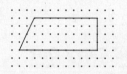

_____

Tell whether the triangles appear to be *congruent*, *similar*, or *neither*.

**7.**

_____

**8.**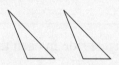

_____

**9.**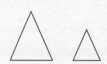

_____

**10.** List the pairs of figures that are similar. If necessary, use a
protractor to measure the angles.

_____

**a.**

**b.**

**c.**

**d.**

**e.**

**f.**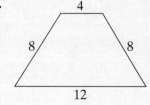

# 8-6 • Guided Problem Solving

**GPS** **Student Page 395, Exercise 17a:**

Triangles *MNO* and *PQR* at the right are similar.

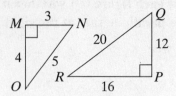

**a.** List the pairs of congruent angles.

## Understand

1. What does it mean to be *congruent*?

   _____

2. How do you know if the angles in triangles *MNO* and *PQR* are right angles?

   _____

   _____

## Plan and Carry Out

3. Name the right angle in each triangle.

   _____

4. Name the angle opposite the shortest side in each triangle.

   _____

5. Name the angle opposite the second-longest side in each triangle.

   _____

## Check

6. How do you know if you paired the correct angles together?

   _____

## Solve Another Problem

7. List the pairs of corresponding sides in the figure above.

   _____

Name _____ Class _____ Date _____

# Practice 8-7

**Tell whether each figure has line symmetry. If it does, draw the line(s) of symmetry. If not, write *none*.**

1.

2.

3.

4.

5.

6.
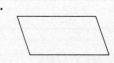

**Complete each figure so that the line is a line of symmetry.**

7.
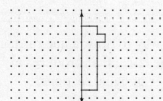

8.
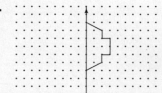

9.
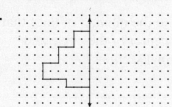

10.
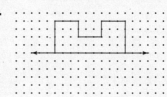

**Is there a line of symmetry for each word? If so, draw it.**

11.
B O X

12.
T O O T

13.
M O M

14. Many logos such as the one at the right have both horizontal line symmetry and vertical line symmetry. Design another logo. What types of symmetry does it have?

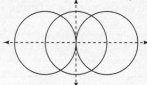

L1 Practice

*Course 1 Lesson 8-7*

# 8-7 • Guided Problem Solving

**GPS** Student Page 401, Exercise 16:

**Reasoning** How many lines of symmetry does a circle have? Explain your reasoning.

## Understand

1. What is a line of symmetry?

   _____

   _____

## Plan and Carry Out

2. Draw a circle with a line through the center.

4. If you had drawn a different line through the center of the circle, would it have produced the same number of equal sections?

   _____

5. Can you find a way to draw a line through the center of the circle that produces a different number of equal sections?

   _____

6. Is there a limit to the number of lines that go through the center of the circle and divide it into equal sections?

   _____

3. Into how many equal parts did your line divide the circle?

   _____

7. How many lines of symmetry does a circle have?

   _____

## Check

8. How do you determine if each line is a line of symmetry?

   _____

   _____

## Solve Another Problem

9. How many lines of symmetry does an equilateral triangle have?

   _____

# Practice 8-8

**Transformations**

**Draw two translations of each figure.**

1.
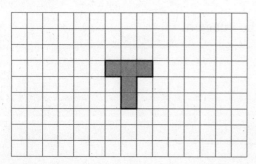

2.
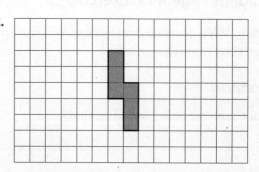

**Draw the reflection of each figure. Use the dashed line as the line of reflection.**

3.
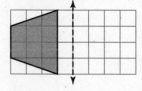

4.
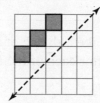

**Tell whether each pair of figures shows a translation or a reflection.**

5.

6.
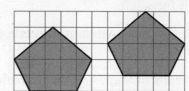

_____                            _____

**Tell whether each figure is a rotation of the shape at the right.
Write *yes* or *no*. If so, state the number of degrees.**

7.

8.

9.

_____          _____          _____

# 8-8 • Guided Problem Solving

**GPS** Student Page 405, Exercise 21:

**Reasoning** What transformations can you use to change the image of the letter C so that it faces left?

## Understand

1. What are you being asked to find?

   _____

   _____

2. What three transformations have you learned how to perform?

   _____

3. In the space at the right, make a sketch of a right triangle. Sketch the image of the triangle after each of the three transformations.

## Plan and Carry Out

4. Draw the letter C in the space at the right. Attempt to make a translation of the letter so that it faces left.

5. Draw the letter C again. Attempt to make a reflection of the letter so that it faces left.

6. Draw the letter C again. Attempt to rotate the letter so that it faces left.

7. Look at the results of Steps 4, 5, and 6. Which transformations can make the letter C face left?

   _____

## Check

8. Which transformation could not make the letter C face left? Why not?

   _____

   _____

   _____

## Solve Another Problem

9. What transformations can you use to change the letter A so that it points down?

   _____

# 8A: Graphic Organizer

**For use before Lesson 8-1**

**Study Skill** Try to read each lesson before your teacher presents it in class. This will help you recognize new terms and understand the material better.

**Write your answers.**

1. What is the chapter title? _____

2. How many lessons are there in this chapter? _____

3. What is the topic of the Test-Taking Strategies page? _____

4. Complete the graphic organizer below as you work through the chapter.
   - In the center, write the title of the chapter.
   - When you begin a lesson, write the lesson name in a rectangle.
   - When you complete a lesson, write a skill or key concept in a circle linked to that lesson block.
   - When you complete the chapter, use this graphic organizer to help you review.

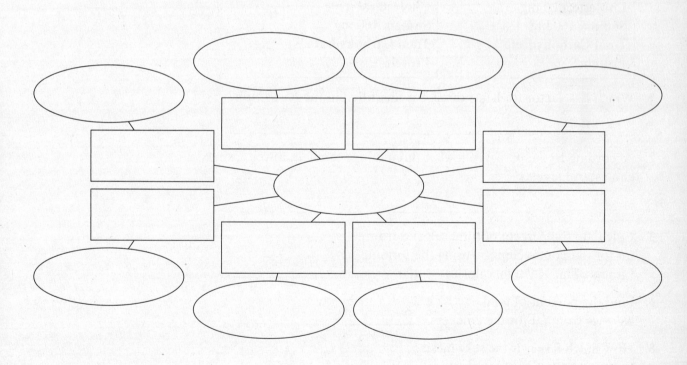

# 8B: Reading Comprehension

**Study Skill** Read problems carefully. Pay special attention to units when working with measurements.

**Use the paragraph and the labels below to answer the questions.**

Healthy eating is important. A high-fat diet can contribute to elevated cholesterol levels, which is a risk factor for heart disease. A low-fat, low-cholesterol diet, as well as exercise, can help lower cholesterol levels. You can determine the amount of fat in packaged foods by looking at the Nutrition Facts Label on the package.

| **Potato Chips**<br>**Nutritional Facts**<br>Serving Size 1 oz (28 g) | **Crackers**<br>**Nutritional Facts**<br>Serving Size 14 g |
|---|---|
| Amount Per Serving<br>*Calories 160* | Amount Per Serving<br>*Calories 70* |
| **Total Fat** 10 g<br>**Cholesterol** 0 mg<br>**Sodium** 160 mg<br>**Total Carbohydrate** 14 g<br>**Protein** 2 g | **Total Fat** 3 g<br>**Cholesterol** 0 mg<br>**Sodium** 160 mg<br>**Total Carbohydrate** 9 g<br>**Protein** 1 g |

1. Which risk factor for heart disease is identified in the paragraph?

   _____

2. According to the paragraph, what three things can help lower cholesterol levels?

   _____

3. Calculate the percent of total calories from fat for the potato chips by using the formula (grams of fat × 9/total calories) × 100. _____

4. Find the percent of total calories from fat for the crackers. _____

5. How much larger is the serving size for potato chips than for crackers? _____

6. Does making the serving sizes equal change the percent of total calories from fat? _____

7. **High-Use Academic Words** In Exercise 3, what does it mean to *calculate?*

   a. to put into a proper order          b. to determine by mathematical processes

# 8C: Reading/Writing Math Symbols

**For use after Lesson 8-2**

**Study Skill** Make a realistic study schedule. Set specific goals for yourself, rather than general ones. For example, read Chapter 12, do problems 1–20, or study for a math test before doing homework.

**Match the symbol in Column A with its meaning in Column B.**

| Column A | Column B |
|---|---|
| 1. $\overrightarrow{AB}$ | **A.** degree |
| 2. $\angle$ | **B.** segment $AB$ |
| 3. ° | **C.** ray $AB$ |
| 4. $\overleftrightarrow{AB}$ | **D.** perpendicular |
| 5. $\perp$ | **E.** angle |
| 6. $\overline{AB}$ | **F.** line $AB$ |

**Write each of the following using appropriate mathematical symbols.**

7. angle $ABC$ _____

8. ray $CD$ _____

9. line $BC$ _____

10. segment $DE$ _____

11. forty-seven degrees _____

12. ray $OA$ _____

**Express the following proportions in division notation.**

13. four to five is equal to sixteen to twenty _____

14. two to three is equal to twelve to eighteen _____

15. one to six is equal to six to thirty-six _____

16. five to ten is equal to one-half _____

17. three to twenty is equal to a number to ten _____

18. twenty-four to a number is equal to two-thirds _____

# 8D: Visual Vocabulary Practice

**For use after Lesson 8-5**

**Study Skill** When learning a new concept, try to draw a picture to illustrate it.

**Concept List**

| | | |
|---|---|---|
| complementary angles | acute triangle | parallel lines |
| perpendicular lines | rhombus | scalene triangle |
| supplementary angles | trapezoid | vertical angles |

**Write the concept that best describes each exercise. Choose from the concept list above.**

**1.**

$m\angle A = 64°$ and $m\angle B = 26°$

_____

**2.**

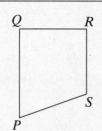

$\overline{PQ}$ is parallel to $\overline{RS}$.

_____

**3.**

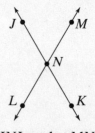

$\angle JNL$ and $\angle MNK$

_____

**4.**

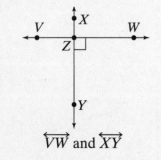

$\overleftrightarrow{VW}$ and $\overleftrightarrow{XY}$

_____

**5.**

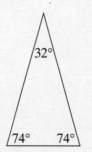

_____

**6.**

$m\angle S = 64°$ and $m\angle T = 116°$

_____

**7.**

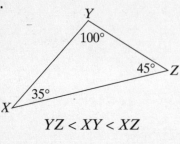

$YZ < XY < XZ$

_____

**8.**

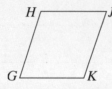

$\overline{GH} \cong \overline{HJ} \cong \overline{JK} \cong \overline{GK}$, $\overline{HG}$ is parallel to $\overline{JK}$, and $\overline{HJ}$ is parallel to $\overline{GK}$.

_____

**9.**

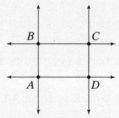

If $ABCD$ is a rectangle, then $\overleftrightarrow{BC}$ and $\overleftrightarrow{AD}$ are these:

_____

# 8E: Vocabulary Check

**For use after Lesson 8-6**

**Study Skill** Strengthen your vocabulary. Use these pages and add cues and summaries by applying the Cornell Notetaking style.

**Write the definition for each word or term at the right. To check your work, fold the paper back along the dotted line to see the correct answers.**

_____

_____

_____ acute angle

_____

_____

_____ congruent angles

_____

_____

_____ rhombus

_____

_____

_____ right angle

_____

_____

_____ perpendicular lines

_____

_____

# 8E: Vocabulary Check (continued)

**Write the vocabulary word or term for each definition. To check your work, fold the paper forward along the dotted line to see the correct answers.**

an angle with measure
between 0° and 90°

_____

angles that have the same
measure

_____

a parallelogram with four
congruent sides

_____

an angle with a measure of
90°

_____

lines that intersect to form
right angles

_____

Vocabulary and Study Skills

# 8F: Vocabulary Review Puzzle

**For use with the Chapter Review**

**Study Skill** Puzzles are a fun way to learn and review vocabulary.

**Complete the crossword puzzle. For help, use the glossary in your textbook.**

## ACROSS

1. lines that intersect to form right angles

5. figures that have the same shape, but not necessarily the same size

8. angle that measures 90°

9. lines that lie in different planes

10. part of a line

12. angle that measures less than 90°

13. a triangle with no congruent sides

## DOWN

2. parallelogram with four right angles

3. a triangle with at least two sides congruent

4. lines that are in the same plane and do not intersect

6. parallelogram with four congruent sides

7. an angle that measures 180°

11. a triangle with three congruent sides

# Practice 9-1

**Metric Units of Length, Mass, and Capacity**

**Choose an appropriate metric unit of length.**

1. the height of an office building

   _____

2. the width of a page of a text

   _____

3. the length of an ant

   _____

4. the depth of a lake

   _____

**Choose an appropriate metric unit of mass.**

5. a grain of rice

   _____

6. a cat

   _____

7. a leaf

   _____

8. an eraser

   _____

**Choose an appropriate metric unit of capacity.**

9. a gasoline tank

   _____

10. a coffee mug

    _____

11. a pitcher of juice

    _____

12. a swimming pool

    _____

**Is each measurement reasonable? Write *True* or *False*.**

13. The mass of the horse is about 500 kg.

    _____

14. Jean drank 5.8 L of juice at breakfast.

    _____

15. A mug holds 250 mL of hot chocolate.

    _____

16. A penny is about 3 kg.

    _____

# 9-1 • Guided Problem Solving

**GPS** **Student Page 419, Exercise 31:**

**Estimation** The width of a door is about 1 meter. How can you estimate the length of a wall that contains the door?

## Understand

1. What are you being asked to do?

   _____

## Plan and Carry Out

2. How wide is the door?

   _____

3. How can you use the width of the door to estimate the length of the wall?

   _____

   _____

   _____

   _____

   _____

## Check

4. What would be an approximate length of a wall in terms of the width of the door if about 6 doors would fit along the length of the wall?

   _____

## Solve Another Problem

5. The height of a window is approximately 3 feet. How can you estimate the height of a wall that contains the window?

   _____

   _____

   _____

# Practice 9-2

**Converting Units in the Metric System**

• • • • • • • • • • • • • • • • • • • • • • • • • • • • • • • • • • • • • • •

**Convert each measurement to meters.**

1. 800 mm

   _____

2. 50 cm

   _____

3. 2.6 km

   _____

4. 35 km

   _____

5. 40 mm

   _____

6. 300 cm

   _____

**Convert each measurement to liters.**

7. 160 mL

   _____

8. 0.36 kL

   _____

9. 0.002 kL

   _____

10. 8 kL

   _____

11. 80 mL

   _____

12. 17.3 mL

   _____

**Convert each measurement to grams.**

13. 4,000 mg

   _____

14. 7 kg

   _____

15. 56,000 mg

   _____

16. 600 mg

   _____

17. 90 kg

   _____

18. 2,800 mg

   _____

**Convert each measurement.**

19. _?_ km = 3,400 m

   _____

20. 420 mL = _?_ cL

   _____

21. 37 cm = _?_ m

   _____

22. 5,100 mg = _?_ cg

   _____

23. 77.8 mm = _?_ cm

   _____

24. 9.5 kL = _?_ L

   _____

25. _?_ m = 400,000 cm

   _____

26. 948 mm = _?_ cm

   _____

• • • • • • • • • • • • • • • • • • • • • • • • • • • • • • • • • • • • • • • • • • **385**

# 9-2 • Guided Problem Solving

**GPS** Student Page 423, Exercise 25:

**Science** Light travels at approximately 299,792,458 meters per second. Approximately how many kilometers does light travel in one second?

## Understand

1. What are you being asked to do?

   _____

   _____

2. Which is larger, a meter or a kilometer?

   _____

   _____

## Plan and Carry Out

3. How many meters does light travel in one second?

   _____

4. Will the number of kilometers light travels in one second be bigger or smaller than the answer in Step 3?

   _____

5. What number do you divide meters by to get kilometers?

   _____

6. Divide the answer in Step 3 by the answer in Step 5.

   _____

7. Approximately how many kilometers does light travel in one second?

   _____

   _____

## Check

8. How can you check your answer?

   _____

## Solve Another Problem

9. A boulder weighs 44,320 grams. Approximately how many kilograms does the boulder weigh?

   _____

Guided Problem Solving

# Practice 9-3

**Perimeters and Areas of Rectangles**

**Find the perimeter and area of each rectangle.**

1.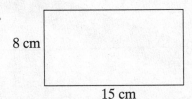

8 cm

15 cm

perimeter: _____

area: _____

2.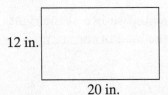

12 in.

20 in.

perimeter: _____

area: _____

3.

6 cm

6 cm

perimeter: _____

area: _____

4. $\ell = 5$ in., $w = 13$ in.

perimeter: _____

area: _____

5. $\ell = 18$ m, $w = 12$ m

perimeter: _____

area: _____

6. $\ell = 3$ ft, $w = 8$ ft

perimeter: _____

area: _____

**Find the area of each square given the side $s$ or the perimeter $P$.**

7. $s = 3.5$ yd

_____

8. $s = 9$ cm

_____

9. $P = 24$ m

_____

**Choose a calculator, paper and pencil, or mental math to solve.**

10. The length of a rectangle is 8 centimeters. The width is 6 centimeters.

   a. What is the area? _____

   b. What is the perimeter? _____

11. The area of a rectangle is 45 square inches.
    One dimension is 5 inches. What is the perimeter?

    _____

12. The perimeter of a square is 36 centimeters.
    What is the area of the square?

    _____

13. The perimeter of a rectangle is 38 centimeters.
    The length is 7.5 centimeters. What is the width?

    _____

# 9-3 • Guided Problem Solving

**GPS** Student Page 429, Exercise 18:

**Stamps** The world's smallest postage stamp, shown at the right, measures 0.31 inch by 0.37 inch. Find the area of the stamp.

## Understand

1. What are you being asked to find?

   _____

2. What is the formula for the area of a rectangle?

   _____

## Plan and Carry Out

3. What is the length of the stamp?

   _____

4. What is the width of the stamp?

   _____

5. Substitute the values into the formula.

   _____

6. What is the area of the stamp?

   _____

## Check

7. Explain how to check your answer.

   _____

   _____

## Solve Another Problem

8. A window measures 28 in. wide by 36 in. tall. What is the area of the window?

   _____

   _____

# Practice 9-4

**Find the area of each triangle.**

1.

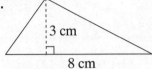

3 cm
8 cm

_____

2.

8 mm
6 mm

_____

**Find the area of each parallelogram.**

3.

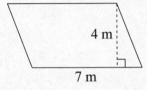

4 m
7 m

_____

4.

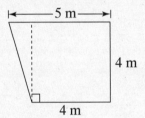

8 in.
5 in.

_____

**Find the area of each complex figure.**

5.

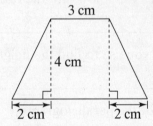

5 m
4 m
4 m

_____

6.

3 cm
4 cm
2 cm   2 cm

_____

7. Draw and label a triangle and a parallelogram that each have an area of 20 square units.

**Tell whether each statement is *true* or *false*.**

8. A parallelogram and triangle can have the same base and area. _____

9. Two triangles that have the same base always have the same area. _____

# 9-4 • Guided Problem Solving

**GPS** Student Page 435, Exercise 19:

**Algebra** A parallelogram has an area of 66 in.$^2$ and a base length of 5 inches. What is the height of the parallelogram?

## Understand

1. What are you being asked to find?

   _____

2. What information are you given?

   _____

   _____

## Plan and Carry Out

3. Write the formula you will use to find the area of a parallelogram.

   _____

4. Substitute the values you know into the formula.

   _____

5. What operation do you use to find the height?

   _____

6. What is the height of the parallelogram?

   _____

## Check

7. Check your answer. Explain your method.

   _____

   _____

## Solve Another Problem

8. A parallelogram has an area of 96 cm$^2$ and a height of 4 cm. What is the base length of the parallelogram?

   _____

# Practice 9-5

**Circles and Circumference**

List each of the following for circle $O$.

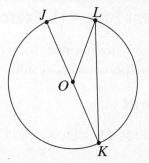

1. three radii _____

2. one diameter _____

3. two chords _____

**Find the unknown length for a circle with the given dimension.**

4. $r = 4$ in.; $d = $ _?_

_____

5. $d = 15$ cm; $r = $ _?_

_____

**Find the circumference of each circle. Round to the nearest unit.**

6.
5 mm

_____

7.
11 in.

_____

8.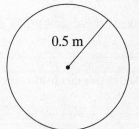
0.5 m

_____

9.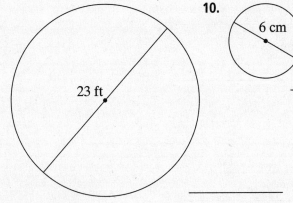
23 ft

_____

10.
6 cm

_____

11.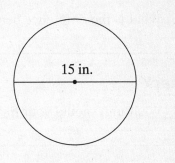
15 in.

_____

**Estimate the circumference of each circle with the given radius or diameter. Use 3 for $\pi$.**

12. $d = 4$ in. _____

13. $r = 10$ ft _____

**Find the diameter of a circle with the given circumference. Round to the nearest unit.**

14. $C = 128$ ft _____

15. $C = 36$ cm _____

# 9-5 • Guided Problem Solving

**GPS** **Student Page 441, Exercise 23:**

**Trainers** A dog trainer uses hoops with diameters of 24 and 30 inches. What is the difference between their circumferences? Use 3 for $\pi$.

## Understand

1. What do you need to know in order to answer the question?

   _____

2. How do you find the circumference of a circle when you know the diameter?

   _____

   _____

## Plan and Carry Out

3. What is the diameter of each hoop?

   _____

4. What is the circumference of the 24-in. hoop?

   _____

5. What is the circumference of the 30-in. hoop?

   _____

6. What is the difference between their circumferences?

   _____

## Check

7. What unit should your final answer have? Why?

   _____

   _____

## Solve Another Problem

8. Included in the china Jill and Ed received for their wedding were dinner plates and salad plates. The dinner plates have a diameter of 10 in. and the salad plates have a diameter of 7 in. What is the difference between their circumferences? Use 3 for $\pi$.

   _____

# Practice 9-6

**Find the area of each circle. Round to the nearest tenth.**

**1.**
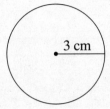
3 cm

_____

**2.**
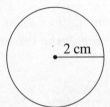
2 cm

_____

**Find the area of each circle. Round to the nearest unit. Use $\frac{22}{7}$ for $\pi$.**

**3.**
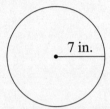
7 in.

_____

**4.**
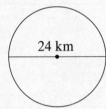
24 km

_____

**Find the area of a circle with the given radius or diameter. Round to the nearest tenth.**

**5.** $r = 12$ cm _____

**6.** $d = 15$ m _____

**7.** $d = 9$ cm _____

**8.** $d = 14$ cm _____

**Solve each problem. Round to the nearest square inch.**

**9.** Find the area of an 8-inch diameter pizza.

_____

**10.** Find the area of a 12-inch diameter pizza.

_____

**11.** The cost of the 8-inch pizza is $7.00. The cost of the 12-inch pizza is $12.50. Which size pizza is the better buy? Explain.

_____

_____

_____

# 9-6 • Guided Problem Solving

**GPS** **Student Page 447, Exercise 24:**

You can pick up the signal of one radio station, within 45 miles of the station. Find the approximate area of the broadcast region.

## Understand

1. What are you being asked to find?

   _____

2. Write the formula you use to find the area of a circle.

   _____

## Plan and Carry Out

3. What is the radius of the broadcast area?

   _____

4. Substitute the values into the area formula.

   _____

5. Evaluate the formula to find the area of the broadcast region to the nearest square mile.

   _____

## Check

6. Use a radius of 50 and 3 for $\pi$ to estimate the area. Then use a radius of 40 and 3 for $\pi$ to estimate the area. Is your answer reasonable? Why?

   _____

   _____

   _____

## Solve Another Problem

7. The lead investigator in a search for a boat tells the coast guard to search everywhere within 5 miles of the last known location of the boat. What is the area of the search region? Use 3.14 for $\pi$.

   _____

   _____

   _____

# Practice 9-7

**Name each three-dimensional figure.**

1.

_____

2.

_____

3.

_____

4.

_____

5.

_____

6.

_____

**Solve the questions below. It may help to draw a sketch of the figure named.**

7. In a square pyramid, what shape are the faces?

_____

8. How many faces does a rectangular prism have? How many edges? How many vertices?

_____

_____

# 9-7 • Guided Problem Solving

Name the figure. Then find the number of faces, vertices, and edges in the figure.

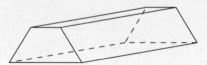

## Understand

1. What is a face?

   _____

2. What is a vertex?

   _____

   _____

3. What is an edge?

   _____

   _____

## Plan and Carry Out

4. How many bases does the figure have? _____

5. Does this make the figure a pyramid or a prism? _____

6. What is the shape of the bases? _____

7. Name the figure. _____

8. How many faces are there total? _____

9. How many vertices are there? _____

10. How many edges are there? _____

## Check

11. How do you know the figure is not a pyramid?

## Solve Another Problem

12. Name the figure. Then find the number of faces, vertices, and edges in the figure.

    _____

    _____

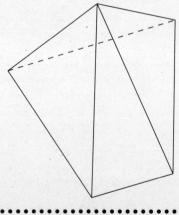

•••••••••••••••••••••••••••••••••••••   Guided Problem Solving

# Practice 9-8

**Draw a net for each prism.**

**1.**

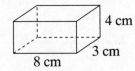

4 cm
3 cm
8 cm

**2.**

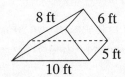

8 ft   6 ft
5 ft
10 ft

**Find the surface area of each figure to the nearest whole number.**

**3.**

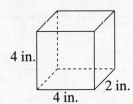

4 in.
4 in.
2 in.

_____

**4.**

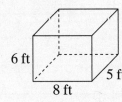

6 ft
8 ft
5 ft

_____

**5.**

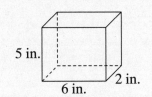

5 in.
6 in.
2 in.

_____

**6.**

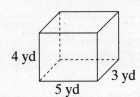

4 yd
5 yd
3 yd

_____

**Find the surface area of the rectangular prism with the given net.**

**7.**

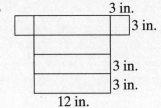

3 in.
3 in.
3 in.
3 in.
12 in.

_____

**8.**

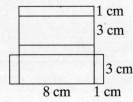

1 cm
3 cm
3 cm
8 cm   1 cm

_____

# 9-8 • Guided Problem Solving

**GPS** **Student Page 455, Exercise 15:**

**Writing in Math** Suppose each dimension of a rectangular prism is doubled. How is the surface area affected?

## Understand

1. Write the formula used to find the surface area of a rectangular prism.

   _____

2. To double a number means to multiply that number by what value?

   _____

## Plan and Carry Out

3. Multiply each dimension by 2 and substitute it into the surface area formula from Step 1.

   _____

4. Simplify the formula.

   _____

5. Instead of multiplying the area of each face by 2, multiply by what number?

   _____

6. How is the surface area affected when each dimension is doubled?

   _____

## Check

7. Explain another way to solve this problem.

   _____

   _____

## Solve Another Problem

8. Suppose each dimension of a rectangular prism is tripled. How is the surface area affected?

   _____

# Practice 9-9

**Find the volume of each rectangular prism.**

**1.**

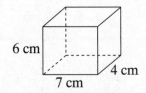

6 cm

7 cm   4 cm

_____

**2.**

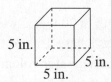

5 in.

5 in.   5 in.

_____

**3.**

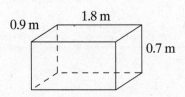

0.9 m   1.8 m

0.7 m

_____

**4.**

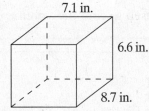

7.1 in.

6.6 in.

8.7 in.

_____

**5.** $\ell = 6$ cm, $w = 5$ cm, $h = 12$ cm

_____

**6.** $\ell = 13$ in., $w = 7$ in., $h = 9$ in.

_____

**7.** $\ell = 2.5$ ft, $w = 1.9$ ft, $h = 11.6$ ft

_____

**8.** $\ell = 48.1$ m, $w = 51.62$ m, $h = 3.42$ m

_____

**Solve.**

**9.** A packing box is 1.2 m long, 0.8 m wide, and 1.4 m high. What is the volume of the box?

_____

**10.** A fish aquarium measures 3 feet long, 2 feet wide, and 2 feet high. What is the volume of the aquarium?

_____

**11.** A swimming pool is 25 feet wide, 60 feet long, and 7 feet deep. What is the volume of the pool?

_____

# 9-9 • Guided Problem Solving

**GPS** Student Page 460, Exercise 14:

A truck trailer has a length of 20 feet, a width of 8 feet, and a height of 7 feet. A second trailer has a base area of 108 square feet and a height of 8 feet. Which trailer has a greater volume? How much greater is it?

## Understand

1. Circle the information you will need to solve the problem.

2. Write the formula used to find the volume of a rectangular solid.

_____

## Plan and Carry Out

3. Substitute the values for the length, width, and height of the first trailer into the formula for the volume of a rectangular solid. What is the volume? _____

4. Repeat Step 3 for the second trailer.

_____

5. What are the units for the volume of this solid? _____

6. Which trailer has the greater volume? _____

## Check

7. How can you check your answer?

_____

_____

_____

## Solve Another Problem

8. A building is 32 feet tall and has a base area of 420 square feet. What is the volume of the building?

_____

Guided Problem Solving

# Practice 9-10

**Surface Areas and Volumes of Cylinders**

**Find the surface area of each figure to the nearest whole number.**

**1.**

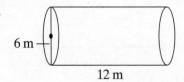

6 m —

12 m

_____

**2.**

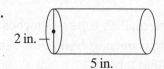

2 in. —

5 in.

_____

**3.**

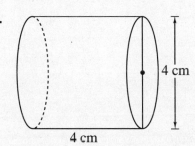

4 cm

4 cm

_____

**4.**

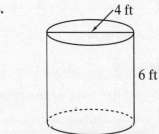

4 ft

6 ft

_____

**Find the volume of each cylinder. Round to the nearest whole number.**

**5.**

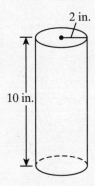

2 in.

10 in.

_____

**6.**

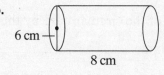

6 cm —

8 cm

_____

**Find the surface area and volume of each cylinder with the measurements listed below. Round to the nearest whole number.**

**7.** $d = 12$ in.; $h = 14$ in.

Surface area: _____

Volume: _____

**8.** $d = 8.4$ m; $h = 9.3$ m

Surface area: _____

Volume: _____

# 9-10 • Guided Problem Solving

**GPS** Student Page 465, Exercise 16:

**Packaging** A cardboard mailing tube is 3 inches in diameter and 20 inches long. The tube is open at both ends. Find the surface area and volume of the mailing tube.

## Understand

1. Circle the information you will need to solve the problem.

2. How will the fact that the ends of the tube are open affect the surface area? How will it affect the volume?

   _____

   _____

## Plan and Carry Out

3. Find the area of the circular base of the tube. $(A = \pi r^2)$

   _____

4. Find the circumference of the circular base of the tube. $(C = 2\pi r)$

   _____

5. Multiply the circumference of the tube's base by the height of the tube to find the tube's surface area. _____

6. Multiply the area of the circular base by the height of the tube to find the tube's volume. _____

7. What are the surface area and the volume of the tube?

   _____

## Check

8. Divide the surface area of the tube by $\pi$ and then divide the quotient by the height of the tube. Is your answer the same as the tube's diameter?

   _____

## Solve Another Problem

9. A drinking cup has a diameter of 4 in. and a height of 8 in. The cup has a base but no lid. What are the surface area and the volume of the cup?

   _____

# 9A: Graphic Organizer

**For use before Lesson 9-1**

**Study Skill** Develop consistent study habits. Block off approximately the same amount of time each evening for schoolwork. Plan ahead by setting aside extra time when you know you have a test or big project coming up.

**Write your answers.**

1. What is the chapter title? _____

2. How many lessons are there in this chapter? _____

3. What is the topic of the Test-Taking Strategies page? _____

4. Complete the graphic organizer below as you work through the chapter.
   - In the center, write the title of the chapter.
   - When you begin a lesson, write the lesson name in a rectangle.
   - When you complete a lesson, write a skill or key concept in a circle linked to that lesson block.
   - When you complete the chapter, use this graphic organizer to help you review.

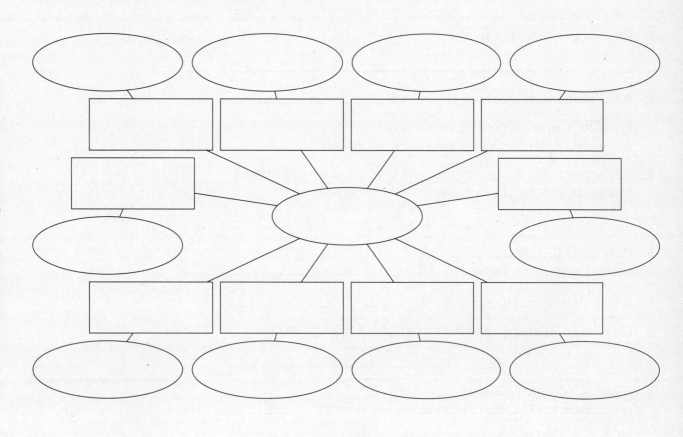

# 9B: Reading Comprehension

**Study Skill** Pay attention in class and when reading so information does not slip out of your "short-term memory."

**Read the paragraph below and answer the questions.**

Elephants are the largest living land animals. There are two species of elephants, the African and the Asian. Elephants are vegetarians and eat up to 440 pounds of plants per day. They use their tusks to strip bark from trees and their trunks to pull up plants and pick leaves. They drink about 26 gallons of water per day. At birth a baby elephant measures about three feet high and weighs approximately 265 pounds. At six years of age, an elephant can weigh as much as 2,200 pounds. Although an elephant consumes a great deal of food, it has only 6 teeth at a time. When a tooth wears away or falls out, another one grows in its place. During a lifetime, four full sets of teeth are lost.

1. What is the paragraph about?

   _____

2. What are the two species of elephants? _____

3. If one lb is equal to 0.454 kg, how many
   kilograms of plants can an elephant eat in one day? _____

4. According to the paragraph, how much weight does an elephant
   gain in the first six years of life?

   _____

5. How many teeth can an
   elephant have in its lifetime? _____

6. Which statistic measures a volume? _____

7. How many quarts of water does an elephant drink in one day?

   _____

8. If one in. is equal to 2.54 cm, how many
   centimeters tall is a baby elephant when it is born? _____

9. **High-Use Academic Words** In Exercise 8, what does it mean to
   be *equal?*

   a. to have the same measure or value       b. to produce an effect upon

# 9C: Reading/Writing Math Symbols
**For use after Lesson 9-9**

**Study Skill** Use flashcards to learn equations, facts, and formulas.

**Specific letters are used to represent parts of formulas for area, perimeter, volume, etc. Identify the type of measurement that each of the following letters typically represents in a geometric formula.**

**1.** *l* _____

**2.** *A* _____

**3.** *C* _____

**4.** *w* _____

**5.** *b* _____

**6.** *r* _____

**7.** *d* _____

**8.** *h* _____

**9.** *V* _____

**10.** *P* _____

**Match the expression in Column A with its meaning in Column B.**

| Column A | Column B |
|---|---|
| **11.** $s^2$ | **A.** perimeter of a rectangle |
| **12.** $bh$ | **B.** circumference of a circle |
| **13.** $\pi r^2$ | **C.** area of a circle |
| **14.** $2l + 2w$ | **D.** area of a square |
| **15.** $\frac{1}{2}bh$ | **E.** area of a parallelogram |
| **16.** $\pi d$ | **F.** area of a triangle |
| **17.** $lwh$ | **G** volume of a rectangular prism |
| **18.** $2lw + 2lh + 2wh$ | **H.** surface area of a rectangular prism |

# 9D: Visual Vocabulary Practice

**For use after Lesson 9-7**

*High-Use Academic Words*

**Study Skill** When you feel you're getting frustrated, take a break.

**Concept List**

| | | |
|---|---|---|
| explain | acronym | illustrate |
| represent | abbreviate | classify |
| property | approximate | dimensions |

**Write the concept that best describes each exercise. Choose from the concept list above.**

| | | |
|---|---|---|
| **1.**<br><br>$0.8, 80\%, \frac{4}{5}$<br><br><br><br><br>_____ | **2.**<br><br>6<br>3 ▢<br><br>The perimeter is<br>$2(3 + 6) = 18$ units.<br><br>_____ | **3.**<br><br>Write in. for inches.<br><br><br><br><br>_____ |
| **4.**<br><br>Pentagons, squares, octagons, and triangles are all polygons; circles are not.<br><br><br>_____ | **5.**<br><br>9.6% of 25.36 ≈ 10% of 25<br><br><br><br><br>_____ | **6.**<br><br>$l \times w \times h$<br><br><br><br><br>_____ |
| **7.**<br><br>$(a + b) + c = a + (b + c)$<br><br><br><br><br>_____ | **8.**<br><br>Write LCM for least common multiple.<br><br><br><br><br>_____ | **9.**<br><br>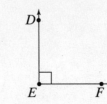<br>$m\angle DEF = 90°$<br><br>_____ |

# 9E: Vocabulary Check

**Study Skill** Strengthen your vocabulary. Use these pages and add cues and summaries by applying the Cornell Notetaking style.

**Write the definition for each word or term at the right. To check your work, fold the paper back along the dotted line to see the correct answers.**

_____  chord

_____

_____

_____  circumference

_____

_____

_____  radius

_____

_____  surface area

_____

_____

_____  cylinder

_____

_____

# 9E: Vocabulary Check (continued)

**Write the vocabulary word or term for each definition. To check your work, fold the paper forward along the dotted line to see the correct answers.**

a segment that has both endpoints on a circle

_____

the distance around a circle

_____

a segment that connects a circle to the center of a circle

_____

the sum of the areas of all the surfaces of a three-dimensional figure

_____

a three-dimensional figure with two congruent parallel bases that are circles

_____

# 9F: Vocabulary Review Puzzle

**For use with the Chapter Review**

**Study Skill** Get plenty of rest before a major quiz or test. If you're well rested, you may be able to concentrate better and retain more of what you hear or see in class.

**Below is a list of words grouped by number of letters. Fit each word into the puzzle grid. Use each word only once.**

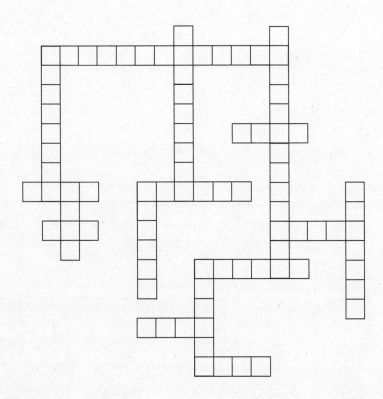

| **3 letters** | **4 letters** | **5 letters** | **6 letters** | **7 letters** |
|---|---|---|---|---|
| net | area | liter | sphere | pyramid |
| | cone | | square | |
| | edge | | vertex | |
| | face | | volume | |
| | gram | | | |

| **8 letters** | **9 letters** | **13 letters** |
|---|---|---|
| cylinder | perimeter | circumference |
| | | perpendicular |

# Practice 10-1

**The rectangle shape in a set of blocks comes in two sizes (small and large), three colors (yellow, red, and blue), and two thicknesses (thick and thin).**

**1.** Draw a tree diagram to find the total number of outcomes. _____

**2.** How many outcomes are possible?

_____

**3.** How many outcomes will be red?

_____

**4.** How many outcomes will be blue and thin?

_____

**5.** How many outcomes will be large?

_____

**Use the counting principle to find the total number of outcomes.**

**6.** You toss a coin 8 times.

_____

**7.** A restaurant offers 12 types of entrees, 6 types of appetizers, and 4 types of rice. How many meals of appetizer, entree, and rice are there?

_____

**8.** You spin the spinner at the right, then toss a coin. Construct a sample space using a tree diagram. How many possible outcomes are there?

_____

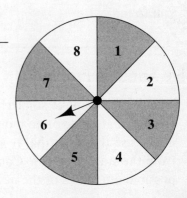

*Course 1 Lesson 10-1*

**411**

# 10-1 • Guided Problem Solving

**GPS** **Student Page 480, Exercise 12a:**

**Games** To play a game, you spin a spinner and draw a card. The spinner tells you to move 1, 2, 3, or 4 spaces. The cards read *Free Turn, Lose a Turn,* or *No Change.* It is your turn.

a.  Construct a sample space for the possible outcomes.

## Understand

1.  What is a sample space? How do you construct a sample space?

   _____

   _____

2.  How many outcomes are possible with the spinner? How many outcomes are possible with the cards?

   _____

## Plan and Carry Out

3.  List all the possible outcomes on the spinner. _____

   List all the possible outcomes with the cards. _____

   _____

4.  In the space at the right, list the first possible spinner outcome three times.

5.  Next to each copy of the first spinner outcome, write one of the possible card outcomes.

6.  Repeat Steps 4 and 5 for each of the other possible spinner outcomes. Now you have a sample space.

## Check

7.  Use a tree diagram to organize the information from the question. Does your tree diagram match the sample space you found?

   _____

## Solve Another Problem

8.  You decide to make some changes to the game. You use a new spinner that tells you to move 1, 2, 3, 4, 5, or 6 spaces. You decide not to use the cards that read *No Change,* and you remove them from the stack of cards. Construct a sample space for the possible outcomes of the new game.

Guided Problem Solving

Name _____ Class _____ Date _____

# Practice 10-2

**Probability**

**A number cube is rolled once. Find each probability. Write your answer as a fraction, a decimal, and a percent.**

**1.** $P(3)$ _____

**2.** $P(\text{even})$ _____

**3.** $P(1, 3, \text{ or } 5)$ _____

**4.** $P(1 \text{ or } 6)$ _____

**A spinner is divided into 5 equal sections. You spin the spinner once.**

**5.** Find the probability that the spinner lands on a white section.

_____

**6.** Find the probability that the spinner lands on a shaded section.

_____

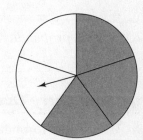

**Use the words *impossible, equally likely,* and *certain* to help you describe each event. Then find the probability.**

**7.** drawing a nickel at random from a bag containing 7 dimes

_____

_____

**8.** choosing a name that starts with *H* from a phone book page that begins with *Hardy* and ends with *Hoffman*

_____

_____

**A stack of cards is placed face down. Each card has one letter of the word *EXCELLENT*. Find each probability. Write as fraction, decimal, and percent.**

**9.** $P(\text{E})$

_____

**10.** $P(\text{N})$

_____

**11.** $P(\text{T or X})$

_____

**12.** $P(\text{consonant})$

_____

# 10-2 • Guided Problem Solving

**GPS** **Student Page 485, Exercise 18:**

**Baseball** A baseball team has the starting and relief pitchers shown in the table. The manager selects a pitcher at random. Find the probability that the pitcher is left-handed.

| Pitchers | Number |
|---|---|
| Left-Handed Starters | 1 |
| Right-Handed Starters | 4 |
| Left-Handed Relievers | 2 |
| Right-Handed Relievers | 1 |

## Understand

1. What are you being asked to do?

   _____

2. What is *probability*?

   _____

## Plan and Carry Out

3. What is the formula for determining probability?

   _____

4. How many left-handed pitchers are there? _____

5. How many total pitchers are there? _____

6. What is the probability that the pitcher will be left-handed?

   _____

7. Write the probability from step 6 as a decimal.

   _____

8. Write the probability from step 6 as a percent.

   _____

## Check

9. How can you check your answer?

   _____

   _____

## Solve Another Problem

10. Find the probability that the pitcher selected will be a starting pitcher.

    _____

    _____

# Practice 10-3

**Mirga and José played a game and completed the table.**

| Mirga wins | 卌 卌 卌 卌 | |
| Jose wins | 卌 | |
| Times played | 卌 卌 卌 卌 卌 卌 || |

1. Find the experimental probability that Mirga wins.

   _____

2. Find the experimental probability that José wins.

**The table below shows the results of spinning a spinner 8 times. Find each experimental probability.**

| Trial | 1 | 2 | 3 | 4 | 5 | 6 | 7 | 8 |
|-------|---|---|---|---|---|---|---|---|
| Outcome | blue | yellow | red | blue | green | red | yellow | blue |

3. $P$(red) _____    4. $P$(yellow) _____    5. $P$(green) _____

**One day, 40 members who came to an athletic club were asked to complete a survey. Use the results below to find each probability.**

| Question | Result |
|----------|--------|
| Are you male or female? | 28 male, 12 female |
| Are you under 26 years old? | 24 yes, 16 no |

6. $P$(male) _____    7. $P$(26 or older) _____

**For exercises 8 and 9, refer to the table, which shows the results of tossing a number cube 20 times. Is each game fair? Explain.**

| Outcome | 1 | 2 | 3 | 4 | 5 | 6 |
|---------|---|---|---|---|---|---|
| Number of Times Rolled | 1 | 2 | 4 | 6 | 2 | 5 |

8. Player A wins if the number is even. Player B wins if the number is odd.

   _____

9. Player A wins if the number is 2. Player B wins if the number is 5.

   _____

# 10-3 • Guided Problem Solving

**GPS** **Student Page 491, Exercise 15:**

**Basketball**  A player makes 4 of 12 free throws. Find the experimental probability of the player missing a free throw.

## Understand

1. What are you being asked to do?

   _____

   _____

2. What is *experimental probability*?

   _____

   _____

## Plan and Carry Out

3. What is the formula for determining experimental probability?

   _____

4. How many trials are there?

   _____

5. How many times did he miss?

   _____

6. What is the experimental probability of the player missing a free throw?

   _____

   _____

## Check

7. Does the basketball player miss more or make more free throws? Does this agree with the probability you found?

   _____

   _____

## Solve Another Problem

8. What is the experimental probability that he makes the free throw?

   _____

# Practice 10-4

**Answer each question with a complete sentence in your own words.**

**1.** What is a *population*?

_____

_____

_____

**2.** What is a *sample*?

_____

_____

_____

**3.** How can you predict the number of times an event will occur?

_____

_____

_____

**The probability of an event is 20%. How many times should you expect the event to occur in the given number of trials?**

**4.** 15 trials          **5.** 40 trials          **6.** 75 trials

_____          _____          _____

**Write and solve a proportion to make each prediction.**

**7.** In a sample of 400 customers at a fast-food restaurant, it was determined that 156 customers ordered a salad. The restaurant typically has 1,200 customers in a day. Predict how many of these customers will order a salad.

_____

**8.** Before a company delivers 600 strings of lights, it tests a sample. A quality inspector examines 75 strings of lights and finds that 3 are defective. Predict how many strings of lights in the delivery are defective.

_____

# 10-4 • Guided Problem Solving

**GPS** Student Page 497, Exercise 19:

A sample of 100 gadgets is selected from one day's production of 5,000 gadgets. In the sample, 7 are defective. Predict the number of gadgets in the day's production that are *not* defective.

## Understand

1. What are you being asked to find?

   _____

2. What do you need to use to solve this problem?

   _____

## Plan and Carry Out

3. Write a ratio of the number of gadgets that are not defective to the number in the sample.

   _____

4. Let *n* represent the number of gadgets that are not defective in the day's production. Write a ratio of the number of gadgets that are not defective to the total number of gadgets in the day's production.

   _____

5. Write a proportion with the two ratios in Steps 3 and 4. Then solve the proportion.

   _____

6. Predict the number of gadgets that are not defective in the day's production.

   _____

## Check

7. Explain how to check your answer.

   _____

## Solve Another Problem

8. A sample of 50 CDs is selected from the day's production of 300 CDs. In the sample, 4 are defective. Predict the number of defective CDs in the day's production.

   _____

# Practice 10-5

**Decide whether or not the events are independent. Explain your answers.**

**1.** You draw a red marble out of a bag. Then you draw a green marble.

_____

**2.** You draw a red marble out of a bag and put it back. Then you draw a green marble.

_____

**You spin the spinner at the right twice. Find each probability.**

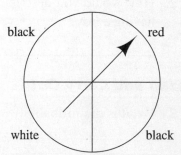

**3.** both red          **4.** both black

_____          _____

**5.** white, then red   **6.** black, then red

_____          _____

**7.** Are the spins independent events? Explain.

_____

**A number cube is rolled three times. Find the probability of each sequence of rolls.**

**8.** 2, 3, 6          **9.** odd, even, odd          **10.** all greater than 1

_____          _____          _____

**Suppose each letter of your name is printed on a separate card.**

**11.** One card is drawn from a container holding first-name letters. Find $P$(first letter of your first name).

_____

**12.** One card is drawn from a container holding last-name letters. Find $P$(first letter of your last name).

_____

# 10-5 • Guided Problem Solving

**GPS** Student Page 503, Exercise 21:

**Biology** Assume that parents are equally likely to have a boy or a girl. Find $P$(girl, then boy).

## Understand

1. What does it mean for two events to be equally likely?

   _____

2. How would you describe the events of having a girl and then having a boy?

   _____

   _____

## Plan and Carry Out

3. What is the probability of a couple having a girl?

   _____

4. What is the probability of a couple having a boy?

   _____

5. Write an expression to find the probability of a couple having a girl and then having a boy.

   _____

6. Find the probability that a couple will have a girl and then have a boy.

   _____

## Check

7. List all of the possible outcomes of a couple having two children. What is the probability that they will have a girl and then a boy? Does your answer check?

   _____

## Solve Another Problem

8. Find the probability that a couple will have a girl, a boy, and then another girl.

   _____

# 10A: Graphic Organizer

**For use before Lesson 10-1**

**Study Skill** When you review your class notes, use a highlighter to mark important information. Pay special attention to the material you have highlighted when you review for tests.

**Write your answers.**

1. What is the chapter title? _____

2. How many lessons are there in this chapter? _____

3. What is the topic of the Test-Taking Strategies page? _____

4. Complete the graphic organizer below as you work through the chapter.
   - In the center, write the title of the chapter.
   - When you begin a lesson, write the lesson name in a rectangle.
   - When you complete a lesson, write a skill or key concept in a circle linked to that lesson block.
   - When you complete the chapter, use this graphic organizer to help you review.

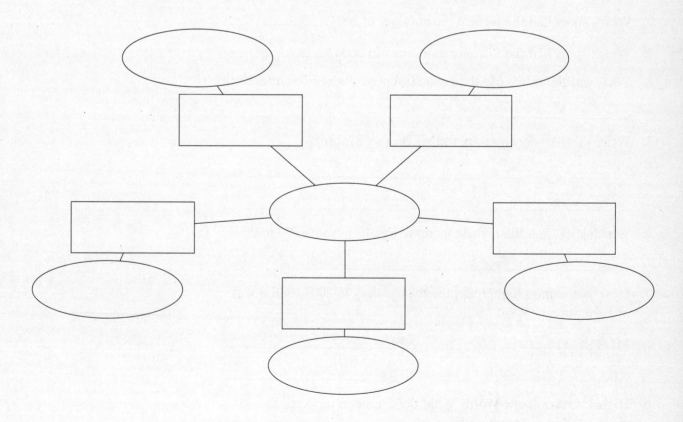

# 10B: Reading Comprehension

**Study Skill** Take short breaks between assignments. You are able to focus on a new assignment better when you take a brief "time out."

**Use the information below to answer the questions.**

Following is a list of the mean salaries in 2004 and 1990 for the four major professional sports: Major League Baseball (MLB), the National Football League (NFL), the National Basketball Association (NBA), and the National Hockey League (NHL).

|  | **2004** | **1990** |
|---|---|---|
| **MLB** | $2,486,609 | $597,537 |
| **NFL** | $1,330,000 | $430,000 |
| **NBA** | $4,900,000 | $823,000 |
| **NHL** | $1,830,000 | $271,000 |

1. What is the information about?

   _____

2. Which sport had the highest mean salary in 2004? _____

3. Which sport had the lowest mean salary in 2004? _____

4. What was the range of salaries in 2004 according to the information?

   _____

5. Write the 2004 mean salary for MLB in word form.

   _____

   _____

6. Which sport had the highest increase in salary from 1990 to 2004?

   _____

7. How many times higher was the mean salary in 2004 than it was in 1990 for each sport?

   MLB _____     NFL _____

   NBA _____     NHL _____

8. **High-Use Academic Words** What does it mean to *focus*, as mentioned in the study skill?

   a. to concentrate                         b. to align

# 10C: Reading/Writing Math Symbols

**For use after Lesson 10-3**

**Study Skill** It is important that you fully understand the basic concepts in each lesson before moving on to more complex material. So, be sure to ask questions when you are not comfortable with the material you have learned.

**Write the meaning of each mathematical expression.**

1. $P(C)$

   _____

2. $P(\text{tails})$

   _____

3. $P(\text{not } C)$

   _____

4. $P(\text{not tails})$

   _____

5. $P(A \text{ and } B)$

   _____

6. $P(A) \times P(B \text{ after } A)$

   _____

**Write each statement using appropriate mathematical symbols.**

7. the probability of event $M$ occurring _____

8. the probability of rolling a number cube
   and getting a number divisible by 2 _____

9. the probability of event $B$ not occurring _____

10. the probability of rolling a number
    cube and not getting a three _____

11. the probability of drawing a spade
    and then drawing a heart _____

# 10D: Visual Vocabulary Practice

**Study Skill** If a word is not in the Glossary, use a dictionary to find its meaning.

**Concept List**

| | | |
|---|---|---|
| counting principle | outcome | dependent events |
| independent events | permutations | population |
| probability of an event | sample space | experimental probability |

**Write the concept that best describes each exercise. Choose from the concept list above.**

| | | |
|---|---|---|
| **1.**  If you roll a six-sided number cube, then rolling the number 2 is an example of this. | **2.**  For these events, $P(A, \text{then } B) = P(A) \times P(B \text{ after } A)$. | **3.** 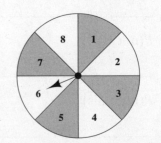 $\{1, 2, 3, 4, 5, 6, 7, 8\}$ |
| **4.**  FLY   LFY   YFL<br><br>FYL   LYF   YLF | **5.**  Marc conducted a survey at his high school. He asked the student athletes how many sports they played. The high school student athletes represent this for the survey. | **6.** <table><tr><td>**Sandwiches**</td><td>**Drinks**</td></tr><tr><td>Turkey</td><td>Apple Juice</td></tr><tr><td>Ham</td><td>Water</td></tr><tr><td>Tuna</td><td>Tea</td></tr><tr><td>Peanut Butter</td><td>Milk</td></tr><tr><td>Roast Beef</td><td>Fruit Punch</td></tr></table> The total number of sandwich and drink combinations is $5 \times 5 = 25$. |
| **7.**  A baseball pitcher has thrown 68 strikes in his last 100 pitches. $\frac{68}{100}$ or 68% may be used to determine the chance that the pitcher will throw a strike in a given pitch. | **8.**  For these events, $P(A, \text{then } B) = P(A) \times P(B)$. | **9.**  $\dfrac{\text{number of favorable outcomes}}{\text{total number of possible outcomes}}$ |

# 10E: Vocabulary Check

**Study Skill** Strengthen your vocabulary. Use these pages and add cues and summaries by applying the Cornell Notetaking style.

**Write the definition for each word or term at the right. To check your work, fold the paper back along the dotted line to see the correct answers.**

_____ permutation

_____

_____

_____ sample

_____

_____

_____ compound event

_____

_____

_____ tree diagram

_____

_____

_____ simulation

_____

_____

# 10E: Vocabulary Check (continued)

**For use after Lesson 10-5**

Write the vocabulary word or term for each definition. To check
your work, fold the paper forward along the dotted line to see the
correct answers.

an arrangement of objects in a
particular order

_____

a part of a population

_____

an event that consists of two or
more events

_____

an organized list of all possible
combination of items

_____

a model of a real-world
situation used to find
experimental probabilities

_____

# 10F: Vocabulary Review

**For use with the Chapter Review**

**Study Skill** Participating in class discussions will help you remember new material. Do not be afraid to express your thoughts when your teacher asks for questions, answers, or discussions.

**Choose the term that best completes each sentence.**

1. A(n) (*event, sample*) is an outcome or group of outcomes.

2. You can use a (*sample, population*) to gather information to make predictions.

3. When two events, such as a tossed coin landing on heads or tails, have the same chance of occurring, the outcomes are (*certain, equally likely*).

4. You can use the (*counting principal, sample*) to find the number of outcomes in a compound event.

5. If the occurrence of one event does not affect the probability of another event, the two are (*independent events, simulations*).

6. The set of all possible outcomes is the (*population, sample space*).

7. The (*probability, equally likely outcome*) of an event is a number that describes how likely it is that the event will occur.

8. A (*population, fair game*) is a group about which you want information.

9. Rolling a number cube and then spinning a spinner are examples of (*independent, dependent*) events.

# Practice 11-1

**Exploring Integers**

**Use an integer to represent each situation.**

1. spent $23 _____

2. lost 12 yards _____

3. deposit of $58 _____

**Write the opposite of each integer.**

4. 16 _____

5. −12 _____

6. 100 _____

**Find each absolute value.**

7. $|-5|$ _____

8. $|13|$ _____

9. $|25|$ _____

10. The temperature in Fargo, North Dakota, was 6°F at noon. By 4 P.M. the temperature dropped to −10°F. What integer represents the change in temperature?

_____

11. Graph these integers on the number line: −4, 9, 1, −2, 3.

**Write an integer for each point on the number line.**

12. *J* _____

13. *K* _____

14. *L* _____

**Write two numbers that have the given absolute value.**

15. 4 _____

16. 38 _____

17. 260 _____

**Think of the days of a week as integers. Let today be 0, and let days in the past be negative and days in the future be positive.**

18. If today is Tuesday, what integer stands for last Sunday? _____

19. If today is Wednesday, what integer stands for next Saturday? _____

# 11-1 • Guided Problem Solving

Starting at the fourth floor, an elevator goes down 3 floors and then up 8 floors. At which floor does the elevator stop?

## Understand

1. Circle the information you will need to solve the problem.

2. What are you being asked to do?

   _____

3. What is a good way to set up the problem visually?

   _____

## Plan and Carry Out

4. At which floor does the elevator start?

   _____

5. When the elevator goes down 3 floors, at which floor does it stop?

   _____

6. When the elevator goes up 8 floors, at which floor does it stop?

   _____

7. At which floor does the elevator stop?

   _____

## Check

8. Write a numerical expression you can use to check your answer.

   _____

## Solve Another Problem

9. A football team is on their opponents' 15-yard line. The quarterback throws a pass, but his team gets a penalty of 10 yards. During the next play, the quarterback passes the ball and the player runs the ball 8 yards. Which yard line is the team on for the next play?

   _____

# Practice 11-2

**Compare, using < or >.**

**1.** 2 ☐ −9

**2.** −5 ☐ −4

**3.** 10 ☐ −10

**4.** −33 ☐ 2

**5.** −50 ☐ −60

**6.** −9 ☐ 0

**Order each set of integers from least to greatest.**

**7.** −7, −5, −12, −4 _____

**8.** 0, −6, 6, 4, −4 _____

**9.** 15, −36, 4, −50 _____

**10.** −3, −12, 9, −27 _____

**11.** Order the temperatures from least to greatest. _____

- The temperature was 25°F below zero.

- The pool temperature was 78°F.

- Water freezes at 32°F.

- The low temperature in December was –3°F.

- The temperature in the refrigerator was 34°F.

**Write an integer that is located on a number line between the given integers.**

**12.** −2, _____, 9

**13.** 3, _____, −12

**14.** 0, _____, −5

**15.** 2, _____, −1

**Complete with an integer that makes the statement true.**

**16.** −9 > _____

**17.** 0 > _____

**18.** 3 < _____

**19.** −5 < _____

**20.** During scuba lessons, Sue dove 30 feet, Harriet dove 120 feet, and Kathy dove 90 feet. What integers represent these depths? Order the integers from least to greatest.

_____

# 11-2 • Guided Problem Solving

**Weather** Order the temperatures below from least to greatest.

- Normal body temperature is about 37°C.

- An average winter day on the polar ice cap is –25°C.

- The warmest day on record in Canada was 45°C.

- The coldest day on record in Texas was –31°C.

## Understand

1. What are you being asked to do?

   _____

2. Are the integers all positive, all negative, or are they a mix of positive and negative?

   _____

## Plan and Carry Out

3. What are the positive integers?

   _____

4. What are the negative integers?

   _____

5. Order each group of integers separately.

   _____

6. Combine the lists, ordering from least to greatest.

   _____

## Check

7. Plot the integers on a number line to check the order.

## Solve Another Problem

8. A porpoise dives 300 meters below the ocean's surface.
   A Weddell seal dives 600 meters below the ocean's surface.
   Which dives farther below the ocean's surface?

   _____

# Practice 11-3

**Write a numerical expression for each model. Find each sum.**

1. _____

2. _____

3. _____

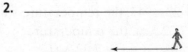

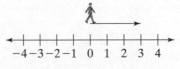
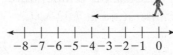
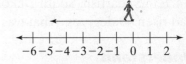

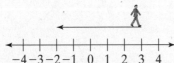
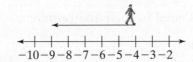

**Use a number line or mental math to find each sum.**

4. $-2 + (-8)$ _____

5. $8 + (-4)$ _____

6. $-2 + (-6)$ _____

7. $6 + (-9)$ _____

**Compare. Write <, =, or >.**

8. $-5 + (-6)$ ☐ $6 + (-5)$

9. $-8 + 10$ ☐ $-3 + 6$

10. $-4 + (-9)$ ☐ $-8 + (-5)$

11. $20 + (-12)$ ☐ $-12 + (-4)$

**Solve.**

12. Bill has overdrawn his account by $15. There is a $10 service charge for an overdrawn account. If he deposits $60, what is his new balance?

_____

13. Jody deposited $65 into her savings account. The next day, she withdrew $24. How much of her deposit remains in the account?

_____

14. The outside temperature at noon was 9°F. The temperature dropped 15 degrees during the afternoon. What was the new temperature?

_____

15. The temperature was 10° below zero and dropped 24 degrees. What is the new temperature?

_____

# 11-3 • Guided Problem Solving

**GPS** Student Page 526, Exercise 25:

**Temperature** At 7:30 A.M. on January 22, 1943, the temperature was −4°F in Spearfish, South Dakota. At 7:32 A.M. the temperature had risen 49 degrees. What was the temperature at 7:32 A.M.?

## Understand

1. Circle the information you will need to solve the problem.

2. What are you being asked to do?

   _____

3. Which word tells you what operation to perform?

   _____

## Plan and Carry Out

4. What was the temperature at 7:30 A.M.?

   _____

5. How many degrees did the temperature rise?

   _____

6. What was the final temperature at 7:32 A.M.?

   _____

## Check

7. What is the difference between 45°F and −4°F?

   _____

## Solve Another Problem

8. Jerry has a golf score of −3, or three under par. Sherry's score is 15 strokes, or points, *worse* than Jerry's score. What is Sherry's score? (*Hint:* In golf, a *low* score is better than a *high* score.)

   _____

# Practice 11-4

**Write a numerical expression for each model. Find each difference.**

**1.**

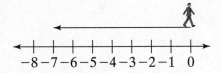

_____

**2.**

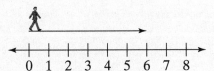

_____

**3.**

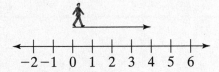    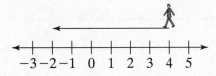

_____

**Find each difference.**

**4.** $2 - 5$ _____    **5.** $-5 - 2$ _____

**6.** $10 - (-3)$ _____    **7.** $-9 - (-2)$ _____

**Compare using <, =, or >.**

**8.** $5 - 12 \ \square\ 5 - (-12)$    **9.** $8 - (-5) \ \square\ -8 - 5$

**10.** $9 - (-4) \ \square\ 4 - (-9)$    **11.** $-12 - 12 \ \square\ 12 - (-12)$

**Solve.**

**12.** The temperature was 48°F and dropped 15° in two hours.
What was the temperature after the change?

_____

**13.** The temperature at midnight is −5°C and is expected to drop 12°
by sunrise. What is the expected temperature at sunrise?

_____

**14.** Catherine has $400 in her checking account. She writes a check for
$600. What is the balance in her account?

_____

# 11-4 • Guided Problem Solving

**Student Page 532, Exercise 23:**

**Hiking** You are at the highest point of Lost Mine Trail. The elevation is 6,850 feet. You hike down the trail to an elevation of 5,600 feet. What is your change in elevation?

## Understand

1. What are you being asked to do?

   _____

2. What operation do you use to represent change?

   _____

## Plan and Carry Out

3. What is the elevation of the highest point?

   _____

4. What is your elevation after hiking down?

   _____

5. Write an expression you can use to find the change in elevation.

   _____

6. What is your change in elevation?

   _____

## Check

7. How can you check your answer?

   _____

   _____

## Solve Another Problem

8. Sarah's savings account had $125 in it before she deposited her $255 paycheck. She then wrote the following checks: $20 for a parking ticket, $35 for her electric bill, $111 for her phone bill, $65 for her cable bill, and $89 for her new cell phone. Does Sarah have enough money left to buy a $50 DVD player? Explain.

   _____

   _____

# Practice 11-5

**Use a number line to find each product.**

**1.** $5 \times 2$

_____

**2.** $-4 \times 3$

_____

**3.** $6 \times (-2)$

_____

**4.** $-3 \times (-2)$

_____

**Find each product.**

**5.** $7 \times 8$

_____

**6.** $-5 \times 7$

_____

**7.** $4 \times (-8)$

_____

**8.** $11 \times (-6)$

_____

**9.** $-7 \times 6$

_____

**10.** $-8 \times (-8)$

_____

**Find each product.**

**11.** $11 \times (\ 9) \times (\ 4)$

_____

**12.** $6 \times (\ 5) \times (\ 1)$

_____

**13.** $5 \times 7 \times (-2) \times 3$

_____

**14.** $-3 \times 6 \times (-4) \times 5$

_____

**Solve.**

**15.** Your teacher purchases 24 pastries for a class celebration, at $2 each. What integer expresses the amount he paid?

_____

**16.** Temperatures have been falling steadily at 5°F each day. What integer expresses the change in temperature in degrees 7 days from today?

_____

**17.** A submarine starts at the surface of the Pacific Ocean and descends 60 feet every hour. What integer expresses the submarine's depth in feet after 6 hours?

_____

# 11-5 • Guided Problem Solving

**GPS** Student Page 537, Exercise 29:

**Ballooning** Hot air balloons generally descend at a rate of 200 to 400 feet per minute. A balloon descends 235 feet per minute for 4 minutes. Write an integer to express the balloon's total movement.

## Understand

1. What are you being asked to do?

    _____

    _____

2. Which word describes the direction of the balloon?

    _____

3. Will the integer be positive or negative?

    _____

## Plan and Carry Out

4. Each minute the balloon descends how many feet?

    _____

5. How many minutes is the balloon descending?

    _____

6. What is $235 \frac{\text{feet}}{\text{minute}} \cdot 4$ minutes?

    _____

7. Write an integer to express the balloon's movement.

    _____

## Check

8. What is $940$ feet $\div 235 \frac{\text{feet}}{\text{minute}}$?

    _____

## Solve Another Problem

9. A submarine dives for 5 seconds at 130 feet per second. Write an integer to express the submarine's movement.

    _____

# Practice 11-6

**Dividing Integers**

**Find each quotient.**

**1.** $14 \div 7$ _____

**2.** $21 \div (-3)$ _____

**3.** $-15 \div 5$ _____

**4.** $45 \div (-9)$ _____

**5.** $-42 \div 6$ _____

**6.** $-105 \div (-15)$ _____

**7.** $108 \div 6$ _____

**8.** $-204 \div 17$ _____

**9.** $240 \div (-15)$ _____

**10.** $-286 \div 13$ _____

**11.** $320 \div 16$ _____

**12.** $-378 \div (-14)$ _____

**Represent each rate of change with an integer.**

**13.** spends $300 in 5 days

**14.** runs 800 feet in 4 minutes

**15.** descends 45 yards in 15 s

**16.** lose 26 ounces of baby fat in 13 months

**Solve.**

**17.** Juan's baseball card collection was worth $800. Over the last 5 years, the collection decreased $300 in value. What integer represents the average decrease in value each year?

**18.** Florence purchased stock for $20 per share. After 6 days, the stock is worth $32 per share. What integer represents the average increase in stock value each day?

**19.** A freight train starts out at 0 miles per hour. After 15 miles the train is traveling 90 miles per hour. What integer represents the average increase in speed per mile?

# 11-6 • Guided Problem Solving

**GPS** **Student Page 542, Exercise 19:**

The value of a share of stock decreased $30 over the last 5 days. Find the average rate of change in dollars per day.

## Understand

1. Circle the information you will need to solve the problem.

2. What are you being asked to do?

   _____

   _____

3. What operation will you perform to find the answer?

   _____

## Plan and Carry Out

4. How much did the stock decrease in total?

   _____

5. How many days did you watch the stock?

   _____

6. What is the average decrease?

   _____

7. What integer represents the average decrease in dollars per day?

   _____

## Check

8. What is $-6 \cdot 5$? Does the answer make sense?

   _____

## Solve Another Problem

9. Emma makes $18 per hour for providing technical support for an Internet provider. Emma works 5 days a week for 6 hours. How much will she make in $2\frac{1}{2}$ months? (*Note*: Assume Emma works 20 days per month.)

   _____

# Practice 11-7

**Solve each equation. Check the solution.**

1. $r + 16 = 8$

2. $-6 + m = -14$

3. $t - 14 = -10$

4. $y - 11 = -4$

5. $h \div 8 = -8$

6. $4z = -96$

7. $-9w = -81$

8. $x \div (-7) = 8$

**Write and solve an equation for each situation.**

9. You have 26 songs on your MP3 player. After you add some, you have 39 songs. How many songs did you add?

10. You earned $32 for baby-sitting for 4 hours. How much did you make per hour?

11. Joe won 24 points for the swim team during the first half of the meet. He won 47 points in all during the meet. How many points did he win during the second half of the meet?

# 11-7 • Guided Problem Solving

**GPS** **Student Page 545, Exercise 23:**

Four friends divided a restaurant bill evenly. Each owed $20. What was the total amount of the bill?

## Understand

1. What are you being asked to determine?

   _____

2. Which word tells you what operation to perform?

   _____

## Plan and Carry Out

3. What will the variable stand for?

   _____

4. What will you divide the variable by?

   _____

5. Write the equation.

   _____

6. Solve the equation by multiplying each side by 4.

   _____

   _____

## Check

7. Substitute your answer for the variable to see if you get a true statement.

   _____

## Solve Another Problem

8. You will make 5 payments on a loan of $75. How much will each payment be?

   _____

# Practice 11-8

**Name the point with the given coordinates in the coordinate plane at the right.**

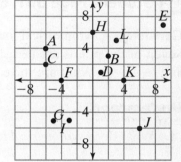

1. $(2, 3)$ _____
2. $(-4, 0)$ _____
3. $(-3, -5)$ _____
4. $(0, 6)$ _____

**Find the coordinates of each point at the right.**

5. $J$ _____
6. $E$ _____
7. $D$ _____
8. $A$ _____

**Graph each point on the coordinate plane at the right.**

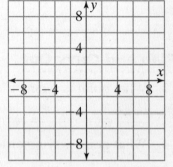

9. $A\,(8, -4)$
10. $B\,(-4, 8)$
11. $C\,(4, 8)$
12. $D\,(-8, -4)$

13. A taxi begins at $(4, -3)$. It travels 3 blocks west and 5 blocks north to pick up a customer. What are the customer's coordinates?

    _____

14. A moving truck fills up a shipment at an old address, at $(-2, 1)$. It travels 7 blocks south and 6 blocks east to the new address. What is the locaiton of the new address?

    _____

15. Use the coordinate plane at the right. Graph four points on the coordinate plane so that when the points are connected in order, the shape is a rectangle. List the coordinates of the points.

    _____

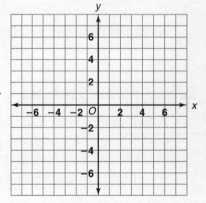

# 11-8 • Guided Problem Solving

**GPS** **Student Page 551, Exercise 31:**

**Geometry** A symmetrical four-pointed star has eight corner points.
Seven of the points are $(-1, 1), (0, 3), (1, 1), (3, 0), (1, -1), (0, -3),$
and $(-1, -1)$. What are the coordinates of the missing point?

## Understand

1.  What does *symmetrical* mean?

    _____

    _____

2.  What is a good way to set up the problem visually?

    _____

## Plan and Carry Out

3.  What point is symmetrical to $(-1, 1)$ over the *y*-axis?

    _____

4.  What point is symmetrical to $(-1, -1)$ over the *y*-axis?

    _____

5.  What point is symmetrical to $(3, 0)$ over the *y*-axis?

    _____

6.  What is the missing point?

    _____

## Check

7.  Does the point $(-3, 0)$ form a four-point star with the other
    seven points?

    _____

## Solve Another Problem

8.  A five-pointed star that is symmetrical over the *y*-axis has ten
    corner points. Eight of the points are $(-1, 1), (0, 3), (1, 1),$
    $(3, 1), (1, -1), (0, -1), (-2, -3),$ and $(-3, 1)$. What are the
    coordinates of the missing points?

    _____

# Practice 11-9

**Use the graph at the right for exercises 1–3.**

1. How many basketballs were sold in the third week?  _____

2. How many basketballs were sold in the fifth week?  _____

3. How many more basketballs were sold in the fourth week than were sold in the third week?  _____

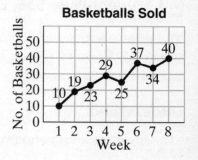

**Basketballs Sold**

4. Find the closing balance for each day.

| Day | Income | Expenses | Balance |
|---|---|---|---|
| Monday | $50 | −$40 | |
| Tuesday | $40 | −$26 | |
| Wednesday | $45 | −$50 | |
| Thursday | $30 | −$35 | |
| Friday | $60 | −$70 | |

5. Draw a line graph to show the balances in exercise 4.

6. On which day did the greatest balance occur?

   _____

7. On which day did the least balance occur?

   _____

8. On which two days was the balance the same?

   _____

   _____

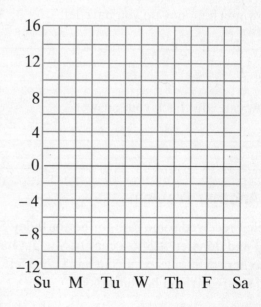

# 11-9 • Guided Problem Solving

**GPS** Student Page 556, Exercise 12:

You receive a total of $125 for your birthday. You spend $20 on a sweater, $15 on a CD, $8 on a book, $12 on a pair of sunglasses, and $35 on a bicycle helmet. How much money do you have left?

## Understand

1. Circle the information you will need to solve the problem.

2. What are you being asked to do?

   _____

## Plan and Carry Out

3. How much money did you receive?

   _____

4. How much money did you spend?

   _____

5. Write an expression for how much you have left.

   _____

6. How much money do you have left?

   _____

## Check

7. How can you check your answer?

   _____

   _____

## Solve Another Problem

8. Helen received some cash for her birthday. She spent $14.30 on a CD and donated $25 to a charity. She put half of what was left into her savings account. She has $17.85 left. How much money did she receive on her birthday?

   _____

# Practice 11-10

**Complete the function table given the rule.**

Rule: Output = Input · 5

**1.**

| Input | 1 | 2 | 3 | 4 | 5 |
|---|---|---|---|---|---|
| Output | 5 | 10 | 15 | | |

Rule: Output = Input + 3

**2.**

| Input | 3 | 4 | 5 | 6 | 7 |
|---|---|---|---|---|---|
| Output | 6 | 7 | 8 | | |

**Make a table and graph each function. Use x-values of −2, −1, 0, 1, and 2.**

**3.** $y = x - 1$

**4.** $y = \frac{x}{2} - 1$

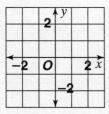

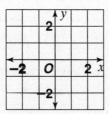

**Graph each function.**

**5.**

| Hours | Wages ($) |
|---|---|
| 1 | 15 |
| 2 | 30 |
| 3 | 45 |
| 4 | 60 |

**6.**

| Gallons | Quarts |
|---|---|
| 1 | 4 |
| 2 | 8 |
| 3 | 12 |
| 4 | 16 |

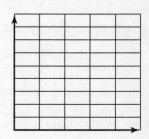

**7.** A parking garage charges $3.50 per hour to park. The function rule = 3.5 h shows how the number of hours h, relates to the parking charge c. Graph the function.

# 11-10 • Guided Problem Solving

**GPS** **Student Page 562, Exercise 18:**

**Business** You start a cookie business. You know that the oven and materials will cost $600. You decide to charge $.75 for each cookie. The function $p = 0.75c - 600$ relates profit $p$ to the number of cookies $c$ that you sell.

**a.** What will be your profit or loss if you sell 400 cookies? If you sell 500 cookies?

**b.** How many cookies must you sell to break even?

## Understand

**1.** What is *profit*?

_____

_____

**2.** How will you use the equation to answer part (a) and part (b)?

_____

_____

_____

## Plan and Carry Out

**3.** Substitute 400 for $c$ and solve for $p$. What is the profit? _____

**4.** Substitute 500 for $c$ and solve for $p$. What is the profit? _____

**5.** What value represents breaking even? _____

**6.** Do you substitute this for $p$ or $c$? _____

**7.** How many cookies must you sell to break even? _____

## Check

**8.** What is $(0.75 \cdot 800) - 600$? _____

## Solve Another Problem

**9.** Distance is a function of time. Suppose you walk at a rate of 2 miles per hour. Write an equation for the distance $d$ you walk in $t$ hours, and use it to determine the distance you will have walked after 10 hours.

_____

# 11A: Graphic Organizer

**For use before Lesson 11-1**

**Study Skill** Develop consistent study habits. Work in a quiet area where you can concentrate. Block off enough time for doing homework, so you do not have to rush through your assignments.

**Write your answers.**

1. What is the chapter title? _____

2. How many lessons are there in this chapter? _____

3. What is the topic of the Test-Taking Strategies page? _____

4. Complete the graphic organizer below as you work through the chapter.
   - In the center, write the title of the chapter.
   - When you begin a lesson, write the lesson name in a rectangle.
   - When you complete a lesson, write a skill or key concept in a circle linked to that lesson block.
   - When you complete the chapter, use this graphic organizer to help you review.

# 11B: Reading Comprehension

**For use after Lesson 11-6**

**Study Skill** Finish one assignment before beginning another. Sometimes it helps to start with the most difficult assignment first.

**Read the paragraph below and answer the questions.**

> The surface temperatures of the solar system's planets vary greatly. The coldest planet is Pluto, where the average temperature is approximately −370°F. The warmest planet is Mercury, where the temperature can reach 950°F. By comparison, the average temperature on Earth is 59°F. Even more amazing is Earth's moon, where the temperature can change more than 700°F from day to night. During the day, the average temperature on the moon is 417°F, while at night the temperature drops to −299°F. Interestingly, the temperature at each of the moon's poles is a constant −141°F.

1. What is the paragraph about?

   _____

   _____

2. What is the average temperature on Earth?

   _____

3. Which of the planets is the warmest?

   _____

4. What is the difference between the highest temperature and the lowest temperature on the moon?

   _____

5. Is the temperature at the moon's poles the mean of its high and low temperature? Explain your answer.

   _____

   _____

6. How much colder is Pluto than Earth? _____

7. **High-Use Academic Words** In Exercise 7, what does it mean to *explain?*

   a. to look for similarities          b. to make understandable

# 11C: Reading/Writing Math Symbols

**For use after Lesson 11-5**

**Study Skill** Prepare a set of flash cards to help you memorize symbols and their meanings.

**Match the symbol in Column A with its meaning in Column B.**

| Column A | Column B |
|---|---|
| 1. $\| \|$ | A. percent |
| 2. $-$ | B. is approximately equal to |
| 3. $\cong$ | C. absolute value |
| 4. $\%$ | D. is congruent to |
| 5. $\sim$ | E. negative |
| 6. $\approx$ | F. is similar to |

**Match the phrase in Column A with the appropriate expression in Column B.**

| Column A | Column B |
|---|---|
| 7. the sum of negative five and two | A. $(-2) - 5$ |
| 8. the product of two and negative five | B. $\|-5\| + 2$ |
| 9. the sum of two and the absolute value of negative five | C. $2(-5)$ |
| 10. the difference of negative two and five | D. $5 - (-2)$ |
| 11. the absolute value of the sum of negative five and two | E. $-5 + 2$ |
| 12. the difference of five and negative two | F. $\|-5 + 2\|$ |

**Match the symbol in Column A with its meaning in Column B.**

| Column A | Column B |
|---|---|
| 13. $\longrightarrow$ | A. line |
| 14. $\longleftrightarrow$ | B. angle |
| 15. $\underline{\quad}$ | C. ray |
| 16. $\angle$ | D. segment |

# 11D: Visual Vocabulary Practice

**For use after Lesson 11-10**

**Study Skill** Math symbols give us a way to express complex ideas in a small space.

## Concept List

| | | |
|---|---|---|
| absolute value | integers | origin |
| coordinate plane | opposites | quadrants |
| function | ordered pair | line |

**Write the concept that best describes each exercise. Choose from the concept list above.**

| | | |
|---|---|---|
| 1.  | 2. A hot dog vendor makes \$1.50 for each hot dog she sells. Let *n* represent the number of hot dogs sold in a day. If *P* represents the profit for the day, this can be represented by $P = 1.5n$. | 3. 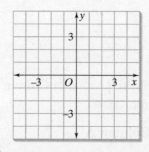 |
| 4. $\|-10\| = 10$ | 5. $\frac{3}{19}$ and $-\frac{3}{19}$ | 6. $(-5, 2)$ |
| 7. 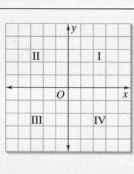 | 8. $(0, 0)$ represents this point. | 9. The numbers 0, 1, 7, and 10 are examples. |

Vocabulary and Study Skills

# 11E: Vocabulary Check

**For use after Lesson 11-10**

**Study Skill** Strengthen your vocabulary. Use these pages and add cues and summaries by applying the Cornell Notetaking style.

**Write the definition for each word or term at the right. To check your work, fold the paper back along the dotted line to see the correct answers.**

_____  absolute value

_____

_____

_____  integers

_____

_____

_____  origin

_____

_____

_____  opposites

_____

_____

_____  function

_____

_____

# 11E: Vocabulary Check (continued)

**Write the vocabulary word or term for each definition. To check your work, fold the paper forward along the dotted line to see the correct answers.**

the distance of a number from 0 on the number line

_____

the set of whole numbers, their opposites, and 0

_____

the point of intersection of the x- and y-axes on a coordinate plane

_____

two numbers that are the same distance from 0 on the number line, but in opposite directions

_____

a relationship that assigns exactly one output value for each input value

_____

# 11F: Vocabulary Review

**Study Skill** Vocabulary is an important part of every subject you learn. You may find it helpful to review new words and their definitions using flashcards.

**Match the word in Column A with its definition in Column B.**

| Column A | Column B |
|---|---|
| 1. absolute value | **A.** two lines in the same plane that never intersect |
| 2. complementary angles | **B.** a parallelogram with four congruent sides |
| 3. origin | **C.** the point where the $x$- and $y$-axes intersect |
| 4. parallel lines | **D.** a three-dimensional figure with two parallel and congruent polygonal faces |
| 5. prism | **E.** the distance a number is from zero on a number line |
| 6. rhombus | **F.** two angles whose sum is 90° |

**Match the word in Column A with its definition in Column B.**

| Column A | Column B |
|---|---|
| 7. integers | **G.** an angle whose measure is less than 90° |
| 8. function | **H.** lines that intersect to form right angles |
| 9. perpendicular lines | **J.** two angles whose sum is 180° |
| 10. supplementary angles | **K.** a pair of numbers that describes the location of a point in a coordinate plane |
| 11. ordered pair | **L.** a rule that assigns exactly one output value to each input value |
| 12. acute angle | **M.** the set of whole numbers and their opposites |

# Practice 12-1

**Explain what was done to the first equation to get the second equation.**

1. $\frac{x}{5} - 3 = 12 \rightarrow x = 75$

   _____

   _____

2. $6x + 7 = 31 \rightarrow x = 4$

   _____

   _____

3. $\frac{x}{3} + 2 = 4 \rightarrow x = 6$

   _____

   _____

**Solve each equation. Check the solution.**

4. $4r + 13 = 57$

   $r =$ _____

   _____

5. $\frac{z}{4} + 16 = 21$

   $z =$ _____

   _____

6. $7 = \frac{t}{6} - 3$

   $t =$ _____

   _____

7. $6q - 18 = 30$

   $q =$ _____

   _____

8. $\frac{w}{15} + 26 = 42$

   $w =$ _____

   _____

9. $15u + 18 = 18$

   $u =$ _____

   _____

**Solve.**

10. Hideki baked 41 cookies. He gave the same number of cookies to each of 5 friends, saving 11 cookies for himself. How many cookies did each friend receive?

    _____

11. Estelle is buying dresses by mail. She pays $65 for each dress, plus a shipping and handling charge of $8 for the entire order. If her order costs $268, how many dresses did she buy?

    _____

Name _____ Class _____ Date _____

# 12-1 • Guided Problem Solving

GPS **Student Page 576, Exercise 27:**

**Choose the correct equation. Then solve the equation.**

**Sales** A sales representative earns weekly base salary of $250 and a commission of 8% on her weekly sales. (A commission is money earned that equals a percent of the sales.) At the end of one week, she earned $410. How much did she sell that week? Let $s$ represent the total sales.

**A.** $250 + 0.08s = 410$     **B.** $250 + 410 = 0.08s$

## Understand

1. What is a commission?

   _____

2. To choose the correct equation, determine which one represents weekly salary + commission = total earned.

   _____

## Plan and Carry Out

3. What is the first step in solving the equation?

   _____

4. Simplify both sides of the equation. _____

5. What is the second step in solving the equation?

   _____

6. Simplify both sides of the equation. _____

7. What are her total sales for the week? _____

## Check

8. How can you check your answer?

   _____

## Solve Another Problem

9. A sales representative earns pay as described above. During a holiday promotion, he earned $650. What were his total sales for that week?

   _____

458 *Course 1 Lesson 12-1*                    Guided Problem Solving

# Practice 12-2

**Graph each inequality on a number line.**

**1.** $x \leq 3$

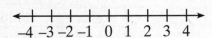

**2.** $t > 1$

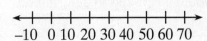

**3.** $q \geq -10$

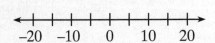

**4.** $m < 50$

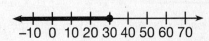

**For each inequality, tell whether the number in bold is a solution.**

**5.** $x < 7; \mathbf{7}$ _____

**6.** $p > -3; \mathbf{3}$ _____

**7.** $z \leq 12; \mathbf{4}$ _____

**8.** $n > 3; \mathbf{6}$ _____

**Write an inequality for each graph.**

**9.** _____

**10.** _____

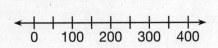

**Write a real-world statement for each inequality.**

**11.** $d \geq 60$

**12.** $p < 200$

_____          _____

**Write and graph an inequality for each statement.**

**13.** You can walk there in 20 minutes or less.

_____

**14.** Each prize is worth over $150.

_____

# 12-2 • Guided Problem Solving

**GPS** Student Page 581, Exercise 16:

**Football**  You must weigh 120 pounds or less to play in a junior football league. Use the table at the right. Who qualifies to play?

| Name | Weight |
|------|--------|
| Aaron | 118 lb |
| Steve | 109 lb |
| Mark | 131 lb |
| James | 120 lb |

## Understand

1.  What are you being asked to determine?

   _____

2.  What is the weight requirement for playing in the junior football league?

   _____

## Plan and Carry Out

3.  Write the weight requirement as an inequality. Use $p$ to represent a player's weight.

   _____

4.  Substitute each player's weight for the inequality's variable to determine if the weight makes the inequality true or false.

   _____

5.  Which players' weights make the inequality true?

   _____

6.  Who qualifies to play?

   _____

## Check

7.  Compare each player's weight to the weight requirement by plotting each weight on a number line.

   _____

## Solve Another Problem

8.  Dave ran less than 5 miles. How many miles could Dave have run? Define a variable and write an inequality.

   _____

   _____

# Practice 12-3

**Solve each inequality.**

**1.** $x - 5 < 15$

**2.** $m + 7 \geq 12$

**3.** $k + 5 < -10$

**4.** $g - (-4) \geq 0$

**5.** $-6 > b - 24$

**6.** $f - 6 < 12$

**Write an inequality for each sentence. Then solve the inequality.**

**7.** Five is greater than a number minus 2. _____

**8.** Twenty is less than or equal to a number plus 4. _____

**9.** A number minus 5 is greater than 25. _____

**Write an inequality for each problem. Then solve the inequality.**

**10.** You and the chess teacher have been playing chess for 18 minutes. To make the chess club, you must win the game in less than 45 minutes. How much time do you have to win the chess game?

_____

**11.** Your phone card allows you to talk long distance for up to 120 minutes. You have been on a long-distance call for 72 minutes. How much longer do you have to talk before your phone card expires?

_____

**Solve each inequality mentally.**

**12.** $x - 28 < 108$

**13.** $s - 18 \geq 12$

**14.** $g + 12 > 20$

**15.** $k - 4 \geq 25$

# 12-3 • Guided Problem Solving

**Budgeting** You want to spend less than $30 on two T-shirts and a pair of shorts. The pair of shorts costs $13. Each of the T-shirts costs the same amount. Write and solve an inequality to find how much money you can spend on each T-shirt.

## Understand

1. What are you being asked to find?

   _____

   _____

2. Which symbol do you need to use in the inequality, < or >? _____

## Plan and Carry Out

3. Given that shorts cost $13, write an expression for the phrase "2 T-shirts and a pair of shorts." Let $t$ represent the cost of one T-shirt.

   _____

4. Use the expression in Step 3 to write an inequality for less than 30. _____

5. What do you do first to both sides of the inequality? _____

6. Simplify both sides of the inequality. _____

7. What do you do to both sides of the inequality to solve for $t$? _____

8. What is the solution? _____

9. How much money can you spend on each T-shirt? _____

## Check

10. Can you spend exactly the amount you found in Step 9? Explain.

    _____

    _____

## Solve Another Problem

11. Suppose you are able to spend $10 more. How much money can you spend on each T-shirt now?

    _____

Name _____ Class _____ Date _____

# Practice 12-4

**Exploring Square Roots and Rational Numbers**

**Determine if each number is a perfect square.**

1. 90 _____

2. 225 _____

3. 28 _____

4. 289 _____

5. 144 _____

6. 1,000 _____

**Find each square root without using a calculator.**

7. $\sqrt{196}$ _____

8. $\sqrt{289}$ _____

9. $\sqrt{16}$ _____

10. $\sqrt{361}$ _____

11. $\sqrt{1}$ _____

12. $\sqrt{25}$ _____

**Use a calculator to find each square root to the nearest hundredth.**

13. $\sqrt{10}$ _____

14. $\sqrt{48}$ _____

15. $\sqrt{28}$ _____

16. $\sqrt{72}$ _____

17. $\sqrt{37}$ _____

18. $\sqrt{86}$ _____

**Tell which consecutive whole numbers each square root is between.**

19. $\sqrt{8}$

20. $\sqrt{3}$

_____

_____

21. $\sqrt{75}$

22. $\sqrt{120}$

_____

_____

**Tell whether each number is rational.**

23. $\frac{2}{9}$ _____

24. $\sqrt{16}$ _____

25. $\sqrt{32}$ _____

26. $\sqrt{48}$ _____

27. $\frac{12}{5}$ _____

28. $8.\overline{65}$ _____

29. The largest pyramid in Egypt, built almost 5,000 years ago, covers an area of about 63,300 square yards. Find the length of each side of the square base. Round to the nearest yard.

_____

30. Square floor tiles frequently have an area of 929 square centimeters. To the nearest tenth of a centimeter, find the length of a side of one of these tiles.

_____

# 12-4 • Guided Problem Solving

**GPS** Student Page 590, Exercise 37:

**Egyptian Pyramids** The area of the square base of the Great Pyramid at Giza is 52,900 square meters. What is the length of each side of the base of the pyramid?

## Understand

1. How do you find the area of a square if you are told the length of the side?

   _____

2. What information are you given? What are you being asked to find?

   _____

   _____

## Plan and Carry Out

3. What is the area of the square?

   _____

4. What is the square root of the answer to Step 3?

   _____

5. What is the length of each side of the square base?

   _____

## Check

6. How can you check your answer?

   _____

   _____

## Solve Another Problem

7. The area of a square table is 1,296 in.$^2$. What is the length of each side of the table?

   _____

# Practice 12-5

**Use the Pythagorean Theorem to write an equation expressing
the relationship between the legs and the hypotenuse for each triangle.**

**1.** _____

**2.** _____

**Find the missing side length of each right triangle.**

**3.** $a = 10, b = 24, c = ?$

_____

_____

**4.** $a = ?, b = 35, c = 37$

_____

_____

**Find the missing side length of each right triangle.**

**5.** $t =$ _____

_____

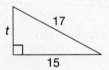

**6.** $d =$ _____

_____

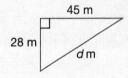

**Solve.**

**7.** The state of Colorado is shaped like a rectangle, with a base
measuring about 385 miles and a height of about 275 miles.
About how far is it from the northwest corner to the southeast
corner of Colorado?

_____

**8.** A drawing tool is shaped like a right triangle. One leg measures
about 14.48 centimeters, and the hypotenuse measures
20.48 centimeters. What is the length of the other leg? Round
your answer to the nearest hundredth of a centimeter.

_____

**9.** An 8-foot ladder is leaned against a wall from 4 feet away. How
high up the wall does the ladder reach? Round your answer to
the nearest tenth of a foot.

_____

# 12-5 • Guided Problem Solving

**GPS** Student Page 593, Exercise 15:

A 10-foot ladder leans against a building. The base of the ladder is 6 feet from the building. How high is the point where the ladder touches the building?

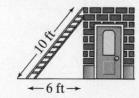

10 ft

← 6 ft →

## Understand

1. Look at the drawing to the right. What kind of triangle is formed by the ladder, the ground, and the building?

_____

2. Circle the part of the triangle whose length you are being asked to find.

## Plan and Carry Out

3. Write the formula for the Pythagorean Theorem.

_____

4. Replace $c$ with the length of the hypotenuse in the drawing.

_____

5. Replace $b$ with the length of the leg given in the drawing.

_____

6. Solve the equation for $a$ to find the missing length.

_____

7. How high is the point where the ladder touches the building?

_____

## Check

8. Substitute your answer along with the other values into the equation $a^2 + b^2 = c^2$ and solve. Does the equation hold true?

_____

## Solve Another Problem

9. The shadow of a polar bear is 24 feet long at dusk. The distance between the top of the bear's head and the end of its shadow is 25 feet. How tall is the bear?

_____

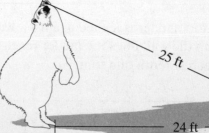

25 ft

24 ft

# 12A: Graphic Organizer

**Study Skill** As your teacher presents new material in the chapter, keep a paper and pencil handy to write down notes and questions. If you miss class, borrow a classmate's notes to catch up.

**Write your answers.**

1. What is the chapter title? _____

2. How many lessons are there in this chapter? _____

3. What is the topic of the Test-Taking Strategies page? _____

4. Complete the graphic organizer below as you work through the chapter.
   - In the center, write the title of the chapter.
   - When you begin a lesson, write the lesson name in a rectangle.
   - When you complete a lesson, write a skill or key concept in a circle linked to that lesson block.
   - When you complete the chapter, use this graphic organizer to help you review.

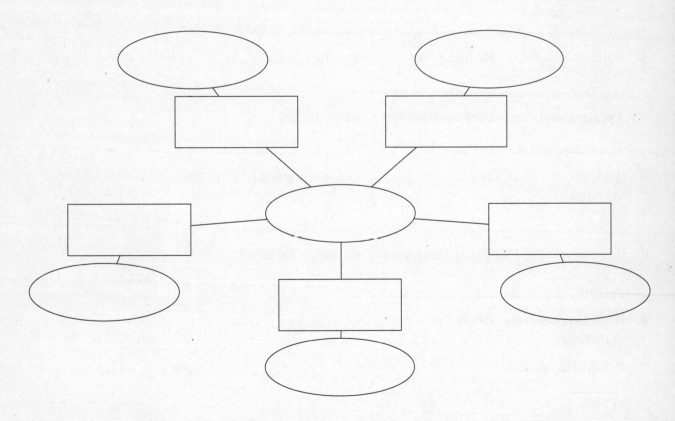

# 12B: Reading Comprehension

**Study Skill** Take a few minutes to relax before and after studying. Your mind will absorb and retain more information if you alternate studying with brief rest intervals.

**Read the paragraph below and answer the questions.**

The first paper money in the United States was printed during a coin shortage in 1862. The denominations of the first bills printed were 1, 5, 25 and 50 cents. In the late 1920s, the size of the paper bills was reduced from 3.1 by 7.4 inches to 2.6 by 6.1 inches. Currently, 50% of the bills printed are one-dollar bills, and they last only about a year and a half. For this reason, approximately 93% of the money printed each year replaces worn-out bills.

1. How many years ago was the first paper money printed?

   _____

2. What was the area of a paper bill before the 1920s?

   _____

3. What was the area of a paper bill after the 1920s?

   _____

4. Write an inequality that relates the old area to the new area.

   _____

5. Approximately how many months does a one-dollar bill last?

   _____

6. What percent of bills printed each year is not for replacing old bills?

   _____

7. What fraction of bills printed each year is not one-dollar bills?

   _____

8. **High-Use Academic Words** In the paragraph, what does it mean to *reduce*?

   a. to make smaller          b. to make more durable

# 12C: Reading/Writing Math Symbols

**For use after Lesson 12-3**

**Vocabulary and Study Skills**

**Study Skill** Use abbreviations, formulas, and symbols to write mathematical statements quickly and with less complicated wording.

**Write the meaning of each mathematical statement.**

1. $y < 5$ _____

2. $(-6 + 4) = -2$

_____

3. $6 - x$ _____

4. $y \geq 4$ _____

5. $\sqrt{64} = 8$ _____

6. $|-4| = 4$ _____

7. $\frac{3}{4} = 75\%$ _____

8. $y \leq 5$ _____

9. $3^2 = 9$ _____

10. $x - 6$ _____

11. $\pi \approx 3.14$ _____

12. $|-6 + 4| = 2$

_____

13. $2 : 3 = 6 : 9$ _____

14. $y > 4$ _____

15. $\frac{2}{3} \approx 66.6\%$

_____

16. $\sqrt{35} \approx 6$

_____

17. $A = bh$

_____

18. $C = 2\pi r$

_____

# 12D: Visual Vocabulary Practice

**For use after Lesson 12-5**

**Study Skill** When interpreting an illustration, look for the most specific concept represented.

## Concept List

| | | |
|---|---|---|
| graph of an inequality | hypotenuse | solution of an inequality |
| leg | perfect square | Pythagorean Theorem |
| rational number | square root | two-step equation |

**Write the concept that best describes each exercise. Choose from the concept list above.**

| | | |
|---|---|---|
| **1.** $-5\frac{2}{3}$ <br><br> _____ | **2.** 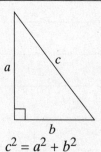 <br> $c^2 = a^2 + b^2$ <br> _____ | **3.** 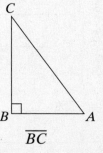 <br> $\overline{BC}$ <br> _____ |
| **4.** $\sqrt{20}$ <br><br> _____ | **5.** 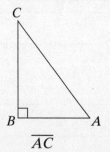 <br> $\overline{AC}$ <br> _____ | **6.** 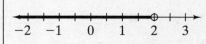 <br><br> _____ |
| **7.** $\frac{x}{2} - 5 = 3$ <br><br> _____ | **8.** 256 because $16^2 = 256$ <br><br> _____ | **9.** $x + 5 < 9$ <br> $x + 5 - 5 < 9 - 5$ <br> $x < 4$ <br><br> The number 3. <br><br> _____ |

# 12E: Vocabulary Check

**Study Skill** Strengthen your vocabulary. Use these pages and add cues and summaries by applying the Cornell Notetaking style.

**Write the definition for each word or term at the right. To check your work, fold the paper back along the dotted line to see the correct answers.**

_____  hypotenuse

_____

_____

_____  perfect square

_____

_____  inequality

_____

_____

_____  square root

_____

_____

_____  rational number

_____

Vocabulary and Study Skills

# 12E: Vocabulary Check (continued)

**Write the vocabulary word or term for each definition. To check your work, fold the paper forward along the dotted line to see the correct answers.**

the longest side of a right triangle, which is opposite the right angle

_____

a number that is the square of an integer

_____

a mathematical sentence that contains $<, >, \leq, \geq,$ or $\neq$

_____

the inverse of squaring a number

_____

any number that can be written as the quotient of two integers where the denominator is not 0

_____

# 12F: Vocabulary Review Puzzle

**For use with the Chapter Review**

**Study Skill** When solving a crossword puzzle, read the clues first.

**Complete the crossword puzzle below. For help, use the glossary in your textbook.**

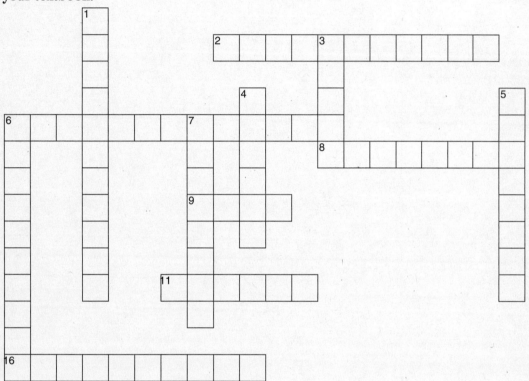

## ACROSS

**2.** The outcome of one event does not depend on the outcome of another event.

**6.** the distance around a circle

**8.** a number that can be written as a quotient of two integers, $\frac{a}{b}$, where $b \neq 0$

**9.** the number of square units inside a figure

**10.** the number of cubic units needed to fill the space inside a figure

**11.** a mathematical phrase containing numbers and operations

## DOWN

**1.** $15 + (23 + 14) = (15 + 23) + 14$ is an example of this property.

**3.** a number expressed with an exponent

**4.** point where edges meet

**5.** a number that makes an equation true

**6.** predicts how a pattern may continue

**7.** a mathematical statement that contains an equal sign